T0306125

ENGAGED DECISION MAKING

In the knowledge economy, teams play a central role in decisions made within and across organisations. The reason why teams with diverse compositions are often used is arguably their ability to develop solutions that none of their members could have produced alone. Systems design, strategy and policy development, risk management, and innovation are just a few of the areas that call for team decisions. Unfortunately, a considerable number of behavioural research studies show that teamwork is fraught with difficulties. Teams often underestimate their fallibility, struggle with conflict, or are unable to share and integrate critical information effectively. Indeed, the evidence shows that two out of three teams do not achieve their goals and half of organisational decisions – many of which are team decisions – fail.

In this book, the authors draw from research in psychology, decision and systems sciences – as well as their own research and consulting work that spans more than 20 years – to show how designed *interventions* can enable team decision making to become rigorous, transparent, and defensible. They cover theory and practice regarding the design, delivery, and evaluation of interventions to support team decision making in situations of varied complexity. Written as an applied resource for researchers and advanced students in particular, this book offers a guide to proven interventions that enhance the process of making team decisions and increase the chances of superior team results.

Etiënne A. J. A. Rouwette is a professor of research and intervention methodology at the Nijmegen School of Management at Radboud University, the Netherlands. He received his PhD from Utrecht University. His research focuses on cognition and communication in group decision support, applying facilitated modelling in domains such as healthcare, sustainability, and security, among others.

L. Alberto Franco is a professor of decision sciences at the University of Bristol Business School, UK. He received his PhD from the London School of Economics and Political Science. His main research interests are centred on the study of group decision support practice, with special attention to evaluating how cognition and behaviour affect, and are affected by, the use of decision aids and facilitated processes.

ENGAGED DECISION MAKING

From Team Knowledge to Team Decisions

Etiënne A. J. A. Rouwette
L. Alberto Franco

Routledge
Taylor & Francis Group

NEW YORK AND LONDON

Cover image: Prostock-Studio

First published 2024
by Routledge
605 Third Avenue, New York, NY 10158

and by Routledge
4 Park Square, Milton Park, Abingdon, Oxon, OX14 4RN

Routledge is an imprint of the Taylor & Francis Group, an informa business

The Open Access version of this book was funded
by DGR Methoden, 2700932.

Library of Congress Cataloging-in-Publication Data
Names: Rouwette, Etiënne Antonio Joseph Alfonso, 1971– author. |
    Franco, A. (Alberto), author.
Title: Engaged decision making : how to transform team knowledge
    into high quality decisions / Etiënne A.J.A. Rouwette and
    L. Alberto Franco.
Description: New York, NY : Routledge, 2024. | Includes
    bibliographical references and index.
Identifiers: LCCN 2023055778 | ISBN 9781032518473 (hardback) |
    ISBN 9781032503516 (paperback) | ISBN 9781003404200 (ebook)
Subjects: LCSH: Decision making. | Teams in the workplace.
Classification: LCC HD30.23 .R6876 2024 | DDC 658.4/03—dc23/
    eng/20240119
LC record available at https://lccn.loc.gov/2023055778

ISBN: 978-1-032-51847-3 (hbk)
ISBN: 978-1-032-50351-6 (pbk)
ISBN: 978-1-003-40420-0 (ebk)

DOI: 10.4324/9781003404200

Typeset in Sabon LT Pro
by Apex CoVantage, LLC

CONTENTS

FIGURES

TABLES

PART I

Are more heads better than one?

Preface

The idea that decisions can be made in a better way will not come as a surprise to many. In fact, plenty of people would agree that decisions – in particular those made by others – leave a lot of room for improvement. Some might even remember occasions on which their own decisions could have been better, in hindsight. In the last four decades, research has shown that people are prone to use quick 'rules of thumb' to make decisions in both everyday life and the work environment, possibly resulting in biased decisions. Decision and behavioural scientists have spent a significant amount of time developing and testing strategies to help people make unbiased decisions. Unfortunately, there are situations in which even unbiased decisions do not achieve the expected results due to factors outside the individual decision maker's control. Specifically, in situations where stakes are high and information is limited, the actions of other parties can affect both the implementation and intended impact of a decision. This is why making decisions in such complex situations often calls for bringing together those with a stake in the outcome of the decision to work as a team and agree on what to do. An effective team takes advantage of its members' diverse experience and knowledge to facilitate the generation of novel ideas and multiple alternatives, and increase members' commitment to the final decision.

However, making a decision as a team does not always guarantee better results. Not only do teams suffer from some of the same biases as individuals, but team decision making can also introduce new challenges. A considerable number of research studies suggest that teams find it difficult to manage conflict or surface relevant information that team members possess. This is

DOI: 10.4324/9781003404200-1

particularly noticeable for complex situations, where members are likely to have strong views about how to formulate the decision problem and which alternative should be chosen. If team discussions are ineffective, dysfunctional team dynamics can arise and lead to errors in judgement or pressures to conform to a premature solution and, ultimately, a decision that nobody supports.

Part I starts with a focus on individual decision making and explains why the personal or work decisions we often make are sometimes suboptimal. We then move on to discuss team decision making and consider the reasons why making a decision as a team, despite its potential benefits, can be fraught with difficulties. Finally, this part ends with a discussion of the potential role that designed interventions can play in improving team decisions.

1

DECISION MAKING TRAPS

Mount Everest is the earth's highest peak above sea level; at an altitude of 8,849 m, ascending to the summit presents a formidable physical and logistical challenge. In preparation for the low levels of oxygen at such a high altitude, climbers have to spend at least six weeks acclimatising their bodies. They follow a gradual climbing routine that takes them through four established camps along the path to the summit, starting with Base Camp at 5,364 m. The final climb starts at Camp IV at 8,000 m, leaving before the sun rises and reaching the summit after nine hours if all goes well – climbers must then return quickly before the sun sets. Without supplemental oxygen, most people would not be able to complete the climb, which creates an additional logistical and physical challenge for the climbers.

Rob Hall and Scott Fisher were two of the world's most experienced high-altitude mountaineers who had their own businesses (Adventures Consultants and Mountain Madness respectively) that specialised in Mount Everest climbing. On 10 May 1996, each led a commercial expedition team that included eight paying clients accompanied by several guides and helpers. Although many members of both expedition teams reached the summit, they were caught in a storm during their descent. Five individuals, including Hall and Fisher, died during the storm. The others barely escaped with their lives after many hours of wandering in the dark at sub-zero temperatures. According to survivors and climbing experts (Boukreev & DeWalt, 1998; Krakauer, 2009; Weathers & Michaud, 2015), Hall and Fisher made a number of poor decisions during the ascent. One of the most critical ones was violating their own 'two o'clock rule': if a climber cannot reach the summit by two o'clock in the afternoon, they should turn around and go back to Camp IV, no matter how close they are. Unfortunately, many of the expedition team members,

DOI: 10.4324/9781003404200-2

including Hall and Fisher, ignored the two o'clock rule and did not reach the summit until later in the afternoon. As a result, the expedition teams found themselves climbing down in darkness during the storm, with five people not able to get back to safety and dying high on the mountain.

The Mount Everest tragedy demonstrates a number of decision making traps caused by cognitive biases that impaired the mountaineers' decision making (Roberto, 2002). In this chapter, we discuss some of the common traps affecting both individual and teams.

1.1 Individual decision making traps

A long-established stream of research in psychology has identified a number of cognitive traps that afflict most of us when making judgements (Hammond et al., 2006; Kahneman, 2003; Plous, 1993). These traps are the result of the mental strategies (heuristics or rules of thumb) we use to simplify complex decisions and prediction tasks. In his book, *Thinking Fast and Slow* (2011), Nobel Prize winner Daniel Kahneman argues that our mental strategies are drawn from a cognitive structure known as System 1, which is based on well-learned, partially unconscious, parallel processing of information. For example, we use System 1 when we tie our shoelaces without a second thought. When using System 1 during problem solving or decision making, an answer suddenly springs to mind: an intuitive hunch that does not come from a defined or recallable process (e.g. we can't stop our brain from completing 2 + 2 = ?). Kahneman also identifies a more developed cognitive structure, known as System 2, that directs our attention to activities that require more difficult information search and processing. This structure uses serial processes which can produce more sound lines of argumentation and arrive at appropriate conclusions. For example, when buying a house, most people would spend considerable effort comparing mortgage packages, going over each one carefully to make sure they do not miss important details. Hence, in this situation, the majority of us would use System 2 rather than System 1. When potential mistakes are not costly and we have the opportunity to learn from them – which for many of us means most circumstances – using System 1 serves us well: it saves us a lot of time and we can still make good decisions. This system is typically used in repeated decisions without major consequences. For other situations, especially those that involve high stakes and are unique or complex, System 2 is required. Unfortunately, we do not always recognise that a situation cannot be handled by System 1 and as a result fail to engage System 2. Additionally, in some instances even System 2 might not be up to the task because it has a limited capacity, meaning that it may not be able to tackle very complex decision making situations. As a consequence, we make mistakes leading to errors in judgement that can go unrecognised. Psychologists call these systematic mistakes 'cognitive biases'

(Bazerman, 2006; Kahneman et al., 1982); we can think of them as hidden decision traps that we fall into with some regularity. A substantial amount of evidence shows that these biases affect experts and novices from a wide variety of backgrounds, in laboratory as well as field research.

There are a considerable number of cognitive biases that have been studied in a variety of disciplines including psychology, economics, and decisions sciences. Our main interest here is team decision making, and thus later we discuss only a selected sample of biases that are most relevant to teams.[1]

1.1.1   Overconfidence bias

Research studies of decision making highlight that people have a natural tendency to be overconfident about their judgements. For example, a 2018 survey by the American Automobile Association reports that 80% of American men consider their driving skills better than average despite the fact that more than 90% of car crashes are the result of human error.[2] Perhaps most worryingly, research also shows that doctors, while being completely certain of their clinical diagnoses, in fact are wrong 40% of the time (Podbregar et al., 2001). These are all examples of an *overconfidence bias*: the tendency for people to hold an exaggerated belief in what they can do, control, or know.

Overconfidence is particularly noticeable when there is a need to provide estimates of quantities (e.g. sales, costs, delays). Authors Edward Russo and Paul Schoemaker asked more than 2,000 managers in different industries to estimate industry-specific quantities in the form of ranges they were 90% confident of containing the true quantity values. They found that fewer than 1% of the quantity values fell within the estimated ranges. However, if managers are asked for job-specific estimates, they do perform better, but overconfidence remains high (about 30% of ranges do not capture the true quantity values). The evidence produced by Russo and Schoemaker is confirmed by a body of similar results from different professions, levels or expertise, ages, and nationalities (Lichtenstein et al., 1977; Wright & Phillips, 1980).

In terms of consequences, overconfidence is perhaps the most significant of the cognitive biases. In the Everest tragedy, the evidence suggests that Fisher and Hall displayed clear signs of overconfidence. Unsurprisingly, they had many reasons to be confident. Both had climbed many of the world's most difficult peaks and had become accustomed to overcoming adverse climbing conditions. They also knew that about 400 individuals had successfully reached the summit in the previous five years, and that most of them were not nearly as skilled and experienced as they were (Roberto, 2002).

Displaying overconfidence is not always bad. Indeed, when persistence in the face of adversity needs to be encouraged, showing a small dose of overconfidence may be a good thing. Overconfident people are by nature stubbornly optimistic, but unwarranted optimism can be costly. A series of studies shows that about half of inventors continue developing their projects even after being told that their chances of success were unequivocally almost zero (Åstebro, 2003). Furthermore, on average these optimistic individuals doubled their initial losses before giving up. Overconfident people are also very persuasive, and this can potentially mislead others. In his memoir, *The Wolf of Wall Street* (Belfort, 2011), former stockbroker Jordan Ross Belfort insists that people who display overconfidence are better able to influence others and gain their trust. Research by Cameron Anderson and colleagues has corroborated this effect; they show that people are considered more competent and attain greater status through the *illusion* that they are competent (Anderson et al., 2012; Kennedy et al., 2013). Even more shocking, another study suggests that when reliable information about individuals is unavailable or costly to obtain, overconfident individuals still wield influence regardless of their performance! (Sah et al., 2013).

1.1.2 Availability bias

Participants in a study heard a list of 19 names of famous women and 20 names of non-famous men (and inversely with 19 famous men and 20 non-famous women). They were then asked to estimate whether there were more males or females in the list. The results show that 80% of participants judged the famous gender to be more frequent (Tversky & Kahneman, 1973). These results are an example of an *availability bias*, which is the tendency to place too much emphasis on the information and evidence that is most readily available when judging frequencies and probabilities. In this case, being famous was more memorable (and thus available) to participants.

The ease with which instances or associations are brought to mind is pervasive when making judgments about unknown events. When assessing the chances that a particular couple will get divorced, we may try to recall similar couples which this question brings to mind. If divorces are more prevalent among the instances recalled, we will judge divorce as probable for this couple. Alternatively, we can try to imagine circumstances that will lead a couple to get divorced. If these circumstances are easily imagined, then divorce will also appear probable.

Availability can be a reliable heuristic if the recalled events have frequently occurred in the past. Frequently occurring events are usually easier to recall, so judging them as more probable should be reliable. However, rare or unusual events are also easier to bring to mind, and this can lead to biased probability estimates. In the case of the Everest tragedy, Rob Hall is likely to have underestimated the probability of a bad storm because he had enjoyed several previous seasons of good weather on summit day (Roberto, 2002).

1.1.3 Sunk-cost bias

The tendency for people to escalate commitment to a failing course of action is known as the *sunk-cost bias* (Staw, 1976, 1981). In a seminal study conducted by researcher Barry Staw, people who choose a course of action that produces negative consequences invest more than people who do not make that choice. Staw argues that people keep on investing in a failing course of action because of the need to justify their previous choice, particularly if they are responsible for losses. Over the years, researchers have identified many other factors that cause escalation behaviour, including economic (e.g. withdrawal costs higher than persistence costs; long delays between expenditures and benefits), social (e.g. 'face-saving'; perceived social rewards of persistent behaviour), and organisational (e.g. institutional inertia; mission and values) factors (Staw & Ross, 1989).

The sunk-cost bias affects decisions in many business and policy settings (Biyalogorsky et al., 2006; Cheng et al., 2003; Keil et al., 2000; Ross & Staw, 1986, 1993; Staw & Ross, 1978; Staw & Hoang, 1995). In the Everest case, the climbers had spent $65,000 plus many months of training and preparing, and thus the sunk costs were substantial. This may explain why they violated the turnaround-time rule and kept climbing even in the face of evidence that things could turn out badly (Roberto, 2002).

1.1.4 Confirmation bias

Researchers have accumulated a significant amount of evidence on what is known as *confirmation bias*, that is, people's built-intendency to favour information that supports their current beliefs or preferred choices and dismiss evidence that challenges them (Klayman, 1995; Klayman & Ha, 1987). Indeed, research shows that we are more than twice as likely to favour confirming than disconfirming information (Hart et al., 2009). For instance, anti-vaccine campaigners are typically most interested in health information that is consistent with their beliefs than that which is not. Another easy-to-identify example is when a consumer buys a particular brand of phone and attempts to justify their decision after purchasing. A study conducted by scholars Mathew Hayward and Donald Hambrick shows that CEOs overpay acquisition premiums by 4.8% every time a favourable article about them appeared in the media (Hayward & Hambrick, 1997). It appears that people see only what they want to see, and this can lead to biased decisions.

In the Everest case, it is worth noting that more than 300 people have died trying to climb Everest since the first summit attempt in 1922, and countless others have experienced serious injuries. Storms on Everest are not unusual and are in fact the norm rather than the exception. For example, there were three consecutive seasons in the mid-1980s when no one climbed the mountain due to ferocious weather conditions. This represents important information that Rob Hall ignored when he chose to break the two o'clock turnaround rule. The information that he focused on was his own beliefs about the situation he was in; he strongly believed he could take his team to the summit and back despite breaking his own rules. The fact that in the past he had taken 39 clients to the summit and back safely, had always enjoyed good weather on summit day, and had never been caught in a storm high on the mountain may have contributed to Hall's biases.

1.1.5 Framing bias

Finally, people tend to hold a narrow view of the decision at hand and assume knowledge is complete, which makes them overlook important objectives, options, and outcomes (Larrick, 2009; Russo & Schoemaker, 1989). Put differently, the *frames* that people use in a decision making situation are often narrow. For example, in 1995, the top management team at Seagate, the world's largest producer of data storage devices at the time, got together to develop a comprehensive list of objectives that encapsulated the company's mission. It turned out that the set each member came up with was only a subset of the collective list of objectives. Perhaps more surprisingly is that, on average, only 36% of the specific objectives they later recognised as relevant were initially listed by team members. This illustrates that the information that comes to mind (i.e. the frames that people use) often seems complete and coherent, reducing the desire for further research (Bond et al., 2008).

Frames are structured ways of thinking that simplify and guide our understanding of reality. A frame forces us to view the world from a particular and limited perspective, and it strongly influences our perceptions of what we see or expect to see. Using a frame is like looking through binoculars: part of the landscape comes into focus, but there is far more that you do not see. Our frames are thus selective and narrow, and affected by expertise and experience. The seminal study by DeWitt Dearborn and Herbert Simon provides further illustration of the use of frames that are consistent with experience and functional background (Dearborn & Simon, 1958; Russo & Schoemaker, 2002). Dearborn and Simon asked managers with different functional backgrounds to read a case about an organisation facing a particular situation. When requested to identify the most important problem in the case, the majority of managers highlighted issues consistent with their backgrounds: sales managers mentioned sales issues, production managers mentioned production issues, and so on. Clearly, functional expertise and experience influence which aspects of a situation are thought to be relevant. Follow-up research modified this picture somewhat, but the overall conclusion is that the department in which a manager works influences their opinion (Beyer et al., 1997; Chattopadhyay et al., 1999; Walsh, 1988).

The frames we use pertaining to a situation are also influenced by how we perceive the context. To illustrate, consider two ways of defining a project brief in the construction industry [cf. 46]. Typically, contractors see a project brief as a kind of insurance against changes in project specifications made by

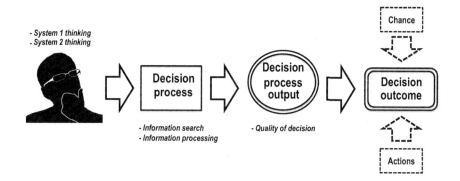

FIGURE 1.1   Individual decision making.

Source: Image of person thinking by OpenClipArt-Vectors from Pixabay

clients, and as a means to prevent costly surprises during the project. On the other hand, clients may frame a project brief as a generic and fluid document that can be updated while the project progresses. It is easy to see how these different motivations and perceived contexts lead to different understandings of a project brief, which in turn may cause difficulties in the interaction between contractors and clients. The problem is not that the frames they use are wrong per se, but that each frame is only a partial picture of reality; some characteristics take centre stage and others are in the wings.

A *framing bias* is caused by associative memory processes that lead people to start with a set of assumptions and then collect evidence in a way that is consistent with the initial view. The information that comes to mind seems complete and coherent, reducing the need for further search. The way a decision problem is framed can have dramatic effects. For example, framing a decision outcome in terms of gains or losses can cause people to reverse their preferences (Kahneman & Tversky, 1979; Tversky & Kahneman, 1981).

To summarise, and as shown in Figure 1.1, research shows that, when faced with a decision making situation, individuals engage in either System 1 or System 2 thinking that involves searching and processing information in simple or complex ways, respectively. When using System 1, people draw on mental strategies to simplify complex decisions and prediction tasks. Although usually effective, these strategies can lead to systematic biases that may go unrecognised and affect the quality of decisions. Figure 1.1 also highlights that, irrespective of whether a decision is biased or not, the long term outcome of a decision after implementation can be affected by things that are outside our control, like chance or the actions of others.

1.1.6   Other biases

There are many other biases that researchers have identified. For example, the *anchoring bias* (Kahneman et al., 1982; Tversky & Kahneman, 1974) refers to the notion that people often allow an initial reference point to distort their estimates. Typically, when we are asked to estimate the value of a quantity (e.g. what next year's sales will be, how long a project will last), we begin at an initial value (a reference point) and then adjust it to obtain the final estimate. Unfortunately, the adjustment is often insufficient. In one study (Northcraft & Neale, 1987), participants received a ten-page booklet describing a house for sale. They then visited the house and neighbourhood for a maximum of 20 minutes. All participants received identical booklets, with the exception of one piece of information: the listing price. They were then asked to value the property using a range of indicators, such as selling price and lowest acceptable offer. Low listing prices consistently led to low estimated property values, while high listing prices yielded high estimates. Both amateurs and professional real estate agents gave significantly biased estimates.

Also, people often judge the chances that a person or an object belongs to a particular category (e.g. how likely is it that this person is a consultant?) by how representative the person or object is of that category. Similarly, the probability that events originate from a particular process (e.g. how likely is it that the peaks and troughs in the sales graph are random?) is judged by how representative the events are of that process. In both cases, our assessments can lead to a *representative bias* (Kahneman et al., 1982; Tversky & Kahneman, 1974) if we ignore relevant statistical information or have misperceptions about the nature of random processes. An example concerns decisions on commercialising inventions (Shane et al., 2015). In many universities, technology licensing officers have a central role in deciding which of a range of inventions should be supported and become a university spinoff. Previous studies show that licensing officers think that spinoff company founders are typically male immigrants with industry experience who are easy to work with. A total of 352 licensing officers participated in a study, conducted online, in which they received information on inventions which were adapted from actual university invention descriptions. If licensing officers use the representativeness heuristic in making their decisions, they would be more likely to favour cases that look like the standard example and disfavour cases that look dissimilar. Invention descriptions were paired with inventor profiles that were carefully manipulated: the inventor was male or female, had an American or a Chinese name, did or did not have industry experience, and was more or less easy to work with. Decisions on whether or not to recommend the inventor to start a company were influenced by gender, industry experience, and how easy it was to work with the person. This indeed shows that the more an inventor looks like the typical inventor, the more likely the person is to get positive advice. This may be defensible for a factor such as industry experience, as it may relate to potential success of a spinoff.[3] It is, however, surprising that gender should influence the decision on who (not) to advise to start a company.

1.2 Team decision making traps

The examples and studies described so far concerned decisions made by individuals. While these clearly may have consequences for others, as was clear from the Mount Everest case, decisions in organisations are often discussed in teams. In this book, we define a team as three or more individuals who are brought together to make a decision, or provide a recommendation, about a situation of interest or concern. Team members socially interact face to face or virtually, may have a stake in the situation, and may be drawn from one or more organisations. The use of teams for decision making has many advantages. They offer greater thinking capacity, expertise, knowledge, and information. They also bring multiple perspectives (or frames) about the situation to team discussions. And team members are more likely to support the decision or recommendation because of their participation in the decision making process.

From our discussion of cognitive biases in the previous section, a key issue is whether teams fall into the same decision traps as individuals. Unfortunately, the empirical evidence suggests that individual errors are often amplified at the team level (Sunstein & Hastie, 2015). Indeed, teams have been found to be suffering from augmented representative biases (Stasser & Dietz-Uhler, 2001), show more unrealistic overconfidence (Sniezek & Henry, 1989), be more vulnerable to framing effects (Kerr et al., 1996), and be even more susceptible to sunk-cost bias (Whyte, 1993), to name a few. Not all teams amplify the errors made by individuals. Indeed, there is some evidence that, compared to individuals, teams are less subject to certain biases such as availability and anchoring (see Sunstein and Hastie 215). However, the central point is that individual biases are not automatically corrected when they work as a team, and they often get worse.

Furthermore, a considerable amount of research studies suggests that teams do not always achieve their potential due to 'losses' in the decision making process (Steiner, 1972). Well-documented process losses include team members working harder to make up for others who 'free-ride' knowing that the team (and not individual team members) is accountable for the decision (Ingham et al., 1974; Jackson & Harkins, 1985; Williams et al., 1981) or team members pressuring others to conform to an early consensus on a particular solution (Festinger et al., 1950; Janis, 1982; Taras, 1991). In the next chapter, we discuss the impact of motivational factors as a potential source of biases and process losses in team decision making.

Notes

1. For more extensive treatments, the interested reader can consult the relevant literature (Arkes, 1991; Gilovich et al., 2002; Kahneman, 2011; Kahneman et al., 1982; Tversky and Kahneman, 1974).

2. See https://newsroom.aaa.com/2018/01/americans-willing-ride-fully-self-driving-cars/
3. It is worth highlighting that the advice given by Shane and colleagues was to pair inventors without experience with those who have experience.

References

Anderson, C., Brion, S., Moore, D. A., & Kennedy, J. A. (2012). A status-enhancement account of overconfidence. *Journal of Personality and Social Psychology*, *103*(4), 718.

Arkes, H. R. (1991). Costs and benefits of judgment errors: Implications for debiasing. *Psychological Bulletin*, *110*(3), 486.

Åstebro, T. (2003). The return to independent invention: Evidence of unrealistic optimism, risk seeking or skewness loving? *The Economic Journal*, *113*(484), 226–239.

Bazerman, M. (2006). *Judgement in managerial decision making* (6th ed.). Wiley.

Belfort, J. (2011). *The wolf of wall street*. Hachette.

Beyer, J. M., Chattopadhyay, P., George, E., Glick, W. H., Ogilvie, D., & Pugliese, D. (1997). The selective perception of managers revisited. *Academy of Management Journal*, *40*(3), 716–737.

Biyalogorsky, E., Boulding, W., & Staelin, R. (2006). Stuck in the past: Why managers persist with new product failures. *Journal of Marketing*, *70*(2), 108–121.

Bond, S. D., Carlson, K. A., & Keeney, R. L. (2008). Generating objectives: Can decision makers articulate what they want? *Management Science*, *54*(1), 56–70.

Boukreev, A., & DeWalt, G. W. (1998). *The climb: Tragic ambitions on Everest*. St Martin's.

Chattopadhyay, P., Glick, W. H., Miller, C. C., & Huber, G. P. (1999). Determinants of executive beliefs: Comparing functional conditioning and social influence. *Strategic Management Journal*, 763–789.

Cheng, M. M., Schulz, A. K. D., Luckett, P. F., & Booth, P. (2003). The effects of hurdle rates on the level of escalation of commitment in capital budgeting. *Behavioral Research in Accounting*, *15*, 63.

Dearborn, D. C., & Simon, H. A. (1958). A note on the departmental identifications of executives. *Sociometry*, *21*(2), 140–144.

Festinger, L., Schachter, S., & Back, K. (1950). *Social pressures in informal groups; a study of human factors in housing*. Harper.

Gilovich, T., Griffith, D., & Kahneman, D. (Eds.). (2002). *Heuristics and biases: The psychology of intuitive judgment*. Cambridge University Press.

Hammond, J. S., Keeney, R. L., & Raiffa, H. (2006). The hidden traps in decision making. *Harvard Business Review*, *84*(1), 118–126.

Hart, W., Albarracín, D., Eagly, A. H., Brechan, I., Lindberg, M. J., & Merrill, L. (2009). Feeling validated versus being correct: A meta-analysis of selective exposure to information. *Psychological Bulletin*, *135*(4), 555.

Hayward, M. L., & Hambrick, D. C. (1997). Explaining the premiums paid for large acquisitions: Evidence of CEO hubris. *Administrative Science Quarterly*, 103–127.

Ingham, A. G., Levinger, G., Graves, J., & Peckham, V. (1974). The Ringelmann effect: Studies of group size and group performance. *Journal of Experimental Social Psychology*, *10*(4), 371–384.

Jackson, J. M., & Harkins, S. G. (1985). Equity in effort: An explanation of the social loafing effect. *Journal of Personality and Social Psychology, 49*(5), 1199.

Janis, I. L. (1982). *Groupthink: Psychological studies of policy decisions and fiascos* (2nd ed.). Houghton Mifflin Company.

Kahneman, D. (2003). A perspective on judgment and choice. Mapping bounded rationality. *American Psychologist, 58*(9), 697–720.

Kahneman, D. (2011). *Thinking, fast and slow.* Farrar, Straus and Giroux.

Kahneman, D., Slovic, P., & Tversky, A. (Eds.). (1982). *Judgement under uncertainty: Heuristics and biases.* Cambridge University Press.

Kahneman, D., & Tversky, A. (1979). Prospect theory: An analysis of decisions under risk. *Econometrica, 47*(2), 263–292.

Keil, M., Mann, J., & Rai, A. (2000). Why software projects escalate: An empirical analysis and test of four theoretical models. *MIS Quarterly,* 631–664.

Kennedy, J. A., Anderson, C., & Moore, D. A. (2013). When overconfidence is revealed to others: Testing the status-enhancement theory of overconfidence. *Organizational Behavior and Human Decision Processes, 122*(2), 266–279.

Kerr, N. L., MacCoun, R. J., & Kramer, G. P. (1996). Bias in judgment: Comparing individuals and groups. *Psychological Review, 103*(4), 687.

Klayman, J. (1995). Varieties of confirmation bias. *Psychology of Learning and Motivation, 32,* 385–418.

Klayman, J., & Ha, Y.-W. (1987). Confirmation, disconfirmation, and information in hypothesis testing. *Psychological Review, 94*(2), 211.

Krakauer, J. (2009). *Into thin air: A personal account of the Mount Everest disaster.* Anchor Books.

Larrick, R. P. (2009). Broaden the decision frame to make effective decisions. In *Handbook of principles of organizational behavior* (pp. 461–480). Wiley.

Lichtenstein, S., Fischhoff, B., & Phillips, L. D. (1977). Calibration of probabilities: The state of the art. In *Decision making and change in human affairs* (pp. 275–324). Springer.

Northcraft, G. B., & Neale, M. A. (1987). Experts, amateurs, and real estate: An anchoring-and-adjustment perspective on property pricing decisions. *Organizational Behavior and Human Decision Processes, 39*(1), 84–97.

Plous, S. (1993). *The psychology of judgment and decision making.* McGraw Hill.

Podbregar, M., Voga, G., Krivec, B., Skale, R., Parežnik, R., & Gabršček, L. (2001). Should we confirm our clinical diagnostic certainty by autopsies? *Intensive Care Medicine, 27*(11), 1750–1755.

Roberto, M. A. (2002). Lessons from Everest: The interaction of cognitive bias, psychological safety, and system complexity. *California Management Review, 45*(1), 136–158.

Ross, J., & Staw, B. M. (1986). Expo 86: An escalation prototype. *Administrative Science Quarterly,* 274–297.

Ross, J., & Staw, B. M. (1993). Organizational escalation and exit: Lessons from the Shoreham nuclear power plant. *Academy of Management Journal, 36*(4), 701–732.

Russo, J. E., & Schoemaker, P. J. (1989). *Decision traps: Ten barriers to brilliant decision-making and how to overcome them.* Doubleday.

Russo, J. E., & Schoemaker, P. J. H. (2002). *Winning decisions: Getting it right the first time.* Crown Business.

Sah, S., Moore, D. A., & MacCoun, R. J. (2013). Cheap talk and credibility: The consequences of confidence and accuracy on advisor credibility and persuasiveness. *Organizational Behavior and Human Decision Processes, 121*(2), 246–255. https://doi.org/10.1016/j.obhdp.2013.02.001

Shane, S., Dolmans, S. A. M., Jankowski, J., Reymen, I. M. M. J., & Romme, A. G. L. (2015). Academic entrepreneurship: Which inventors do technology licensing officers prefer for spinoffs? *The Journal of Technology Transfer, 40*, 273–292.

Sniezek, J. A., & Henry, R. A. (1989). Accuracy and confidence in group judgment. *Organizational Behavior and Human Decision Processes, 43*(1), 1–28.

Stasser, G., & Dietz-Uhler, B. (2001). Collective choice, judgment, and problem solving. In *Blackwell handbook of social psychology: Group processes* (pp. 31–55). Wiley.

Staw, B. M. (1976). Knee-deep in the big muddy: A study of escalating commitment to a chosen course of action. *Organizational Behavior and Human Performance, 16*(1), 27–44.

Staw, B. M. (1981). The escalation of commitment to a course of action. *Academy of Management Review, 6*(4), 577–587.

Staw, B. M., & Hoang, H. (1995). Sunk costs in the NBA: Why draft order affects playing time and survival in professional basketball. *Administrative Science Quarterly*, 474–494.

Staw, B. M., & Ross, J. (1978). Commitment to a policy decision – multi-theoretical perspective. *Administrative Science Quarterly, 23*(1), 40–64.

Staw, B. M., & Ross, J. (1989). Understanding behavior in escalation situations. *Science, 246*(4927), 216–220.

Steiner, I. D. (1972). *Group process and productivity*. Academic Press.

Sunstein, C. R., & Hastie, R. (2015). *Wiser: Getting beyond groupthink to make groups smarter*. Harvard Business Press.

Taras, D. G. (1991). Breaking the silence: Differentiating crises of agreement. *Public Administration Quarterly*, 401–418.

Tversky, A., & Kahneman, D. (1973). Availability: A heuristic for judging frequency and probability. *Cognitive Psychology, 5*(2), 207–232.

Tversky, A., & Kahneman, D. (1974). Judgment under uncertainty. Heuristics and biases. *Science, 185*, 1124–1131.

Tversky, A., & Kahneman, D. (1981). The framing of decisions and the psychology of choice. *Science, 211*(4481), 453–458.

Walsh, J. P. (1988). Selectivity and selective perception: An investigation of managers' belief structures and information processing. *Academy of Management Journal, 31*(4), 873–896.

Weathers, B., & Michaud, S. G. (2015). *Left for dead: My journey home from Everest*. Bantam.

Whyte, G. (1993). Escalating commitment in individual and group decision making: A prospect theory approach. *Organizational Behavior and Human Decision Processes, 54*(3), 430–455.

Williams, K., Harkins, S. G., & Latané, B. (1981). Identifiability as a deterrant to social loafing: Two cheering experiments. *Journal of Personality and Social Psychology, 40*(2), 303.

Wright, G. N., & Phillips, L. D. (1980). Cultural variation in probabilistic thinking: Alternative ways of dealing with uncertainty. *International Journal of Psychology, 15*(1–4), 239–257.

2

MOTIVATED TEAM DECISION MAKING

The use of teams for decision making pervades contemporary organisational practice. Within and across organisations, teams are formed to tackle situations that require a decision to be made, whether it is simple or complex, routine or one-off, short or long-term. They do this by using the diversity of perspectives, knowledge, information, and expertise within the team to develop an understanding of, and responses to, a situation that no team member could have produced alone (Fraidin, 2004; Hill, 1982). Indeed, team decisions can produce remarkable results: for example, when a team of NASA engineers found a way to bring the crew of the damaged Apollo 13 spacecraft back to earth (Kranz, 2001), or when a global team comprised of representatives of multiple organisations worked together to rescue all 33 miners trapped in the San Jose copper mine in Chile (Franklin, 2011).

Unfortunately, considerable research shows that team decision making often fails to deliver on its promises (e.g. Hackman, 2002; Kerr & Murthy, 2004; Nutt, 2002). Scholars have found that teams suffer process losses (Steiner, 1972) and fall into the same decision traps individuals do (see Chapter 1) – sometimes even more so (e.g. Argote et al., 1990; Smith et al., 1998; Whyte, 1993). Others have reported that teams sometimes underestimate their vulnerability and fallibility (Janis, 1982; Janis & Mann, 1977), are unable to share and integrate critical information effectively (Schulz-Hardt et al., 2000; Stasser & Titus, 1985), or struggle to manage conflict (Amason, 1996; De Dreu & Weingart, 2003). Notable examples of failed team decision making include the launch of the Challenger space shuttle (Aldag & Fuller, 1993; Esser & Lindoerfer, 1989), the Bay of Pigs invasion (Rasenberger, 2012; Schlesinger, 2002), and the disposal of the Brent Spar oil storage and tanker (Grint, 2005; Jordan, 2001). These, and related analyses of team decision

DOI: 10.4324/9781003404200-3

making, share the notion that teams act as *information processors* (Hinsz et al., 1997; Levine & Moreland, 1998; Tindale & Kameda, 2000); they process and integrate relevant information to reach a collective agreement on what to do about the situation of interest. We use the term 'information' here to refer to all relevant knowledge, data, facts, goals, and interests pertaining to the situation, including taken-for-granted assumptions and frames (see Chapter 1) which team members may bring to the table.

In this chapter, we discuss two critical factors that affect the ability of teams to share and integrate information effectively. To this end, we will draw on Motivated Information Processing in Groups (MIP-G) theory, developed by social psychology scholar Carsten de Dreu and colleagues (De Dreu et al., 2008; Nijstad & De Dreu, 2012). MIP-G theory sheds light on the role of different motivations in teams and extends the notion of teams as information processors to teams as *motivated* information processors. Broadly, the theory posits that both cognitive and social motives drive the sharing and integration of information within teams. *Cognitive motivation* (also known as 'epistemic' motivation) refers to "the willingness to expend effort to achieve a thorough, rich and accurate understanding of the world, including the group task or decision problem at hand" [27, p. 23]. *Social motivation*, on the other hand, is defined as "the individual preference for outcome distributions between oneself and other group members" [27, p. 23]. Furthermore, social motivation can be proself (i.e. the individual is concerned with their own outcomes) or prosocial (i.e. the individual is concerned with joint outcomes and fairness). Cognitive motivation affects the depth of information processing whereas social motivation biases the type of information that is processed.

Cognitive and social motivation captures the influence of a host of cognitive style variables such as the need for cognition (Cacioppo & Petty, 1982), need for closure (Kruglanski & Webster, 1996), and personality traits such as openness to experience and agreeableness (Costa & McCrae, 2000). They also capture the influence of situational factors such as time pressure, accountability, and incentive schemes. Increasingly, research shows that cognitive and social motivation interacts to influence the nature of information exchange and integration within teams, which in turn determine the extent to which teams are able to fulfil their synergistic potential (e.g. De Dreu et al., 2008; Nijstad & De Dreu, 2012; Resick et al., 2014; Steinel et al., 2010; Toma & Butera, 2015; Van Ginkel & Van Knippenberg, 2008). In what follows, we first introduce the core elements of MIP-G theory, and then extend its original formulation to explore the role of cognitive and social motivation in the management of team conflict.

2.1 Cognitive motivation and information processing

Developing appropriate responses to a situation of concern often requires bringing together a team of people with different expertise, experiences, and views pertaining to the situation. For example, up until 2005, teenage pregnancy rates in the UK had remained similar to those in the 1970s, while most of Western Europe had halved them. The severity of the problem led the UK government to advocate 'joined-up working' policies to break the long-term, reinforced cycles of social exclusion such as those resulting from teenage pregnancy. One of these policies was a requirement that all local authorities in England create a Teenage Pregnancy Strategy Group (TPSG) to make decisions about how to tackle the problem. These teams involved representatives from local authorities, the National Health Service, the education authorities, faith groups, and other stakeholders such as the voluntary sector, which included young parents' representatives (cf. Franco & Lord, 2011). The expected benefit of bringing people from different organisations together as a team was that the differences in team members' views and knowledge about the teenage pregnancy rate problem would become a valuable asset, enabling them to develop a shared understanding of the problem before they reach agreement on how to act. In this way, a team like the TPSG would be able to make progress which could have not been possible by any team member working alone.

When team members get together to address a situation of concern, they are likely to have different views. Initially, team members will bring their own implicit frames to the discussion, each highlighting different parts of the situation as important. For example, when the TPSG had to decide which projects to fund to alleviate the problems associated with teenage pregnancy, team members had different opinions about the value and impact of candidate projects for funding. Sharing the multiple frames that team members hold is critical to gaining a better understanding of the situation. However, as discussed in Chapter 1, this is often difficult as people are often blind to their own and others' frames (Cannon-Bowers et al., 1993; Russo & Schoemaker, 1989).

Beyond individual frames, team members will also bring different types of information to the discussion such as knowledge, data, facts, and assumptions pertaining to the situation. Furthermore, the distribution of information within the team will often be asymmetric. This suggests, at least in principle, the potential for synergetic benefits from sharing and integrating the information that team members possess. Yet in practice, such benefits are not always realised. Extensive research has shown that teams are prone to discuss information held by all members (shared information) much more than unique information (unshared) that is often critical to deal with the situation. Team members, deeply engaged in the discussion, often fail to recognise the salience of unshared information for the issues under consideration, and thus this information never surfaces, remaining hidden.

This phenomenon is best illustrated by studies of hidden profile tasks (Lu et al., 2012). In the original study, developed by psychology scholars Garold Stasser and William Titus, a team has to choose among two candidates, A and B, for a job position (Stasser & Titus, 1985). Table 2.1 shows the design of the study. In the columns are committee members X, Y, and Z. The rows indicate which information on two candidates is known to a member: a_1 to a_7 refer to information items on candidate A; b_1 to b_4 refer to information items on candidate B. All information items are positive. The upper panel refers to a situation in which all information is shared: all items are known to X, Y, and Z. In the lower panel, some information items are shared and others are unshared. The full information set about the candidates would clearly identify A as the best candidate for the job. Indeed, if information is divided as in the upper panel of Table 2.1, almost all groups identify the best candidate in a matter of minutes.

However, the lower panel shows a different situation. Here, prior to discussion, some information about the candidates is known to all team members (shared information), and other information is unique to team members (unshared information). The combination of shared and unshared information held by any one member would identify B as the best candidate (as there are only three positive items on A compared to four positive items on B). Thus, the optimal choice is hidden from the team as a whole and can only be discovered by disseminating and processing the unshared information among team members. However, it turns out that teams have a natural tendency to focus on shared information. In fact, only about 20% of teams had members ask whether there is any additional information not yet known to others. Hidden profile studies not only highlight the tendency of team members to talk primarily about shared information and ignore unshared information but also indicate that whether or not team members actively and systematically process the exchanged information is, at least, as important (Greitemeyer & Schulz-Hardt, 2003; Winquist & Larson, 1998).

Different explanations for why teams show a preference towards shared information have been offered (Faulmüller et al., 2010, 2012; Greitemeyer & Schulz-Hardt, 2003; Stasser, 1992; Stasser & Titus, 1987). MIP-G theory postulates that teams find it difficult to uncover hidden profiles because team

TABLE 2.1 Hidden profile task

	Member X	Member Y	Member Z
	All information shared		
Pro-A	$a_1a_2a_3a_4a_5a_6a_7$	$a_1a_2a_3a_4a_5a_6a_7$	$a_1a_2a_3a_4a_5a_6a_7$
Pro-B	$b_1b_2b_3b_4$	$b_1b_2b_3b_4$	$b_1b_2b_3b_4$
	Biased distribution		
Pro-A			
• shared	a_1	a_1	a_1
• unshared	a_2a_3	a_4a_5	a_6a_7
Pro-B (all shared)	$b_1b_2b_3b_4$	$b_1b_2b_3b_4$	$b_1b_2b_3b_4$

Note. see also Stasser et al. (1989)

members may have low levels of cognitive motivation (De Dreu et al., 2008). When team members' cognitive motivation is low, they will be less willing to search or generate new information pertaining to the situation being discussed, and less willing to actively and systematically process the information that is exchanged. Consequently, in a team with low levels of cognitive motivation, team members are more likely to be blind to their own and others' frames, unwilling to develop an appropriate frame that fits the situation under consideration, and only focus on discussing information they recognise and share in common.

If teams cannot always deal effectively with simple decision making situations such as the hidden profile task, what can we expect for more complex situations? On the one hand, the need to draw on a wide range of stakeholders who have different views and perspectives of a complex situation should make the possibility of processing information in depth more likely. On the other hand, the pressures under which stakeholders tend to work may lower cognitive motivation within the team and thus hinder the depth of information processing (De Dreu et al., 2008). If situation-relevant frames, knowledge, assumptions, or data fail to surface during team discussions, it will affect the decision outcome. By not discussing all pertinent information, the team is likely to adopt a narrow frame, lose sight of important objectives, overlook plausible responses to the situation, and fail to appreciate the full consequences of different options.

Research showing that higher levels of cognitive motivation promote high-quality decisions implicitly assumes that team members also share a motivation to develop shared goals and a joint decision by consensus, and have little or no incentives to achieve personal gains at the expense of others (cf. De Dreu et al., 2008). However, the empirical evidence suggests that the positive effects of high cognitive motivation on team decision making are limited to decision making situations in which team members show a concern with fairness and collective outcomes (de Dreu et al., 2008). Unfortunately, this is not always the case in practice. Though team members need one another to develop effective ways to tackle the situation of concern, they may not want the joint effort to be successful at the cost of losing sight of their personal or constituency interests. We turn to this issue in the next section.

2.2 Social motivation and information processing

Teams wishing may experience difficulties when discussing aspects of a situation in which team members have competing interests. Here, we use the term 'competing interests' to refer to the goals and objectives that team members wish to achieve regarding the situation of concern. Although the need for cooperation is central to team decision making, often team members have other competing incentives (Davis et al., 1976). This was most evident in the

TPSG case, where team members were all competing for funds to support their preferred projects. As the funds were limited, only those projects that would provide the best value would be funded. Consequently, a pound spent on a project that helps young parents to go back into education would not be spent on funding clinics offering contraception services. In this respect, the TPSG members had competing interests.

Many decision making situations can be thought of as 'mixed-motive' negotiations in which team members may both cooperate to achieve shared goals and compete to advance their own individual interests (Bazerman et al., 1988; Lax & Sebenius, 1986). In practice, the extent to which interests compete within a team is likely to vary across situations. A source of variation is often a differential access to knowledge, expertise, resources, or authority to make decisions, which makes some team members more powerful than others. Teams from a single organisational department may often work together in a clear hierarchy, but in collaborations across departments or organisations, authority and power are often more diffused. However, those collaborations are often necessary to get work done.

An example is the criminal justice chain, which in most countries involves a cooperation between police, public prosecution, judges, and prison services. Prosecutors typically have a central role in this chain, as they set priorities for police investigations and have a major responsibility in the processing of cases. Similarly, in the Netherlands, the public prosecution had a large influence on what type of cases would be shelved or processed. The Dutch police, however, could decide where to deploy its resources. In the early 2000s, the Dutch government decided to set a higher target for prosecuted cases. At the time, there was a concern in the press that an increased target in the number of cases processed would lead the police to bring in more cases but focus on less serious crimes (e.g. traffic violations instead of burglaries). Thus, even though stakeholders depend on one another to make progress in a situation of mutual concern (Davis et al., 1976; Edmondson, 2016; Gray, 1989; Grint, 2005), they may at the same time look for ways to advance their own agendas and interests. When competitive interests are high among team members representing powerful organisational constituencies or divisions that seek to maintain or strengthen their positions, the team decision process and outcome will be significantly affected.

The concept of social motivation can help to explain the behaviours that arise when team interests are symmetric or asymmetric (e.g. Beersma & De Dreu, 2002; De Dreu & Van Lange, 1995; Giebels et al., 2000; Weingart et al., 1993). When interests are aligned, team members are more likely to exhibit *prosocial* behaviours, meaning that they are motivated to seek consensus and collective goals by reaching agreements that integrate all team members' aspirations. By contrast, when interests are not aligned, team members may adopt a *proself* orientation to act and thus be mostly concerned with achieving their own goals, reducing the potential for mutual gains and the development of appropriate responses to the situation of concern.

When proself behaviours occur at the expense of prosocial behaviours, team members become strong advocates of their own positions and consequently only mention information that is consistent with that position. As a result, the information that team members share will be biased: advocates may only share information that supports their position or undermines others' positions, even if they may also possess information that does the opposite. Research shows that this is likely to impact the team decision process in at least three ways (cf. De Dreu et al., 2008). First, the more team members exhibit or adopt proself behaviours, the less likely it is that the team will advance joint goals, which limits the potential for mutual gains. Second, because the information shared by proself team leaders is biased, this precludes the team from developing creative solutions or responses that integrate all the relevant information pertaining to the situation at hand. Finally, the occurrence of proself behaviours is likely to produce 'winners' and 'losers', meaning the latter group will feel less committed to implementing the team decision.

MIP-G theory posits that the generation, dissemination, and processing of information by team members is a function of the interaction between cognitive and social motivation within the team, and that this interaction will affect the quality of team decision making. This dynamic aspect of motivated team decision making is discussed next.

2.3   Dynamics of motivated team decision making

There is increasing research evidence that lends support for MIP-G theory (e.g. Bechtoldt et al., 2010; De Dreu, 2007; De Dreu et al., 2006; De Dreu et al., 2008; Nijstad & De Dreu, 2012; Resick et al., 2014; Steinel et al., 2010; Toma & Butera, 2015; Van Ginkel & Van Knippenberg, 2008). Specifically, compared with proself team members, prosocial team members are more likely to input information conducive to collective goals and performance, they are more likely to communicate information in an accurate way, and they are less likely to spin information conducive to personal goals, to strategically withhold information, and to engage in lying and deception. Furthermore, according to MIP-G theory, these tendencies amplify when cognitive motivation among team members is high rather than low. The reason for these tendencies is twofold. Firstly, high cognitive motivation brings about a stronger disposition to deliberately and systematically process information that is or becomes available during team discussion. Secondly, high cognitive motivation reduces in-group tendencies (Janis, 1982; Kruglanski et al., 2006) and associated preference for autocratic leadership and reduced participative decision making (De Dreu et al., 2008).

According to MIP-G theory, four patterns of behaviour are possible according how cognitive and social motivation interact.[1] Low levels of cognitive motivation leads proself team members to engage in as little information exchange as possible to safeguard their personal interests. On the other hand, low levels of cognitive motivation prompts prosocial team members to reach early consensus in order to preserve team harmony and cohesion. In contrast, high levels of cognitive motivation leads proself team members to engage in heated debate and argument, effortful deception, and selective sharing of information in a self-serving way, and it leads prosocial team members to engage in collaborative problem solving behaviour to develop the best possible way forward for the entire team (De Dreu et al., 2008).

The interaction between cognitive motivation and social motivation, and how it impacts both the team decision process and outcome, is aptly illustrated by the decision to launch the space shuttle Challenger. On the morning of 28 January 1986, the Challenger was launched from the Kennedy Space Center and the temperature that morning was around −5 °C, well below the temperatures at which the shuttle engines had been tested before. Seventy-three seconds after launch, the Challenger exploded, resulting in the deaths of all seven astronauts aboard, and becoming the worst disaster in space flight history. The catastrophe shocked the whole world, and for many Americans it was the most tragic event since the assassination of John F. Kennedy in 1963. The findings of the Presidential Commission on the Space Shuttle Challenger Accident[2] pointed to a flawed decision making process as a primary contributory cause.

Very few machines rival the space shuttle in terms of its sheer complexity. Manufactured by Rockwell International and managed by NASA, the 250-ton machine operated at the very limit of human engineering. The launch of the Challenger was originally scheduled for 22 January 1986, but was postponed three times. The first two postponements occurred because the previous space mission was late, and the third postponement was based on an unacceptable weather forecast. Finally, a launch attempt on 27 January was cancelled because of high crosswinds. On the evening before the actual launch on 28 January, NASA and Morton Thiokol (MT) managers and engineers held a teleconference to discuss the issue of launching the shuttle despite near-freezing temperatures expected for the next morning. Morton Thiokol was the contractor that produced the solid rocket boosters responsible for the shuttle's primary propulsion and had grave concerns that low temperatures would prevent the shuttle booster's O-rings from sealing, leading to leakage of hot gases that could cause a catastrophic accident during launch. Roger Boisjoly was the key engineer expressing concerns.

All participants in the teleconference were probably acutely aware of a sense of public pressure to launch. Prior delays, along with interest in the presidentially backed project to send a civilian teacher to space would have further contributed to this.[3] Furthermore, the evidence suggests that both NASA and MT held divergent interests pertaining to the launch decision. MT managers were concerned about disappointing NASA and potentially losing a valuable contract with a major client. In turn, NASA managers wanted to avoid further embarrassment and more delays. There were three key players present in the teleconference who held divergent interests: MT engineer Roger Boisjoly wanted to convince others that the O-rings were unreliable at lower temperatures and to ensure that his dissenting opinion was registered; NASA manager Larry Mulloy wanted to launch on time the following day unless he had credible information for not doing so; and MT manager Barry Lund wanted to manage the tension between supporting his engineers and not angering his client.

Roger Boisjoly had been looking at the relationship between low temperatures and erosion in the O-rings for previous shuttle flights prior to the teleconference. The evidence suggests that all participants in the meeting had access to the same data that Boisjoly had prepared. The data were inconclusive as the combination of O-ring erosion and low temperatures had been observed only in a very small number of previous shuttle launches. Boisjoly thus found himself lacking sufficient data to prove his case and was relying on his intuition to come to the conclusion that cold temperatures were problematic. Without sufficient data, he could not persuade the top managers. On the other hand, data about the temperature at the launch of those flights in which the O-rings did not experience erosion did not surface during discussions, even though these data were also known to many participants in the room.

Clearly, all parties in the teleconference wanted to make the best possible decision, but NASA managers framed the situation in such a way that launching the shuttle was the default option unless they were persuaded by a counterargument. For NASA managers, the decision was about whether the data presented suggested that the shuttle would fail, and they spent significant cognitive effort scrutinising the data (high cognitive motivation) supporting the claim that low temperatures and O-ring erosion were correlated. The findings of the Presidential Commission indicate that NASA managers were not open to being influenced by arguments from the MT engineers, and instead tried to win the argument at all costs, presenting their views forcefully, and seeing the other party as an opponent (proself behaviours). For MT managers and engineers, the decision was about whether it was safe to launch the shuttle. However, while Roger Boisjoly spent significant cognitive effort in collecting and examining different types of evidence suggesting a relationship between temperature and O-ring erosion (high cognitive motivation), he also downplayed the gaps in the data he presented by giving a positive spin to his arguments through making moral claims (proself behaviour).[4]

Had all the parties involved been willing and able to spend their cognitive efforts in jointly understanding whether there was a correlation between

O-ring failure and temperature, they might have recognised that they did have access to data that was not shared during discussions, and which could have convinced everyone to delay the launch. Indeed, if data about previous flights that had not experienced O-ring erosion were added to the data that Boisjoly presented to NASA, it would have become apparent that O-ring erosion and temperature were indeed correlated, and that a launch delay was thus necessary.

The preceding discussion identifies specific behaviours that are likely to affect the effectiveness of team decision making. In actual practice, team members may differ in the level of cognitive and social motivation they bring to their discussions. As De Dreu et al. note: "because of temperament, socialisation, or differences in environmental pressures, some group members may have high and others low cognitive motivation and some may have a proself and others a prosocial motivation" (De Dreu et al., 2008, p. 42). Research highlights that high levels of cognitive motivation combined with a prosocial orientation foster effective team decision making. This is because of better information dissemination and integration that leads to high-quality insights, agreements, consensus, and commitment. This will happen only when there is enough time to make the decision (i.e. low urgency) and team members represent all the key stakeholders in the situation (De Dreu et al., 2008; Nijstad et al., 2014).

The actual differences in the levels of cognitive and social motivation within the team will manifest themselves during team discussions and may lead to conflict that could potentially derail the entire team decision making effort. Furthermore, the actual nature of the conflict experienced by team members will be contingent on team members' cognitive and social motivations, as explained next.

2.4   Motivation and team conflict

A team exhibiting high levels of cognitive motivation will be able to surface the diversity of information and interests distributed within the team. This means that some level of conflict is likely to be experienced by the team. For example, team members may have framed the situation of concern in different ways, and this greatly influences what they would ultimately like to do. This likely means that options satisfying individual needs and interests will have been identified and be favoured prior to a team discussion. Differences in frames and interests can lead to conflict within a team, but how conflict develops is contingent on team members' social motivation. If the team embraces a prosocial orientation, then it is more likely that conflict will remain at a 'cognitive' level, and this type of conflict can be beneficial. An important stream of research has produced evidence that when the conflict experienced is only 'cognitive', it often has positive effects on team decision making because it encourages better understanding of the issues being considered (Amason & Schweiger, 1997; Eisenhardt et al., 1997; Jehn, 1995;

Pelled, 1996; Van de Vliert & De Dreu, 1994). Cognitive conflict can be beneficial because it enables team members to pay close attention to both shared and unshared information, and can lead to debates that critically examine key assumptions, alternative frames of the situation of concern, and expose the risks or weaknesses of certain options.

By contrast, if the team adopts proself behaviours, cognitive conflict can become dysfunctional and deteriorate into interpersonal or *affective* conflict (Amason, 1996; Jehn, 1995), which may prevent team members from working together effectively. Affective conflict arises when team members feel that their ideas, arguments, and preferences are challenged by others, or even refuted on the basis of facts and new evidence, making them feel upset or hurt and reacting defensively. When differences of opinion emerge and are difficult to reconcile, team members spend their efforts focusing on each other rather than on understanding the situation of concern. As team members begin to experience affective conflict, emotions and stress run high and winning the argument becomes more important than finding a good solution. Team members are likely to strongly advocate their positions and use flexible (even deceitful) ways to get their way. Research shows that if affective conflict is not managed effectively, it can seriously erode social relations within the team (Eden & Ackermann, 2010).

On the other hand, when teams have low levels of cognitive motivation and a prosocial motivation, then conflict is likely to be tabled to preserve group harmony, leading to lazy compromises or effortless concessions (De Dreu et al., 2008; Nijstad & De Dreu, 2012). An example of the latter is a situation known as 'groupthink' (Janis, 1972; Turner & Pratkanis, 1988). In this situation, there is already a preferred course of action that has become the group norm which nobody wants to question. Having an 'elephant in the room' is another example. To an outsider, it seems as if the team carefully avoids certain topics, even though these stand out as important to the task at hand (the elephant). Team norms, social roles, and status differences can lead team members to tailor what they say to what they think others want to hear (Argyris, 1997; Gladwell, 2008), hence impeding free information exchange and team decision making. By contrast, when teams have low levels of cognitive motivation and a proself orientation, then team members will engage in low-effort, selfish behaviour, such as 'free-riding' and being unwilling to understand each other's positions. Consequently, team members will not give in and, instead, engage in vetoing that will be experienced as affective conflict. This in turn may lead to stalemates and indecision.

Obviously how conflict is experienced within the team (cognitive, affective, tabled) is complex, and multiple conflict trajectories are possible within a team (e.g. Franco et al., 2016; Poole & Dobosh, 2010; Sambamurthy & Poole, 1992). The Challenger case discussed earlier illustrates this complexity; team members may display both prosocial and proself behaviours during their discussions. Furthermore, cognitive motivation may be higher or lower during team members' interactions, depending on individual differences and situational factors. Additionally, it is often the case that heterogeneous teams are likely to have an asymmetric distribution of cognitive and social motivation. For example, it may be possible to have teams with only a minority of members with high cognitive motivation and proself orientation. Whether this distribution of motivations will enable conflict to remain cognitive, escalate to become affective, or simply be tabled, is a research question to be addressed (De Dreu et al., 2008; Nijstad & De Dreu, 2012).

The notion of teams as motivated information processors (De Dreu et al., 2008; Nijstad & De Dreu, 2012) rests on the assumption that personality and situational variables affect a team's cognitive and social motivation. Furthermore, increasing evidence shows that prosocial teams with high levels of cognitive motivation are more likely to process information in a deep and systematic manner, engage in beneficial cognitive conflict, and avoid affective conflict, which in turn enables them to reach higher-quality decisions. As mentioned, several factors need to be in place if this potential is to be reached: adequate time to discuss the matter, presence of all key stakeholders, and avoiding the tendency of prosocial teams to protect group harmony, thereby ignoring alternative views (Jordan, 2001; Parks & Cowlin, 1996). The question is, then, how to increase levels of cognitive motivation and foster prosocial behaviours within the team while reducing or managing proself behaviours effectively. Research by Kathleen Eisenhardt and colleagues describes a number of strategies that leaders can use to raise the levels of cognitive motivation within their teams, and get team members to surface the cognitive conflict required to debate their differences properly (Eisenhardt et al., 1997). Unfortunately, high levels of cognitive conflict often lead to affective conflict, and the dilemma then becomes how to elicit cognitive conflict while maintaining low levels of affective conflict. The work of scholars Amy Edmondson and Dianne McLain Smith identifies specific actions that team members can take to manage affective conflict effectively when it rises (Edmondson & McLain Smith, 2006), and some of these will be discussed in Chapter 15.

In sum, the extent to which team members are willing to search and process information thoroughly (cognitive motivation), and whether they do this in a truthful or deceptive manner (social motivation), will determine if they are more or less likely to engage in productive conflict and realise the synergetic benefits presumably offered by team decision making. That is, arriving together at a better solution that no individual team member could have produced alone. This argument, supported by MIP-G theory and research, is summarised in Figure 2.1.

In the next chapter, we introduce the notion of using structured procedures to both benefit and mitigate from the effects of motivational influences on team decision making. These procedures, which we call 'interventions',

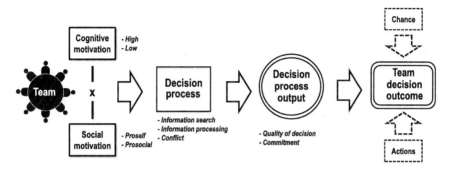

FIGURE 2.1   Team decision making.

Source: Adapted from De Dreu et al. (2008). Image of team by Ricarda Mölck from Pixabay

can be applied to decision situations of varied complexity to help teams transform their collective knowledge into superior team results.

Notes

1. It should be noted that MIP-G theory considers these patterns as idealised behaviours, given that the situation of concern may have both competitive and cooperative features, and raise both higher and lower levels of cognitive motivation.
2. Presidential Commission on the Space Shuttle Challenger Accident. (1986). *Report of the presidential commission on the space shuttle challenger accident.*
3. Christa McAuliffe had been selected from among more than 11,000 applicants to be the first teacher carried into space on the Teacher In Space Program. The plan specified that McAuliffe would teach two lessons from space: The first would include an introduction to the crew members and their jobs, the cockpit, and human conditions on the shuttle. The second would explain how the shuttle flew, technological advances made through space exploration, and why space exploration is important.
4. Roger Boisjoly arguably said during the teleconference: "launching [the shuttle] below freezing is an act away from goodness".

Literatures

Ackoff, R. L. (1974). *Redesigning the future: A systems approach to societal problems.* John Wiley & Sons.

Ackoff, R. L. (1981). The art and science of mess management. *Interfaces, 11*(1), 20–26.

Aldag, R. J., & Fuller, S. R. (1993). Beyond fiasco: A reappraisal of the groupthink phenomenon and a new model of group decision processes. *Psychological Bulletin, 113*(3), 533.

Amason, A. C. (1996). Distinguishing the effects of functional and dysfunctional conflict on strategic decision making: Resolving a paradox for top management groups. *Academy of Management Journal, 39*(1), 123–148.

Amason, A. C., & Schweiger, D. M. (1997). The effects of conflict on strategic decision making effectiveness and organizational performance. In C. K. De Dreu & E. Van de Vliert (Eds.), *Using conflict in organizations* (pp. 101–115). SAGE.

Argote, L., Devadas, R., & Melone, N. (1990). The base-rate fallacy: Contrasting processes and outcomes of group and individual judgment. *Organizational Behavior and Human Decision Processes, 46*(2), 296–310.

Argyris, C. (1997). Learning and teaching: A theory of action perspective. *Journal of Management Education, 21*(1), 9–26.

Bazerman, M. H., Mannix, E. A., & Thompson, L. L. (1988). *Groups as mixed-motive negotiations*. National Institute for Dispute Resolution.

Beersma, B., & De Dreu, C. K. (2002). Integrative and distributive negotiation in small groups: Effects of task structure, decision rule, and social motive. *Organizational Behavior and Human Decision Processes, 87*(2), 227–252.

Boos, M., Schauenburg, B., Strack, M., & Belz, M. (2013). Social validation of shared and nonvalidation of unshared information in group discussions. *Small Group Research, 44*(3), 257–271.

Bratton, J., Grint, K., & Nelson, D. (2004). *Organizational leadership*. Thomson/Southwestern.

Cacioppo, J. T., & Petty, R. E. (1982). The need for cognition. *Journal of Personality and Social Psychology, 42*, 116–131.

Cannon-Bowers, J., Salas, E., & Converse, S. (1993). Shared mental models in expert team decision making. In N. J. Castellan (Ed.), *Individual and group decision making: Current issues* (pp. 221–246). Erlbaum.

Costa, P. T., Jr., & McCrae, R. R. (2000). *Neo personality inventory*. Oxford University Press.

Davis, J. H., Laughlin, P. R., & Komorita, S. S. (1976). The social psychology of small groups: Cooperative and mixed-motive interaction. *Annual Review of Psychology, 27*(1), 501–541.

De Dreu, C. K. W., Nijstad, B. A., & Van Knippenberg, D. (2008). Motivated information processing in group judgment and decision making. *Personality and Social Psychology Review, 12*(1), 22–49.

De Dreu, C. K. W., & Van Lange, P. A. (1995). The impact of social value orientations on negotiator cognition and behavior. *Personality and Social Psychology Bulletin, 21*(11), 1178–1188.

De Dreu, C. K. W., & Weingart, L. R. (2003). Task versus relationship conflict, team performance, and team member satisfaction: A meta-analysis. *Journal of Applied Psychology, 88*(4), 741–749.

Dienst Justitiële Inrichtingen. (2002). *Terugblik en toekomst DJI Jaarverslag 2002*. Dienst Justiële Inrichtingen.

Eden, C., & Ackermann, F. (2010). Decision making in groups: Theory and practice. In P. C. Nutt & D. C. Wilson (Eds.), *Handbook of decision making* (pp. 231–272). Wiley-Blackwell.

Edmondson, A. C. (2016). Wicked problem solvers. *Harvard Business Review, 94*(6), 52–59, 117.

Edmondson, A. C., & McLain Smith, D. (2006). Too hot to handle? How to manage relationship conflict. *California Management Review, 49*(1), 6–31.

Eisenhardt, K. M., Kahwajy, J. L., & Bourgeois, L. J. I. (1997). How management teams can have a good fight. *Harvard Business Review, 75*(4), 77–85.

Esser, J. K., & Lindoerfer, J. S. (1989). Groupthink and the space shuttle challenger accident: Toward a quantitative case analysis. *Journal of Behavioral Decision Making, 2*(3), 167–177.

Faulmüller, N., Kerschreiter, R., Mojzisch, A., & Schulz-Hardt, S. (2010). Beyond group-level explanations for the failure of groups to solve hidden profiles: The individual preference effect revisited. *Group Processes & Intergroup Relations, 13*(5), 653–671.

Faulmüller, N., Mojzisch, A., Kerschreiter, R., & Schulz-Hardt, S. (2012). Do you want to convince me or to be understood? Preference-consistent information sharing and its motivational determinants. *Personality and Social Psychology Bulletin, 38*(12), 1684–1696.

Fraidin, S. N. (2004). When is one head better than two? Interdependent information in group decision making. *Organizational Behavior and Human Decision Processes, 93*(2), 102–113.

Franco, L. A., & Lord, E. (2011). Understanding multi-methodology: Evaluating the perceived impact of mixing methods for group budgetary decisions. *Omega, 39,* 362–372.

Franco, L. A., Rouwette, E. A., & Korzilius, H. (2016). Different paths to consensus? *The impact of need for closure on model-supported group conflict management European Journal of Operational Research, 249*(3), 878–889.

Franklin, J. (2011). *33 Men: Inside the miraculous survival and dramatic rescue of the Chilean miners.* Penguin.

Giebels, E., de Dreu, C. K. W., & van de Vliert, E. (2000). Interdependence in negotiation: Effects of exit options and social motive on distributive and integrative negotiation. *European Journal of Social Psychology, 30,* 255–272.

Gladwell, M. (2008). *Outliers: The story of success.* Penguin Books.

Gray, B. (1989). *Collaborating: Finding common ground for multiparty problems.* Jossey-Bass.

Greitemeyer, T., & Schulz-Hardt, S. (2003). Preference-consistent evaluation of information in the hidden profile paradigm: Beyond group-level explanations for the dominance of shared information in group decisions. *Journal of Personality and Social Psychology, 84*(2), 322–339.

Grint, K. (2005). Problems, problems, problems: The social construction of 'leadership'. *Human Relations, 58*(11), 1467–1494.

Grint, K. (2010). Wicked problems and clumsy solutions: The role of leadership. In S. Brookes & K. Grint (Eds.), *The public leadership challenge* (pp. 169–186). Palgrave Macmillan.

Hackman, J. R. (2002). Why teams don't work. In R. S. Tindale, L. Heath, J. Edwards, E. J. Posavac, F. B. Bryant, Y. Suarez-Balcazar, E. Henderson-King, & J. Myers (Eds.), *Theory and research on small groups* (pp. 245–267). Kluwer Academic Publishers.

Heifetz, R. A. (1994). *Leadership without easy answers.* Harvard Business School Press.

Heifetz, R. A., & Laurie, D. L. (2001). The work of leadership. *Harvard Business Review, 79*(11), 131–141.

Henningsen, D. D., & Henningsen, M. L. M. (2004). The effect of individual difference variables on information sharing in decision-making groups. *Human Communication Research, 30*(4), 540–555.

Hill, G. W. (1982). Group versus individual performance: Are n+1 heads better than one? *Psychological Bulletin, 91*(3), 517–539.

Hinsz, V. B., Tindale, R. S., & Vollrath, D. A. (1997). The emerging conceptualization of groups as information processors. *Psychological Bulletin, 121*(1), 43.

Janis, I. (1972). *Victims of groupthink. A psychological study of foreign-policy decisions and fiascoes.* Houghton Mifflin Company.

Janis, I. L. (1982). *Groupthink: Psychological studies of policy decisions and fiascos* (2nd ed.). Houghton Mifflin Company.

Janis, I. L., & Mann, L. (1977). *Decision making: A psychological analysis of conflict, choice and commitment.* The Free Press.

Jehn, K. A. (1995). A multimethod examination of the benefits and detriments of intragroup conflict. *Administrative Science Quarterly, 40,* 256–282.

Jehn, K. A., & Mannix, E. A. (2001). The dynamic nature of conflict: A longitudinal study of intragroup conflict and group performance. *Academy of Management Journal, 44*(2), 238–251.

Jordan, G. (2001). *Shell, Greenpeace and the Brent Spar.* Springer.

Kerr, D. S., & Murthy, U. S. (2004). Divergent and convergent idea generation in teams: A comparison of computer-mediated and face-to-face communication. *Group Decision and Negotiation, 13*(4), 381–399.

Kranz, G. (2001). *Failure is not an option: Mission control from Mercury to Apollo 13 and beyond.* Simon and Schuster.

Kruglanski, A., & Webster, D. M. (1996). Motivated closing of the mind: "Seizing" and "freezing". *Psychological Review, 103*(2), 263–283.

Lax, D. A., & Sebenius, J. K. (1986). *Manager as negotiator: Bargaining for cooperation and competitive gain.* Free Press.

Levine, J. M., & Moreland, R. L. (1998). Small groups. In D. Gilbert, S. Fiske, & H. Lindzey (Eds.), *The handbook of social psychology* (4th ed., Vol. 2, pp. 415–469). McGraw-Hill.

Lu, L., Yuan, Y. C., & McLeod, P. L. (2012). Twenty-five years of hidden profiles in group decision making: A meta-analysis. *Personality and Social Psychology Review, 16*(1), 54–75.

Mojzisch, A., Schulz-Hardt, S., Kerschreiter, R., Brodbeck, F. C., & Frey, D. (2008). Social validation in group decision-making: Differential effects on the decisional impact of preference-consistent and preference-inconsistent information. *Journal of Experimental Social Psychology, 44*(6), 1477–1490.

Nijstad, B. A., Berger-Selman, F., & De Dreu, C. K. (2014). Innovation in top management teams: Minority dissent, transformational leadership, and radical innovations. *European Journal of Work and Organizational Psychology, 23*(2), 310–322.

Nijstad, B. A., & De Dreu, C. K. (2012). Motivated information processing in organizational teams: Progress, puzzles, and prospects. *Research in Organizational Behavior, 32,* 87–111.

Nutt, P. (2002). *Why decisions fail. Avoiding the blunders and traps that lead to debacles.* Berrett-Koehler.

Parks, C. D., & Cowlin, R. A. (1996). Acceptance of uncommon information into group discussion when that information is or is not demonstrable. *Organizational Behavior and Human Decision Processes, 66*(3), 307–315. https://doi.org/10.1006/obhd.1996.0058

Pelled, L. H. (1996). Demographic diversity, conflict, and work group outcomes: An intervening process theory. *Organization Science, 7,* 615–631.

Poole, M. S., & Dobosh, M. (2010). Exploring conflict management processes in jury deliberations through interaction analysis. *Small Group Behavior, 41*(4), 408–426.

Postmes, T., Spears, R., & Cihangir, S. (2001). Quality of decision making and group norms. *Journal of Personality and Social Psychology, 80*(6), 918–930.

Rasenberger, J. (2012). *The brilliant disaster: JFK, Castro, and America's doomed invasion of Cuba's Bay of Pigs.* Simon and Schuster.

Resick, C. J., Murase, T., Randall, K. R., & DeChurch, L. A. (2014). Information elaboration and team performance: Examining the psychological origins and environmental contingencies. *Organizational Behavior and Human Decision Processes, 124*(2), 165–176.

Russo, J. E., & Schoemaker, P. J. (1989). *Decision traps: Ten barriers to brilliant decision-making and how to overcome them.* Doubleday.

Sambamurthy, V., & Poole, M. S. (1992). The effects of variations in GDSS capabilities on management of cognitive conflict in groups. *Information Systems Research, 3*(3), 224–251.

Schlesinger, A. M. (2002). *A thousand days: John F. Kennedy in the White House.* Houghton Mifflin Harcourt.

Schulz-Hardt, S., Frey, D., Lüthgens, C., & Moscovici, S. (2000). Biased information search in group decision making. *Journal of Personality and Social Psychology, 78*(4), 655.

Smit, J. (2008). *De prooi: blinde trots breekt ABN Amro [The prey: Blind pride destroys ABN Amro].* Prometheus.

Smith, C. M., Tindale, R. S., & Steiner, L. (1998). Investment decisions by individuals and groups insunk cost' situations: The potential impact of shared representations. *Group Processes & Intergroup Relations, 1*(2), 175–189.

Stasser, G. (1992). Information salience and the discovery of hidden profiles by decision-making groups: A "thought experiment". *Organizational Behavior and Human Decision Processes, 52*(1), 156–181.

Stasser, G., Taylor, L. A., & Hanna, C. (1989). Information sampling in structured discussions of three- and six-person groups. *Journal of Personality and Social Psychology, 57*(1), 57–67.

Stasser, G., & Titus, W. (1985). Pooling of unshared information in group decision making: Biased information sampling during discussion. *Journal of Personality and Social Psychology, 48*, 1467–1478.

Stasser, G., & Titus, W. (1987). Effects of information load and percentage of shared information on the dissemination of unshared information during group discussion. *Journal of Personality and Social Psychology, 53*(1), 81–93.

Steinel, W., Utz, S., & Koning, L. (2010). The good, the bad and the ugly thing to do when sharing information: Revealing, concealing and lying depend on social motivation, distribution and importance of information. *Organizational Behavior and Human Decision Processes, 113*(2), 85–96.

Steiner, I. D. (1972). *Group process and productivity.* Academic Press.

Tindale, R. S., & Kameda, T. (2000). 'Social sharedness' as a unifying theme for information processing in groups. *Group Processes & Intergroup Relations, 3*(2), 123–140.

Toma, C., & Butera, F. (2015). Cooperation versus competition effects on information sharing and use in group decision-making. *Social and Personality Psychology Compass, 9*(9), 455–467.

Turner, M. E., & Pratkanis, A. R. (1988). Twenty-five years of groupthink theory and research: Lessons from the evaluation of a theory. *Organizational Behavior and Human Decision Processes, 73*(2–3), 105–115.

Uhl-Bien, M., & Marion, R. (2011). Complexity leadership theory. In A. Bryman, D. Collinson, K. Grint, M. Uhl-Bien, & B. Jackson (Eds.), *The SAGE handbook of leadership* (pp. 468–482). SAGE.

Uhl-Bien, M., Marion, R., & McKelvey, B. (2007). Complexity leadership theory: Shifting leadership from the industrial age to the knowledge era. *The Leadership Quarterly*, *18*(4), 298–318.

Van de Vliert, E., & De Dreu, C. (1994). Optimizing performance by stimulating conflict. *The International Journal of Conflict Management*, *5*.

Van Ginkel, W. P., & Van Knippenberg, D. (2008). Group information elaboration and group decision making: The role of shared task representations. *Organizational Behavior and Human Decision Processes*, *105*(1), 82–97.

Verweij, M., & Thompson, M. (2006). *Clumsy solutions for a complex world: Governance, politics and plural perceptions*. Springer.

Weingart, L. R., Bennett, R. J., & Brett, J. M. (1993). The impact of consideration of issues and motivational orientation on group negotiation process and outcome. *Journal of Applied Psychology*, *78*(3), 504–517.

Whyte, G. (1993). Escalating commitment in individual and group decision making: A prospect theory approach. *Organizational Behavior and Human Decision Processes*, *54*(3), 430–455.

Winquist, J. R., & Larson, J. R., Jr. (1998). Information pooling: When it impacts group decision making. *Journal of Personality and Social Psychology*, *74*(2), 371.

Wittenbaum, G. M., Hubbell, A. P., & Zuckerman, C. (1999). Mutual enhancement: Toward an understanding of the collective preference for shared information. *Journal of Personality and Social Psychology*, *77*(5), 967.

3

INTERVENTIONS TO SUPPORT TEAM DECISIONS

In practice, launching a team decision making process often comes down to organising and running team meetings that follow a predefined agenda guided by a chairperson (Doyle & Straus, 1976; Schwartzman, 1989). In a traditional meeting procedure, the chairperson is responsible for the agenda but typically also has an opinion on the topic under discussion, which requires managing the process and content of the meeting in parallel. Although used very often, it is difficult to find any reference on the benefits or joys of team meetings. Many team members seem to regard meetings as some sort of necessity and then go on to lament about time wasted, the lack of clear conclusions, or the feeling that the more important things were said in the hallway rather than the meeting itself. That being said, well-managed team meetings can be efficient and productive, and there may even be people who enjoy attending them. However, in addressing important decision situations, the usual drawbacks of meetings are likely to become even more apparent. Because team members are likely to have different views and goals regarding the situation of concern, specific meeting procedures must be designed and implemented to both elicit team members' inputs and manage any conflict that may arise.

Procedures to improve systems or processes of any kind are often referred to as *interventions*. The term 'intervention' can mean many different things. For example, intervention is used to describe individual and group therapy (Snijders, 2006), training to enhance teamwork (Lacerenza et al., 2018), medical or technological procedures, the interference of one nation in the affairs of another, and humanitarian aid in disaster or emergency situations. In this book, we reserve the term 'intervention' to describe a structured decision making process comprised of *designed facilitated activities carried out*

DOI: 10.4324/9781003404200-4

in order to help a team achieve its goals. In this context team goals include generating a better and shared understanding of the decision situation, producing a recommendation on how to respond to the situation, or simply making a choice.

An intervention typically requires that team members are drawn from within or across organisations, and act on behalf of the constituencies they represent (e.g. a unit, department, division, organisation). Interventions of this type represent opportunities for entering "into an ongoing system of relationship, to come between or among persons, groups or objects for the purpose of helping them" (Argyris, 1970, p. 15). Our definition of intervention also implies that facilitation plays a critical role in the intervention process. Specifically, a facilitated process is central to encouraging the active participation of team members in discussions, so that a mutual understanding within the team can be achieved. In addition, a facilitated process also plays a critical role in fostering the development of integrative solutions that create a sense of shared responsibility for their implementation (Kaner, 2007).

Throughout an intervention, team members engage in *divergent* and *convergent* thinking processes (cf. Guilford, 1959). Broadly, the former involves a process of generating ideas in a developmental fashion. For example, surfacing team members' different perspectives on the situation of concern requires divergent thinking. This process is also used in articulating the objectives that team members wish to realise in a situation, as well as generating creative and feasible alternatives for action. On the other hand, convergent thinking refers to the process of organising the set of ideas and information generated by divergent thinking, and transforming it into a small set, where the resulting set may consist of ideas of a higher order, ideas typical for a category, or central ideas. Thus, a convergent thinking process will, for instance, consolidate the best ideas into a set of decision options, which would then be evaluated against a prioritised set of objectives. We will discuss further aspects of divergent and convergent processes in Chapter 14.

An important assumption in the intervention literature is that effective team decision making requires both divergent and convergent thinking to take place. Lack of divergence can result in a too-narrow view of the situation under consideration, leading to a premature consensus that can result in inferior decisions. However, lack of convergence may mean that no way forward is identified (Kaner, 2007). In addition, divergent and convergent processes do not follow a linear sequence. Rather, they tend to operate in an iterative fashion, enabling team members to cycle between divergent and convergent thinking. We will discuss further aspects of divergent and convergent processes in Chapter 14.

In this chapter, the notion of intervention to support team decisions is further elaborated. We begin by introducing simple intervention approaches such as debiasing strategies, brainstorming, nominal group technique, clustering, and prioritising, which have been developed to support divergent thinking, convergent thinking, or both. Next, we introduce more advanced interventions suitable for the case in which the communication and processing of information about the situation of concern represents a very difficult challenge, even for prosocial teams with high levels of cognitive motivation (see Chapter 2). These advanced interventions incorporate some or all of the simple interventions procedures and tools and, in addition, make use of formal representations of the situation as a core decision support tool.

3.1   Simple interventions to support team decision making

3.1.1   Debiasing strategies

How can we avoid cognitive biases when making decisions? A number of debiasing strategies have been developed and tested over many years, from simple to more sophisticated ones, with a view to reducing or eliminating biased decisions. The simplest strategies involve raising awareness about the possibility of bias and providing feedback. However, these strategies have yielded minimal success (see, e.g. Alpert & Raiffa, 1982; Fischoff, 1982). More sophisticated strategies aim to help people move away from System 1 thinking and instead engage in System 2 thinking. These fall into three broad categories (Arkes, 1991; Larrick, 2004): *motivational, cognitive,* and *technological.* The motivational approach assumes that people will engage in System 2 thinking if the stakes are high enough. Put differently, the premise is that an individual possesses an appropriate (i.e. normative) strategy for the decision task at hand and will use it when the benefits exceed the costs. Research on using financial incentives as a motivational strategy has produced little empirical evidence that it is effective in reducing bias (Camerer & Hogarth, 1999; Larrick, 2004). By contrast, making people accountable for the process and outcome of their decisions appears to be a more effective motivational strategy. Accountability relies on the motivational effects of perceived social benefits such as making a good impression and avoiding embarrassment. Its impact on various cognitive biases has been tested extensively, with particular success in cases where decision processes and outcomes have to be justified to an audience whose preferences are unknown to the decision maker (Larrick, 2004).

Cognitive strategies can be clustered into two groups. The first group consists of instructions or prompts to 'think harder', 'consider the opposite', or 'use more information'. This approach has produced impressive results in reducing a number of biases including overconfidence (e.g. Walters et al., 2017), availability (e.g. Dubé-Rioux & Russo, 1988), anchoring (e.g. Epley & Gilovich, 2005), and representativeness (e.g. Lee, 2019). Broadly, the strategy involves asking oneself: "What are some reasons that my initial judgment might be wrong?" (Larrick, 2004, p. 323). The strategy is effective because it encourages people to direct their attention to opposite evidence that would not otherwise be considered. Similarly, prompting decision makers to consider alternative hypotheses has been shown to reduce confirmation biases in seeking and evaluating new information (Hirt & Markman, 1995; Lord et al., 1984).

The second group of cognitive strategies involves formal training in basic disciplines such as statistics, economics, and logical reasoning. The use of training is based on the assumption that people often have a rudimentary knowledge about basic statistical, economic, and logical principles, but have difficulty in knowing how and when to apply them (Larrick, 2004). For example, people have been successfully trained to ignore sunk costs (e.g. Larrick et al., 1990), use relevant statistical information (e.g. Fong et al., 1986), and seek disconfirming evidence (e.g. Cheng et al., 1986). Interestingly, there is some evidence showing that people trained in more quantitative disciplines (e.g. economics) as opposed to more qualitative ones (e.g. humanities) are more likely to apply rational norms to avoid biases (Larrick et al., 1990). Evaluation studies of the debiasing effect of training have typically measured impact just after the training. More recently, however, researchers have begun to examine whether the effects of training can lead to enduring changes in people's behaviour and transfers to other situations beyond the specific training environment or context. The emerging picture is encouraging (e.g. Korteling et al., 2021), particularly when training is based on the use of games (e.g. Bessarabova et al., 2016; Dunbar et al., 2014; Lee et al., 2016), but more research is still needed before reaching a final conclusion.

While the aim of the cognitive approach is to improve our mental strategies, the technological approach aims to expand possible strategies to include external support in the form of information presented in various formats, different elicitation protocols, or formal decision aids. For example, it has been shown that an effective technological strategy to reduce biases is to present information as frequencies rather than probabilities (Gigerenzer & Hoffrage, 1995; Sedlmeier, 1999) or in graphical rather than text form (Cook & Smallman, 2008; Ohlert & Weißenberger, 2015; Roy & Lerch, 1996). Similarly, a wide variety of knowledge elicitation techniques have been successfully tested to reduce biases such as overconfidence (e.g. Abbas et al., 2008; Ferretti et al., 2022; Jain et al., 2013). Surprisingly, a notable shortcoming in debiasing research to date is the lack of empirical evidence on whether formal decision technologies such as those developed in the decision and system sciences are effective debiasing tools. We think this is a shortcoming that must be addressed but there is some evidence available. For example, it has been found that people de-escalate commitment to a failing course of action (thus ignoring sunk costs) when they use a decision aid that shows means–ends relations among important factors affecting the situation under consideration. This type of decision aids has also been used to reduce availability and framing biases (Bond et al., 2010; Hodgkinson et al., 1999; Meissner & Wulf, 2013). Clearly, more research is needed in this area.

In conclusion, we have a number of debiasing strategies at our disposal to move away from System 1 thinking and engage in System 2 thinking to avoid falling into the traps discussed in Chapter 1. A notable exception is a debiasing approach that focuses on leveraging System 1 thinking proposed by behavioural science experts Richard Thaler and Cass Sunstein. Rather than helping people to engage in System 2 thinking using the strategies discussed previously, Thaler and Sunstein's approach involves adapting the decision making environment to people's biases so that the chances that they will make wise choices are maximised (Thaler & Sunstein, 2008). For example, the status quo bias creates a preference for default options (Ritov & Baron, 1992), and this insight is used to ensure that the available default is the option that is likely to be best for individuals and/or society (e.g. making enrolment in a retirement savings plan a default option). The approach has been proven to be effective in a number of situations, but it is not without its critics. This is because the 'one-size-fits-all' nature of many defaults could leave some people with an outcome ill-suited to their personal preferences (for a critique, see Smith et al., 2013).

3.1.2 Brainstorming and nominal group technique

The simplest and perhaps most used intervention to support team decisions is *brainstorming*, a well-known approach that encourages divergent thinking within a team. First described by Alex F. Osborn in his book *Applied imagination: Principles and procedures of creative problem-solving* (Osborn, 1957), the aim of brainstorming is to note down all ideas that may be of interest when thinking about the decision situation at hand, in order to prevent missing anything that might be considered important. Brainstorming is expected to counter a number of human tendencies that stifle creativity: a tendency to evaluate (often focused on negative aspects), a focus on habits, self-discouragement, timidity, and so on. In a standard meeting, original ideas often seem unusual or strange, so that the person thinking of them may not even say them out loud. Even when brought up, criticism by others may prevent the idea from being analysed further. Osborn (1957, p. 227) reports applications in several organisations where brainstorming resulted in more and better ideas than were generated using traditional means. The popularity of brainstorming, its claims on effectiveness, and variations on the original approach have inspired over 30 years of empirical research (Stroebe et al., 2010). Further details about how to conduct a brainstorming intervention can be found in Appendix A.

Despite its popularity and apparent benefits, brainstorming as an approach to team decision making has at least two obvious limitations. One relates to the content of the situation of concern, and the other one to the team decision process. Regarding the former, the production of long lists of mostly unconnected ideas does not fully capture the relations between the different elements comprising the situation (i.e. its content). With respect to decision process, brainstorming can make the team suffer process losses (Steiner, 1972). For example, it could cause some team members to engage in unhelpful behaviours such as sit back and wait for others to complete the task ('freeriding'), or stop searching for novel ideas because of the need to attend to what others are saying ('production blocking') (Diehl & Stroebe, 1987; Stroebe et al., 2010).

Research into the effectiveness of brainstorming has led to the development of alternative approaches such as the nominal group technique, or NGT for short (Delbecq et al., 1975). This technique is used with groups comprised of individuals who do not interact, which contrasts with brainstorming in which group members do interact. Appendix A describes how to conduct the NGT. Research into brainstorming shows that the number and quality of ideas generated in an interacting group are lower than in an NGT group. Research studies have examined three alternative explanations for this finding. The first is social inhibition: the fact that the presence of others inhibits airing of new ideas. Second is social loafing: not participating in the generation of ideas because you expect that others are doing the work anyway. Third is production blocking. Since, in a group setting, typically only one person speaks at a time, others are forced to wait while trying to remember their contributions. While they are remembering their ideas, they cannot at the same time think of new ideas. Further research eventually showed that production blocking explained most of the difference between brainstorming and NGT groups (Diehl & Stroebe, 1987; Stroebe et al., 2010).

Both brainstorming and NGT can be implemented using traditional means such as whiteboards, flipcharts, and pens. Alternatively, they can be used in a computer-supported environment (e.g. Nunamaker et al., 1991). Computers have been used to support team decision making since at least the 1980s (DeSanctis & Gallupe, 1987). This support is in the form of a computer-based group decision support system (GDSS), defined as "a set of software components, hardware components, language components, and procedures that support a group of people engaged in decision-related meetings" (1984, p. 197).[1]

When a computer-based GDSS is used to support a face-to-face team meeting, members will gather in a so-called group decision room. This room contains a series of networked computers arranged in a U-shape. Every team member is seated behind a computer and faces a projection screen. The GDSS software enables the meeting leader to send out questions to the individual computers, collect and project answers on both a central screen and team members' personal screens, and categorise and prioritise ideas in various ways. Team members contribute to the meeting largely by typing in responses to questions on their computer screen.

While in most applications, team members gather in one place at the same time, a computer-based GDSS may also support meetings in which team members come together in different places and at different times. GDSS technology allows meeting participants to log on to a meeting from their own workspace. Communication via computers has a number of additional benefits. In a traditional face-to-face meeting, team members have to wait to make a contribution until others finish speaking. By contrast, in a GDSS meeting everyone is able to work in parallel. Contributions can be made anonymously, which increases the chance that sensitive issues are brought to the table. Finally, computer-based GDSSs such as GroupSystems[2] or MeetingSphere[3] make a report of the session immediately available. The fact that a computer-based GDSS enables parallel work, anonymity and fast reporting may increase the productivity of meetings in comparison to traditional brainstorms.

3.1.3   Clustering and prioritising

Few sessions end after a brainstorm, with dozens of ideas in an unstructured list. Usually, the team wants to organise their ideas in some way, by grouping similar ideas together, by identifying central ideas, or by choosing the most important or effective ideas. In this section, we present basic approaches for convergence and prioritisation.

Decision making teams usually have a natural need to go from divergence to convergence. Brainstorming, NGT, and other methods supporting divergence result in a multitude of ideas. The output of this creative phase may look like chaos to some participants in the team process, but a broad understanding of the problem at hand is needed to prevent too narrow of a focus. Divergence prevents potential problems discussed in the previous chapters, such as the framing error or anchoring bias. The creative, divergent phase is usually followed by a phase of convergence. Approaches to convergence range from formal to more informal methods. Taxonomies are on the formal end and use formal rules to place concepts into a category. They 'categorize phenomena into mutually exclusive and exhaustive sets with a series of discrete decision rules' (Doty & Glick, 1994, p. 232). Typologies, while still formal, are developed using less strict rules and represent ideal types. Each ideal type is a unique combination of characteristics. An example is Porter's (1985) typology of organisational types that maximise competitive advantage.

A more informal approach to categorisation is clustering, which is essentially grouping similar ideas. Clustering can be used to report results, and with participants in a session. Convergence tasks can be supported by the computer-based GDSS discussed earlier.

Finally, after divergence and convergence, decision making teams often wish to prioritise results in one way or another. Prioritisation is in essence ordering ideas on a single criterion, such as importance, feasibility, urgency, effort, and so forth.[4] As with divergent and convergent tasks, prioritisation tasks can also be supported by GDSS. Consequently, these computer based systems can support the team during the entire decision making process, from ideas to recommendations on actions. Some simple prioritisation approaches are further discussed in Appendix A.

3.2   Advanced interventions to support team decisions

Consider the following situation. In the Dutch criminal justice chain, crimes investigated by the police end up as case reports on a public prosecutor's desk, leading to a suspect being brought before a judge in court. If the suspect is found guilty, they are sentenced to pay a fine, spend time in prison or perform community services. During much of the late 1990s, the Dutch prison services were faced with a shortage of prison capacity. In 2000, prisoners serving time for less serious crimes, and who had completed 90% of their sentence, were made eligible for early release. Three years later this figure was decreased to 70%. This dramatically increased the number of prisoners released: from a total of 200 prisoners released early in 2000, to 446 in 2001, and then 4,837 in 2002 (Dienst Justitiële Inrichtingen, 2002). This policy of early release was successful in solving the problem of prison capacity shortage. However, it also created problems elsewhere in the Dutch criminal justice chain. Judges noted that several people they had recently convicted and imprisoned for an earlier crime were reappearing in their court. They recognized some suspects as individuals they had seen earlier and who in fact should still be serving their sentences. Judges then became concerned that sentences passed for earlier crimes were not served to completion. To compensate, they started to pass longer sentences to both old and new offenders. The short term effect of the judges' actions was to increase the demand for prison capacity, going directly against the goal of the prison services' early release policy.

The above case is a typical illustration of a complex situation in which there are multiple interconnected problems that need to be managed (Ackoff, 1974, 1981). One reason why complex situations are challenging is because decisions about a problem that is only a part of the situation cannot be made without considering the other problems in that situation. Put differently, local solutions to a particular problem tend to generate problems elsewhere, as illustrated in the Dutch prison case. Indeed, the interconnectedness between the different problems in a situation makes complex situations systemic and thus particularly challenging. Complex situations can also exhibit high levels of uncertainty. In the Dutch prison services case, future levels of crime can never be predicted with complete certainty. In addition, the services did not foresee the reaction of the judges to their early release policy, nor length of sentences and the speed at which they would be given. What is clear is that the Dutch prison services focused on one part of the situation (shortage of prison capacity), while the judges attended to another (sentences served to completion). This example only covers two of the central stakeholders in the justice system, which as mentioned, spans police, public prosecution, judiciary, and prison services. A decision of any of these stakeholders will likely affect all others. Much like a ball of wool, pulling on one strand will bring with it the entire ball. Furthermore, the uncertainty of stakeholders' responses to any such attempt makes it impossible to guarantee that the intended impact is fully realised.

Here is another example showing the impact of stakeholders' actions in situations that appear simple, but are in fact complex. In discussing the lessons to be learned from the attempted takeover of ABN Amro, the Dutch government considered several actions aimed at preventing major banks from getting into problems again (Smit, 2008). One issue was the high salaries paid out to the banks' top managers. A measure thought to be effective in lowering excessive salaries was to force Dutch financial institutions to make the salaries of their top managers public. This was expected to lead to the naming and shaming of those perceived to be receiving disproportionate salaries and thus create pressure for change. While this did happen, the now-publicly available information enabled managers to learn about how much their peers were earning at competing institutions. In at least one bank, a manager who found himself in the lower range of salaries was offered a higher salary by his human resources department. Their justification was that the bank needed to be seen as paying competitive salaries. We can see here that something perceived as a well-defined problem situation (top managers' salaries are too high) was messier than the Dutch government initially thought, because there were many stakeholders involved in the situation, each with different perspectives, goals and power. For a bank's human resource manager, salaries and the bank's competitive position are interdependent. Other banks adopted a similar policy of increasing salaries. Thus the act of making salaries public set in motion a series of unanticipated and interconnected effects, increasing salaries year after year instead of lowering them!

To summarise, there are situations in which a number of interacting problems interact, diverse stakeholders are involved, and where stakeholders' responses cannot be anticipated. These features make it difficult for the team to choose where to focus their decision making efforts. And even if a clear focus is set, attempts to improve the situation may produce unintended results due to uncertainty around developments in the situation, or the actions and reactions of other parties (Nutt, 2002). So, how can we maximise the chances of a team successfully tackling these complex situations?

There is an extensive management literature that approaches team decision making in complex situations as the domain of leadership (Bratton et al., 2004; Grint, 2005, 2010; Heifetz, 1994; Heifetz & Laurie, 2001; Uhl-Bien & Marion, 2011; Uhl-Bien et al., 2007; Verweij & Thompson, 2006). Specifically, most authors in this area highlight that successful leaders in complex situations facilitate a collaborative team decision making process involving key stakeholders, and ask the kind of questions that open up useful ways to make progress in a complex situation. However, note that these prescriptions rest on the important assumption that the leader will be able to foster high levels of cognitive motivation and prosocial behaviours within the team. Yet people faced with a complex situation may or may not have high levels of cognitive motivation, which can lead to strong disagreements about how to address the situation (Jehn & Mannix, 2001). Complex situations are also typically associated with competing perspectives and interests of team members, which in turn can trigger proself rather prosocial behaviours.

Management and decision scientists have long argued that successful team decision making in situations such as the ones described earlier require a thorough understanding of the issues and goals pertaining to the decision making situation, and of the relationships between these issues and goals (e.g. Eden & Ackermann, 2010). Research shows that this is often achieved through the creation and use of an external and explicit representation of the situation – a 'model' (Pidd, 2010) – as seen by team members. The model is built by the team, with or without the assistance of modelling experts or computer support, and its content typically includes team members' knowledge, frames, assumptions, goals, and expectations about the situation. This can refer to, elements of its past, present, and perceived future, or its desired or ideal state.

Model content is organised in particular ways in order to increase team members' motivation to engage in systematic and deep processing of information about the situation of concern (i.e. to increase their cognitive motivation). Furthermore, because a model is an external and explicit representation of the situation as perceived by team members, the model will not only surface a diversity of information but also interests within the team. Thus, disagreements and conflict about knowledge claims, facts, and values pertaining to the situation will often emerge (Kaplan, 2008). Furthermore, the levels of affective conflict that the team might experience when using models will be contingent on the asymmetry of interests and within the team.[5] Thus, models to support team decision making must be built and implemented using a process that enables both deep information processing and, at the same time, the effective management of conflict.

In this book, our focus is thus on interventions that are *model-driven* (Morton et al., 2003; Rouwette & Franco, 2021), that is, interventions designed to support team decision making in situations of varied complexity and uncertainty, and where the construction and use of models is a core element. A model-driven intervention approach offers specific guidelines for managing model content as well as the interaction process between team members. Models are the core intervention tool through which a wide variety of facts and judgments are captured and integrated; the process guidelines act as a facilitative mechanism intended to help team members work towards a collective solution while dealing with conflict in a constructive manner.

In Part II, we will provide an overview of a selected sample of model-driven intervention approaches. We had three considerations in selecting this particular set of interventions. First, we chose approaches aligned with the notion of facilitated modelling developed within the discipline of operational research, namely, interventions in which a facilitated process is used to construct and analyse models 'on-the-spot' (Franco & Montibeller, 2010, 2011). The second consideration was accessibility, that is, we chose approaches that would-be intervention practitioners could use by themselves without having to buy specific software or equipment.[6] Our final consideration was to choose interventions with a substantive body of research evidence regarding their practical use and effectiveness. Below, we briefly introduce our chosen approaches, in no particular order.

3.2.1   Group model building

The *group model building* approach was developed primarily for examining the performance of a 'system' by looking at the system's past behaviour (Vennix, 1996). The system under study is one that encapsulates the issue or problem that needs to be understood. A visual model of the system is built with the relevant stakeholders and used as a learning tool to explain past performance by separating causes from symptoms. The model also serves as a visual memory of the team's discussions and can be further developed into a form that is amenable to quantitative analyses via computer-based simulations.

3.2.2   Group causal mapping

Developed within the 'soft' operational research tradition (Ackermann, 2012; Rosenhead & Mingers, 2001), *group causal mapping* is an intervention approach that supports exploration of the complexity of the issues constituting the entire decision space as perceived by the team[7] (Bryson et al., 2004). By closely examining means–ends relationships between issues that demand attention from the perspective of team members, implied goals and options emerge during team discussions, which then inform the prioritisation of issues, goals, and subsequently, actions. The approach can be undertaken with basic and computer-supported technology.

3.2.3 Decision conferencing

Belonging to the family of multi-criteria decision analysis (MCDA) approaches (Belton & Stewart, 2002), *decision conferencing* is an intervention approach concerned with the evaluation of options against multiple decision criteria (Phillips, 2007; Phillips & Bana e Costa, 2007). The approach involves a process of structuring the objectives, options, preferences, and trade-offs that are relevant to the decision situation at hand. Decision conferencing is associated with the facilitated modelling approach (Franco & Montibeller, 2010) in general, and with the value-focused thinking approach in particular (Keeney, 1996), and can be deployed with simple computer-based technology (e.g. spreadsheets).

3.2.4 Participatory scenario development

The term 'scenario planning' encompasses a family of intervention approaches designed to improve the understanding of a current situation by exploring possible alternative futures that are pertinent to how the situation is tackled now (Van der Heijden et al., 2002). *Participatory scenario development* starts by eliciting ideas and data about the future from team members, and then integrating the collated information into one or more narratives.[8] Different possible futures, or scenarios, are captured in these narratives. For example, one narrative might be a story covering a day in the life of a person ten years from now. Team members can then place themselves in the scenarios to gain a better appreciation of what seems appropriate in terms of actions that can be taken in the present.

All the approaches above represent alternative ways of dealing with situation-relevant information. Teams that use group model building and group causal mapping spend most of their time clarifying the causal relations between different aspects of the situation of concern. Participatory scenario development approaches structure information in another way, by writing a story on what a future world would look like. Decision conferencing also looks at the future, but not as a possible context that we might find ourselves in, but as the anticipated consequences of decisions we might make now.

The four approaches covered in this book can be, and have been, combined in practice. For example, decision conferencing is often used together with group causal mapping (e.g. Bana e Costa et al., 1999; Franco & Lord, 2011; Franco & Montibeller, 2011b). In addition, participatory scenario development has been supported by group model building and decision conferencing interventions (e.g. Montibeller et al., 2006; Strohhecker, 2005). Furthermore, some forms of brainstorming, NGT, clustering and voting are typically deployed within all the four approaches. Despite this flexibility, in this book we describe each intervention approach in isolation from the rest.

Our reason for doing so is that every single approach constitutes a complex set of theoretical foundations, step-by-step procedures and particular ways to guide the team decision making process. Therefore, we think that understanding and building experience with each of these approaches separately is easiest when practising them for the first time. For a would-be intervention practitioner, the lack of familiarity with team members or their domain-specific knowledge, the conflicts that can arise during team discussions and the need to simultaneously manage both process and content poses enormous demands. In addition, the more advanced use of approaches, in challenging circumstances or with a more complex intervention process resulting from combining methods is, in our opinion, best tried after some experience with more simple situations has been gained.

In the next eight chapters, we will describe the four model-driven intervention approaches in more detail. In the last section of the book, we will assess whether model-driven interventions do a good job in practice, and if so, why.

Notes

1. Whilst many scholars reserve the term 'group decision support system' to refer to decision environments that are computer-based, other scholars (mostly in Europe) use the term also to include decision support environments that do not use computers (Eden, 1992; Eden & Radford, 1990).
2. *GroupSystems* was originally developed by a team of researchers led by Jay Nunamaker at the University of Arizona.
3. MeetingSphere is a facilitation software that has been transformed into a virtual facilitation tool called Xleap (visit www.xleap.net).
4. More sophisticated prioritisation approaches involve the use of a set of criteria (see Chapter 10).
5. When the situation to be addressed is perceived as complex, then interest asymmetry is likely to be at its highest level within the team.
6. Some of the model-driven intervention approaches covered in this book have the option of using specific software and equipment.
7. Group causal mapping is also referred to by its original name, *strategic options development and analysis* (Ackermann & Eden, 2010). The approach has been further developed into a comprehensive strategy making methodology called *journey making* (Ackermann & Eden, 2011).
8. Narratives are models in the sense that they depict the relationships between factors pertaining to a particular future, as well as their consequences. The format of these narratives is typically text-based, although some scenario planning approaches express the narratives visually as a cause-and-effect network (Cairns & Wright, 2017; Wright & Cairns, 2011).

References

Abbas, A., E., Budescu, D. V., Yu, H.-T., & Haggerty, R. (2008). A comparison of two probability encoding methods: Fixed probability vs. fixed variable values. *Decision Analysis*, 5(4), 190–202. https://doi.org/10.1287/deca.1080.0126

Ackermann, F. (2012). Problem structuring methods 'in the dock': Arguing the case for Soft OR. *European Journal of Operational Research*, 219(3), 652–658.

Ackermann, F., & Eden, C. (2010). Strategic options development and analysis. In M. Reynolds & S. Holwell (Eds.), *Systems approaches to managing change: A practical guide* (pp. 135–190). Springer.

Ackermann, F., & Eden, C. (2011). *Making strategy: Mapping out strategic success.* SAGE.

Alpert, M., & Raiffa, H. (1982). A progress report on the training of probability assessors. In D. Kahneman, P. Slovic, & A. Tversky (Eds.), *Judgment under uncertainty: Heuristics and biases* (pp. 294–305). Cambridge University Press.

Argyris, C. (1970). *Intervention theory and method: A behavioral science view.* Addison Wesley.

Arkes, H. R. (1991). Costs and benefits of judgment errors: Implications for debiasing. *Psychological Bulletin, 110*(3), 486.

Bana e Costa, C. A., Ensslin, L., Correa, E. C., & Vansnick, J. C. (1999). Decision support systems in action: Integrated application in a multi-criteria aid process. *European Journal of Operational Research, 113*(2), 315–335.

Belton, V., & Stewart, T. (2002). *Multiple criteria decision analysis: An integrated approach.* Kluwer Academic Publishers.

Bessarabova, E., Piercy, C. W., King, S., Vincent, C., Dunbar, N. E., Burgoon, J. K., Miller, C. H., Jensen, M., Elkins, A., & Wilson, D. W. (2016). Mitigating bias blind spot via a serious video game. *Computers in Human Behavior, 62*, 452–466.

Bond, S. D., Carlson, K. A., & Keeney, R. L. (2010). Improving the generation of decision objectives. *Decision Analysis, 7*(3), 238–255.

Bryson, J. M., Ackermann, F., Eden, C., & Finn, C. B. (2004). *Visible thinking: Unlocking causal mapping for practical business results.* Wiley.

Cairns, G., & Wright, G. (2017). *Scenario thinking: Preparing your organization for the future in an unpredictable world.* Springer.

Camerer, C. F., & Hogarth, R. M. (1999). The effects of financial incentives in experiments: A review and capital-labor-production framework. *Journal of Risk and Uncertainty, 19*(1), 7–42.

Cheng, P. W., Holyoak, K. J., Nisbett, R. E., & Oliver, L. M. (1986). Pragmatic versus syntactic approaches to training deductive reasoning. *Cognitive Psychology, 18*(3), 293–328.

Cook, M. B., & Smallman, H. S. (2008). Human factors of the confirmation bias in intelligence analysis: Decision support from graphical evidence landscapes. *Human Factors, 50*(5), 745–754. https://doi.org/10.1518/001872008x354183

Delbecq, A., Van de Ven, A., & Gustafson, G. (1975). *Group techniques for program planning: A guide to nominal group and Delphi processes.* Scott, Foresman and Co.

DeSanctis, G., & Gallupe, R. B. (1987). A foundation for the study of group decision support systems. *Management Science, 33*(5), 589–609.

Diehl, M., & Stroebe, W. (1987). Productivity loss in brainstorming groups: Toward the solution of a riddle. *Journal of Personality and Social Psychology, 53*(3), 497.

Doty, D. H., & Glick, W. H. (1994). Typologies as a unique form of theory building: Toward improved understanding and modeling. *Academy of Management Review, 19*(2), 230–251.

Doyle, M., & Straus, D. (1976). *How to make meetings work.* Jove Books.

Dubé-Rioux, L., & Russo, J. E. (1988). An availability bias in professional judgment. *Journal of Behavioral Decision Making, 1*(4), 223–237.

Dunbar, N. E., Miller, C. H., Adame, B. J., Elizondo, J., Wilson, S. N., Lane, B. L., Kauffman, A. A., Bessarabova, E., Jensen, M. L., Straub, S. K., Lee, Y.-H., Burgoon, J. K., Valacich, J. J., Jenkins, J., & Zhang, J. (2014). Implicit and explicit training in the mitigation of cognitive bias through the use of a serious game. *Computers in Human Behavior*, *37*, 307–318. https://doi.org/10.1016/j.chb.2014.04.053

Eden, C. (1992). A framework for thinking about group decision support systems (GDSS). *Group Decision and Negotiation*, *1*, 199–218.

Eden, C., & Ackermann, F. (2010). Decision making in groups: Theory and practice. In P. C. Nutt & D. C. Wilson (Eds.), *Handbook of decision making* (pp. 231–272). Wiley-Blackwell.

Eden, C., & Radford, J. (1990). *Tackling strategic problems: The role of group decision support*. SAGE.

Epley, N., & Gilovich, T. (2005). When effortful thinking influences judgmental anchoring: Differential effects of forewarning and incentives on self-generated and externally provided anchors. *Journal of Behavioral Decision Making*, *18*(3), 199–212.

Ferretti, V., Montibeller, G., & von Winterfeldt, D. (2022). Testing the effectiveness of debiasing techniques to reduce overprecision in the elicitation of subjective continuous probability distributions. *European Journal of Operational Research*, *304*(2), 661–675.

Fischoff, B. (1982). Debiasing. In D. Kahneman, P. Slovic, & A. Tversky (Eds.), *Judgment under uncertainty: Heuristics and biases* (pp. 422–444). Cambridge University Press. https://doi.org/10.1017/CBO9780511809477.032

Fong, G. T., Krantz, D. H., & Nisbett, R. E. (1986). The effects of statistical training on thinking about everyday problems. *Cognitive Psychology*, *18*(3), 253–292. https://doi.org/10.1016/0010-0285(86)90001-0

Franco, L. A., & Lord, E. (2011). Understanding multi-methodology: Evaluating the perceived impact of mixing methods for group budgetary decisions. *Omega*, *39*, 362–372.

Franco, L. A., & Montibeller, G. (2010). Facilitated modelling in operational research (invited review). *European Journal of Operational Research*, *205*(3), 489–500.

Franco, L. A., & Montibeller, G. (2011a). 'On-the-spot' modelling and analysis: The facilitated modelling approach. In J. J. Cochran, L. A. Cox Jr, P. Keskinocak, J. P. Kharoufeh, & J. C. Smith (Eds.), *Wiley encyclopedia of operations research and management science*. Wiley.

Franco, L. A., & Montibeller, G. (2011b). Problem structuring for multi-criteria decision analysis interventions. In J. J. Cochran, L. A. Cox Jr, P. Keskinocak, J. P. Kharoufeh, & J. C. Smith (Eds.), *Wiley encyclopedia of operations research and management science*. Wiley.

Gigerenzer, G., & Hoffrage, U. (1995). How to improve Bayesian reasoning without instruction: Frequency formats. *Psychological Review*, *102*(4), 684.

Guilford, J. P. (1959). Three faces of intellect. *American Psychologist*, *14*(8), 469–479.

Hirt, E. R., & Markman, K. D. (1995). Multiple explanation: A consider-an-alternative strategy for debiasing judgments. *Journal of Personality and Social Psychology*, *69*(6), 1069–1086.

Hodgkinson, G. P., Brown, N. J., Maule, A. J., Glaister, K. W., & Pearman, A. D. (1999). Breaking the frame: An analysis of strategic cognition and decision making under uncertainty. *Strategic Management Journal*, *20*(10), 977–985.

Huber, G. (1984). Issues in the design of group decision support systems. *MIS Quarterly*, *8*, 195–204.

Jain, K., Mukherjee, K., Bearden, J. N., & Gaba, A. (2013). Unpacking the future: A nudge toward wider subjective confidence intervals. *Management Science*, *59*(9), 1970–1987. https://doi.org/10.1287/mnsc.1120.1696

Kaner, S. (2007). *Facilitator's guide to participatory decision making* (2nd ed.). Jossey-Bass.

Kaplan, S. (2008). Framing contests: Strategy making under uncertainty. *Organization Science*, *19*(5), 729–752.

Keeney, R. L. (1996). Value-focused thinking: Identifying decision opportunities and creating alternatives. *European Journal of Operational Research*, *92*(3), 537–549.

Korteling, J., Gerritsma, J. Y., & Toet, A. (2021). Retention and transfer of cognitive bias mitigation interventions: A systematic literature study. *Frontiers in Psychology*, 3402.

Lacerenza, C. N., Marlow, S. L., Tannenbaum, S. I., & Salas, E. (2018). Team development interventions: Evidence-based approaches for improving teamwork. *American Psychologist*, *73*(4), 517.

Larrick, R. P. (2004). Debiasing. In P. Simon & M. De Laplace (Eds.), *Blackwell handbook of judgment and decision making* (p. 316). Wiley.

Larrick, R. P., Morgan, J. N., & Nisbett, R. E. (1990). Teaching the use of cost-benefit reasoning in everyday life. *Psychological Science*, *1*(6), 362–370.

Lee, K. K. (2019). An indirect debiasing method: Priming a target attribute reduces judgmental biases in likelihood estimations. *PLoS One*, *14*(3), e0212609.

Lee, Y. H., Dunbar, N. E., Miller, C. H., Lane, B. L., Jensen, M. L., Bessarabova, E., Burgoon, J. K., Adame, B. J., Valacich, J. J., Adame, E. A., Bostwick, E., Piercy, C. W., Elizondo, J., & Wilson, S. N. (2016). Training anchoring and representativeness: Bias mitigation through a digital game. *Simulation & Gaming*, *47*(6), 751–779. https://doi.org/10.1177/1046878116662955

Lord, C. G., Lepper, M. R., & Preston, E. (1984). Considering the opposite: A corrective strategy for social judgment. *Journal of Personality and Social Psychology*, *47*(6), 1231.

Meissner, P., & Wulf, T. (2013). Cognitive benefits of scenario planning: Its impact on biases and decision quality. *Technological Forecasting and Social Change*, *80*(4), 801–814.

Montibeller, G., Gummer, H., & Tumidei, D. (2006). Combining scenario planning and multi-criteria decision analysis in practice. *Journal of Multi-Criteria Decision Analysis*, *14*(1–3), 5–20.

Morton, A., Ackermann, F., & Belton, V. (2003). Technology-driven and model-driven approaches to group decision support. Focus, research philosophy, and key concepts. *European Journal of Information Systems*, *12*(2), 110–126.

Nunamaker, J., Dennis, A., Valacich, J., Vogel, D., & George, J. (1991). Electronic meeting systems to support group work. *Communications of the ACM*, *34*(7), 40–61.

Ohlert, C. R., & Weißenberger, B. E. (2015). Beating the base-rate fallacy: An experimental approach on the effectiveness of different information presentation formats. *Journal of Management Control*, *26*(1), 51–80.

Osborn, A. F. (1957). *Applied Imagination: Principles and procedures of creative problem-solving*. Charles Scribner's Sons.

Phillips, L. D. (2007). Decision conferencing. In W. Edwards, R. Miles Jr, & D. von Winterfeldt (Eds.), *Advances in decision analysis: From foundations to applications* (pp. 375–399). Cambridge University Press.

Phillips, L. D., & Bana e Costa, C. A. (2007). Transparent prioritisation, budgeting and resource allocation with multi-criteria decision analysis and decision conferencing. *Annals of Operations Research*, 154(1), 51–68. https://doi.org/10.1007/s10479-007-0183-3

Pidd, M. (2010). Why modelling and model use matter. *Journal of the Operational Research Society*, 61(1), 14–24.

Porter, M. E. (1985). *Competitive advantage: Creating and sustaining superior performance*. Free Press.

Ritov, I., & Baron, J. (1992). Status-quo and omission biases. *Journal of Risk and Uncertainty*, 5(1), 49–61.

Rosenhead, J., & Mingers, J. (Eds.). (2001). *Rational analysis for a problematic world revisited: Problem structuring methods for complexity, uncertainty and conflict*. Wiley.

Rouwette, E. A. J. A., & Franco, L. A. (2021). Technologies for improving group decision making. In S. J. Beck, J. Keyton, & M. S. Poole (Eds.), *The Emerald handbook of group and team communication research* (pp. 209–228). Emerald Publishing Limited. https://doi.org/10.1108/978-1-80043-500-120211014

Roy, M. C., & Lerch, F. J. (1996). Overcoming ineffective mental representations in base-rate problems. *Information Systems Research*, 7(2), 233–247.

Schwartzman, H. B. (1989). *The meeting: Gatherings in organizations and communities*. Plenum.

Sedlmeier, P. (1999). *Improving statistical reasoning: Theoretical models and practical implications*. Psychology Press.

Smith, N. C., Goldstein, D. G., & Johnson, E. J. (2013). Choice without awareness: Ethical and policy implications of defaults. *Journal of Public Policy & Marketing*, 32(2), 159–172.

Snijders, J. A. (2006). *Interventies in behandelgroepen [Interventions in treatment groups]*. Bohn Stafleu van Loghum.

Steiner, I. D. (1972). *Group process and productivity*. Academic Press.

Stroebe, W., Nijstad, B. A., & Rietzschel, E. (2010). Beyond productivity loss in brainstorming groups: The evolution of a question. *Advances in Experimental Social Psychology*, 43, 157–203.

Strohhecker, J. (2005). Scenarios and simulations for planning Dresdner Bank's E-day. *System Dynamics Review: The Journal of the System Dynamics Society*, 21(1), 5–32.

Thaler, R. H., & Sunstein, C. R. (2008). *Nudge: Improving decisions about health, wealth and happiness*. Yale University Press.

Van der Heijden, K., Bradfield, R., Burt, G., Cairns, G., & Wright, G. (2002). *The sixth sense: Accelerating organizational learning with scenarios*. Wiley.

Vennix, J. A. M. (1996). *Group model building. Facilitating team learning using system dynamics*. Wiley.

Walters, D. J., Fernbach, P. M., Fox, C. R., & Sloman, S. A. (2017). Known Unknowns: A critical determinant of confidence and calibration. *Management Science*, 63(12), 4298–4307. https://doi.org/10.1287/mnsc.2016.2580

Wright, G., & Cairns, G. (2011). *Scenario thinking: Practical approaches to the future*. Palgrave Macmillan.

PART II

An overview of selected interventions

Preface

In this part, we describe a set of distinct intervention approaches developed to support teams facing decision situations of varied complexity. There are so many intervention approaches to support team decision making that we had to be selective. In this book, we are considering intervention approaches that use a model or external representation of the situation of interest, as seen by team members, that is, we are concerned with model-driven interventions.

The four intervention approaches will be presented in pairs of chapters. The first of the pair will describe the approach using the framework shown in the following table.

Background	The origin, main assumptions, and theoretical concepts that inform and justify an intervention's procedures, techniques and tools
Procedure, technique and tool	Procedure: a structured set of activity guidelines to assist people in undertaking a particular intervention Technique: a specific activity that has a clear and well-defined purpose within the context of a procedure Tool: an object used to facilitate the application of a technique (e.g. flipcharts, software); or the outcome of applying a technique (e.g. a model; a ranking of options)
Versions	Alternative forms of the approach reported in the relevant literature
Applications	Summary evidence of use

DOI: 10.4324/9781003404200-5

The second chapter in each pair will describe a practical application. These chapters first sketch the background and central issue in the case. The steps followed by the team are then described. They shows how the intervention approach outlined in the previous chapter is put into practice. Two types of results are then described: first the visible product, in the form of workbooks and final reports describing models and other analytical tools. The final section covers the less visible products, such as reactions and insights, which form the basis for implementation and results achieved. In our case descriptions, we tried to capture the realities of intervention practice, instead of offering a sanitised version that is neat and successful. In our view, the former is more helpful than the latter to someone seeking to understand what intervention approaches do and accomplish.

4

GROUP MODEL BUILDING

Understanding complex behaviour

This chapter describes group model building, an approach that supports decision making by guiding team members through a process of joint model construction. The starting point for the intervention is a problem expressed in a graph over time. This can for instance be a graph showing how greenhouse gases in the atmosphere increased or a company's revenues decreased over the last profits over the last years. Team members start building the model by generating a list of problem elements and then iteratively build the model, one element at a time. Before a new element is added to the model, the facilitator checks for the team's agreement. Group model building uses a particular approach to modelling: system dynamics. System dynamics originated as a quantitative, formal modelling approach and has since developed a strand of qualitative, conceptual modelling as well. In the section on procedure later, we sketch the qualitative version of group model building. The quantitative mode is introduced in the section on (alternative) versions.

4.1 Background

Group model building is a facilitated modelling method that has its origins in system dynamics. System dynamics is a simulation approach that stems from the work of Jay Forrester at MIT in the 1950s. He started out by applying system dynamics to the study of industrial organisations, initially referring to his new approach as industrial dynamics and only later adopting the broader name of system dynamics. Forrester's later applications included topics such as urban growth, markets, world dynamics, and national economies. Since the 1950s the use of the method quickly spread to other institutes and application areas. System dynamics conferences have been held annually since

DOI: 10.4324/9781003404200-6

1985 and attract researchers, consultants, and practitioners from all over the world, working on topics in diverse fields such as management, economics, health policy, sustainability, biophysical systems, psychology, and sociology, among others. In these applications, Forrester's original focus on the interaction between problem elements, instead of singling out separate elements, is still evident. Forrester's early description of the field can be generalised to the wide range of present-day applications.

> Industrial dynamics is a way of studying the behaviour of industrial systems to show how policies, decisions, structure, and delays are interrelated to influence growth and stability. It integrates the separate functional areas of management – marketing, investment, research, personnel, production, and accounting.
>
> *(Forrester, 1961, p. vii)*

In a similar fashion, a recent application of system dynamics to understand Alzheimer's disease (Uleman et al., 2021) integrates brain, physical, and psychosocial domains.

A basic premise of system dynamics is therefore that the characteristics of the whole are more important than the characteristics of individual parts. The behaviour of a system follows from the interaction between its elements, or in other words: 'structure drives behaviour' (Richardson & Pugh, 1981; Vennix, 1996). This implies that everything essential for the causes and symptoms of the particular behaviour being explored is included in the model (Forrester, 1975). When studying a social system, this means the modeller needs to think carefully about two questions: what drives decisions of actors in the system and what are the consequences of decisions? At first sight, the answers to these questions may seem obvious. A decision is driven by a problem, and the result of the decision is that the problem is solved. Imagine a shop owner who wants to keep her inventory up to a certain level. Once she realises the number of items in stock is below the desired level, she orders new items. After some time, these arrive and the problem is solved. What this simple example shows is that time plays a central role in decision making: it takes time before new items are received and added to the inventory. The shop owner knows this and takes this into account in her decisions. What the shop owner does not do is to compare actual inventory to desired inventory every day and order the difference, as this does not take into account orders that are already placed and would lead to excess inventory. Another way of saying this is that it is often too simple to think of drivers causing decisions, decisions leading to consequences, and then the problem is dealt with (Forrester, 1992). Drivers, decisions, and consequences are not linked in a linear, open fashion, but in a closed feedback loop. Figure 4.1 shows how the gap

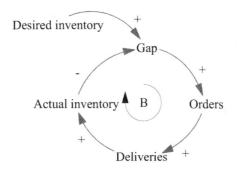

FIGURE 4.1   Example negative (balancing) feedback loop.

between desired and actual inventory is the basis for the shop owner's orders. Eventually, these result in deliveries, which are added to the inventory, and in turn impact the gap.

If the gap is then reduced to zero, the process would end there, but the example can be made more realistic in a number of ways. Inventory is depleted by sales to customers, meaning a gap is created, orders are placed again, and so on. Typically, ordering is not a one-off decision but a continuous process or policy. Figure 4.1 shows a qualitative system dynamics model in the form of a causal loop diagram. The concepts in the diagrams are variables: entities that can change over time. These are connected by arrows that refer to two types of influence of one variable on another. A positive relation means that if the variable at the tail (the cause) changes, the variable at the head (the effect) changes in the same direction. An increase will lead to an increase, and a decrease to a decrease. A negative relation means that variables change in opposite directions: an increase in the cause leads to a decrease in the effect; a decrease leads to an increase. Relations can combine to form feedback loops, meaning that if we start anywhere in the loop and trace the effects we arrive at the starting variable again.

> The essence of the concept . . . is a circle of interactions, a closed loop of action and information. The patterns of behavior of any two variables in such a closed loop are linked, each influencing, and in turn responding to the behavior of the other.
>
> *(Richardson, 1991, p. 1)*

When system dynamicists refer to 'structure', they mean the interactions between variables such as shown in Figure 4.1. Feedback loops are an important element of this structure. 'Dynamics' or 'behaviour' of a system refers to the change of one or more variables over time.

Forrester (1975) noted the importance of feedback for decisions and system behaviour in the early days of exploring dynamic systems. Actors use the information about the value of particular variables (such as the gap between desired and actual inventory in the example before) as input to their decisions and by implementing their decision influence system behaviour. In the negative or balancing loop in Figure 4.1, a change in any variable 'travels' around the loop and eventually results in a change in the original variable in the opposite direction. The loop therefore tends towards stability. In contrast, a positive or reinforcing loop (see Figure 4.2) tends to increase the initial difference. An example is a bank account with a positive interest rate. The balance on the account will increase with interest received, generating more interest next year, increasing the account balance, and so on.

Organisational issues, in particular, complex issues that touch upon multiple functional areas, are likely to be driven by multiple interacting feedback loops. These loops cross-departmental boundaries and show how decisions in one functional area have consequences for another. An example in Figure 4.3 shows a causal loop diagram developed in a project for the Dutch Ministry of Justice (Rouwette & Vennix, 2007). The lower part shows required detention capacity, which is calculated by multiplying the number of prison sentences with the average time served. If required detention capacity is greater than available detention capacity, a shortage of capacity results. In 2000, the Dutch Prison Administration initiated a policy that made prisoners who are serving time for infractions and have completed 90% of their sentence eligible for early release. In 2003, the strictness of norms for early release was reduced, and prisoners who had completed 70% of their sentence were eligible for early release. This increased the potential number of early releases and actual releases. By reducing the average time served by a reduction time, the early release policy frees up capacity for new prisoners. A judge participating in the modelling project recalled that he became aware of the policy after he recognised a suspect as someone recently convicted and imprisoned for an earlier crime. He then became concerned that the suspect's sentence passed for the earlier crime was not served to completion. He foresaw that when judges would perceive an increase in the difference between duration of the sentence

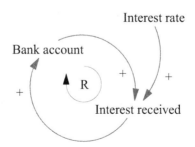

FIGURE 4.2 Example positive (reinforcing) feedback loop.

and time served (upper part of Figure 4.3), they would compensate by increasing the duration of sentences. Thus, there are three main balancing feedback loops in the causal loop diagram. In the loop at the bottom of the figure, an increase in required detention capacity leads to more prisoners released early. This reduces the average time served and thereby reduces required detention capacity. In this way, an initial increase is compensated by a decrease.

The model shows how a problem in one organisational department leads to a local solution (shortage of detention capacity leads to early release of prisoners) which then creates an unanticipated negative side effect in another department (widening the gap between sentence duration and time served). The other department then develops a local solution to address their local problem, going against the intent of the first department. This is a clear example of a 'mixed-motive' situation discussed in Chapter 2, in which team members have to cooperate to achieve shared goals and at the same time compete to advance their own individual interests. The model in Figure 4.3 was developed in the early stages of a project investigating the increase over time in the number of crimes with a known suspect that were not investigated further (Rouwette et al., 2007). This so-called prosecution gap was the result of a lack of capacity in the criminal justice system, but exactly where to intervene in the system to increase capacity was unclear. The model in Figure 4.3 zooms in on (part of) the interaction between judges and prison administration. The criminal justice system also includes police, public

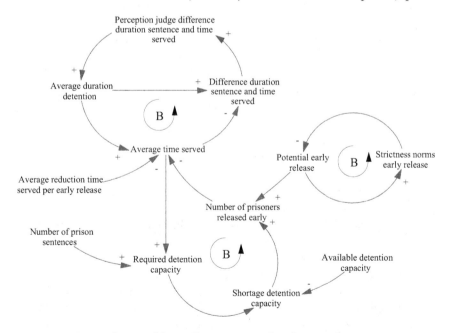

FIGURE 4.3 Example causal loop diagram on early release policy.

Source: From Rouwette & Vennix (2007)

prosecution, and a range of other organisations. The model above therefore depicts only a small subset of the decisions of stakeholders and their interactions that in combination result in the prosecution gap. How does the modeller find information on decisions, drivers, and consequences, and determine its relevance?

A major task of a system dynamics modeller is to identify feedback loops responsible for the behaviour that is studied. This comes down to identifying loops and testing their contribution to overall behaviour. This has led system dynamicists to emphasise two tasks that at first sight may seem contradictory: getting access to mental rather than documentary or quantitative data, and the construction of a quantitative (formal) model. On the first topic, Forrester (e.g. 1992) highlights the importance of mental data over other data sources in an organisation. The mental database, so information stored in people's heads, includes the largest set of data available in any organisation. In contrast, both the written and numerical databases are much smaller. The latter is also more narrow in scope, as it does not reveal the causal relations between variables directly. The importance of mental data becomes clear when we imagine a situation in which only documentary and numerical information are available (Forrester, 1992). Suppose everyone at a university is fired today and new staff starts tomorrow. The new team can only access data stored in documents and information systems. What is the chance that lectures will be given, exams taken, and PhD students supervised? Without mental data, or 'knowing how things are done here', chances are quite small. The modeller therefore needs access to mental data and needs to work with experts and stakeholders to find out how decisions are made. However, such information is likely to reveal many drivers and consequences of a range of decisions, resulting in many different feedback loops that contribute to a smaller or larger extent of the problem of interest. How can the relevance of feedback loops to overall behaviour be tested? System dynamics posits that for systems including more than one or a few feedback loops, it is impossible to predict behaviour. The human mind lacks the ability to trace the dynamic consequences of a complex system structure. It needs support to be able to do so. System dynamics therefore posits that mathematical models are necessary to infer the dynamic consequences of system structure, which includes the contribution of particular feedback loops to (episodes of) behaviour. Mathematical models require a further specification of variables into either stocks or flows, and capturing relations in equations. A mathematical (also referred to as formal or computer) model simulates behaviour over time and can therefore be used to test consequences of changes in structure. We return to this type of models at the end of this chapter. We note here that models can serve multiple purposes in working with stakeholders, which has consequences for their nature and role. So far we described system dynamics models as a tool for understanding an issue external to the team of decision makers, depicting data and relationships in their organisational environment. Zagonel coined the term micro-world for this use of models (Zagonel et al., 2004). However, an alternative purpose of modelling can also be to capture the consensus view of group of stakeholders about a problem. In that case, the model serves as a boundary object (see Chapter 13). When models are used to capture the subjective understanding of a particular situation, quantification is of little use (De Gooyert et al., 2019). When there are significant uncertainties about data and the issue involves many variables that are difficult to quantify, the added value of formal models is also questioned (Coyle, 2000, 2001; Homer & Oliva, 2001).

While working with decision makers and other stakeholders has been a part of system dynamics since its inception (Lane, 2022), an explicit facilitated approach to system dynamics modelling emerged only in the 1980s. Around that time, involving clients directly in the modelling process was greatly simplified by the development of visual software such as Stella (Andersen et al., 2007). While different terms for facilitated system dynamics modelling were and are used, the version known as group model building emerged more or less simultaneously in Albany, New York, and Nijmegen in the Netherlands. In the 1980s, in the Netherlands, Vennix and Gubbels were experimenting with involving clients in model construction, building on experiences with questionnaire approaches (delphi), workshops, and interactive gaming simulations (Vennix et al., 1990). Several ways of working with client groups emerged (Vennix, 1996), resulting in either quantitative or qualitative models. In Albany, New York, group model building was developed as part of the work of the Decision Techtronics Group (DTG). Initiated by John Rohrbaugh, a social psychologist working in small group processes, DTG combined insights from social science research on small group process, facilitation and the use of a variety of Operational Research modelling approaches (Andersen et al., 2007). DTG used a portfolio of modelling approaches in facilitated face-to-face meetings of client groups with projected computer support in the room. The first use of system dynamics with clients comes with a story involving David Andersen and John Rohrbaugh, who were involved in a debate over whether or not it was even possible to build system dynamics models in direct interaction with a client group.

Andersen maintained that the formulation and coding of a system dynamics model (at that time done in DYNAMO) was a task that could not, in principle, involve clients. Rohrbaugh persisted in demonstrating through several pilot projects (typically involving having the facilitation and modelling team work through the night) that such group modelling projects were technically feasible. When Richardson, a seasoned system dynamicist, joined the faculty at Albany, Andersen did not have time to warn him of Rohrbaugh's folly before Rohrbaugh invited Richardson to work on the project. Rohrbaugh and Richardson's success launched GMB at Albany.

(Andersen et al., 2007, p. 692)

The next section outlines the steps in building a qualitative system dynamics model with a team.

4.2   Procedure, technique, and tools

Group model building is generally conducted with a group of between six and 15 people (Rouwette & Vennix, 2009). The group is guided by at least two persons: a facilitator and a modeller/recorder (Richardson & Andersen, 1995). Together these guide the group through the steps outlined in Table 4.1.

The facilitator's task is to elicit relevant knowledge from the group members and to help translate elicited knowledge into system dynamics modelling terms. Chapter 13 covers facilitation in more depth. The modeller builds the model with the aid of system dynamics modelling software with a graphic interface such as Vensim or online tools such as Miro and Kumu. Participants in a modelling session are seated in a semi-circle in front of a whiteboard and/ or projection screen. The model under construction is shown on the screen and visible to all in the room. In this way, it acts as a group memory which documents the model under construction. A separate part of the group memory is used as a parking lot for all kinds of unresolved issues which surface during the deliberations of the group. In combination, the visualised model

TABLE 4.1 Elements of group model building

Procedure

---

1. identify problem variable and reference mode of behaviour
2. identify variables using nominal group technique
3. identify causal relations
4. check feedback loops
5. check validity
6. identify control and target variables

Activity/technique:
• Causal loop diagramming technique

Tool:
• Board and pens and system dynamics modelling software
• *Optional*: System dynamics software such as Vensim or online software such as Kumu or Miro

---

and parking lot reflect at each moment the content of the discussion up to that point.

Group model building starts by identifying the issue of interest. At the beginning of a modelling project, this issue is no more than a label for a problem that the client group is interested in. The work on structuring the problem, so finding symptoms, causes and solutions that all somehow interact to form the problem, starts after that. The central issue is usually depicted in the form of a reference mode of behaviour (see Figure 4.4).

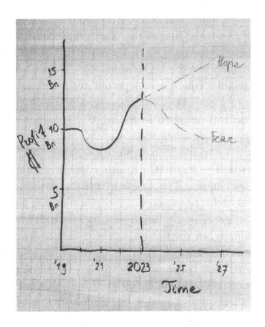

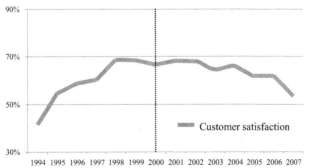

FIGURE 4.4 Examples of a reference mode of behaviour.

Source: See Rouwette (2016)

The reference mode of behaviour is a plot of the behaviour of the most important problem variable(s) over the time horizon studied. It summarises the level of abstraction chosen for the model, the time period the group is interested in as well as the most important behaviour to be simulated, and provides a focus throughout the modelling process. The data for the reference mode may be obtained from a database of the client organisation. For example, the lower pane in Figure 4.4 is based on quantitative data from annual surveys. Alternatively, participants make a sketch of the problem over time and use that as a starting point. For example, the upper pane in Figure 4.4 is a sketch of how team members thought their issue of interest had developed until the present, and their feared and hoped-for development into the future. In both cases, the idea is that this graph over time represents the behaviour we are interested in. The task for the group then becomes to find the structure responsible for the behaviour.

The problem variable, which was depicted in the reference mode, is noted down in the centre of a board or projection screen. This again serves to focus the group on the central question in the next step: which variables (causes, consequences, elements of) relate to this problem variable? Participants are asked to write down variables on a piece of paper, after which these are brought to the board. The facilitator in other words uses the nominal group technique (NGT; see Chapter 3) to come to a list of variables that play a role in the problem. It is useful to explain to the group at this point that variables are entities that can grow or decline over time, such as water in a bathtub, personnel in a company, or the national debt.

The third phase is the heart of group model building and asks participants to relate variables to each other. When drawing relations with a group, the rule that applies to all convergent activities also applies here: changes on the board need to be checked and agreed upon by all participants in the room. Once people agree to a proposed arrow, it is added to the model. In this way, the model structure grows as new variables and relationships are added. The model purpose and system boundary operate as a limit to the addition of new variables. An element should be left out of the model if model purpose or behaviour is not affected by its inclusion (Forrester, 1975). After working on causes, it is useful to switch to effects of the problem variable (see Figure 4.5).

As discussed, a central assumption in system dynamics is that feedback loops are the most important part of the structure of a system. Adding relations as done in the previous phase is likely to close feedback loops. It is worthwhile, when feedback loops are found, to check the loop as a whole. It may be that the team members agree on each relation in the loop, but think the loop as a whole does not make sense or is not important.

Model validity concerns the adequacy of the model for representing the problem under study and the confidence the user may have in the model and recommendations on the basis of the model. Ideally modelling proceeds until participants have sufficient confidence that this model structure captures

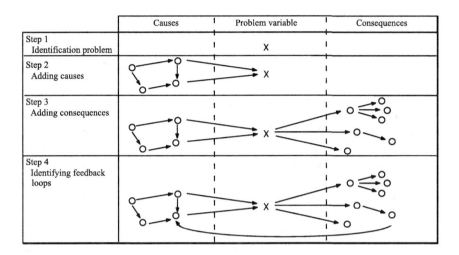

FIGURE 4.5   Steps in building a causal loop diagram.

Source: Vennix (1996, p. 120)

everything that is essential to explain the reference mode of behaviour. Validity is a topic for discussion both in the modelling sessions and in reporting. If the model is used as a boundary object, its aim is to depict the consensus view of team members. Validity then concerns the question: 'is this model a good representation of how these participants give meaning to their reality?' (De Gooyert et al., 2019). On the other hand, if the model aims to capture data and relations external to the participating group, validity is about to what extent the model is a good representation given the goal of the model. System dynamics offers a range of tests to check model validity (Barlas, 1996; Forrester & Senge, 1980; Lane, 2015). These concern the model structure, checking, for instance, whether each variable in the model has a real-world equivalent. Structure is then related to the behaviour of the model. Ultimately, the structure identified in the group model building sessions needs to be adequate to explain the behaviour depicted in the reference mode of behaviour. This is difficult when the model remains at the stage of a causal loop diagram, as we then still rely on the human brain to infer the dynamics consequences of the structure captured by the model. Not surprisingly, system dynamics modellers feel that when using a model to understand an external problem, going through the additional steps of building a formal model adds important insights that cannot be gained from a qualitative model. Formal models, while grounded in mental and documentary data, also allow for the use of quantitative data. This allows for triangulation of conclusions, which may correct partial or biased interpretations brought forward by group members (Van Nistelrooij et al., 2015). Triangulation does, however, not need to take the form of full quantification. Testing crucial model relations against other data (independent from the group conversation) is another option. For instance, when constructing a model on child protection, team members suggested that professionals in child care left their organisation because of a too high administrative burden. This was then tested against information from exit interviews (Lane et al., 2016).

Once sufficient confidence in the model is reached, the last phase in group model building works towards solutions to the issue at hand. This comes down to identifying those levers for change that steer the problematic behaviour in the right direction, while avoiding negative consequences for other important variables. Levers or control variables are those variables that decision makers can control, for instance, hiring new recruits or increasing the marketing budget. Target variables are those variables decision makers would like to change in a preferred direction. Examples are global temperature, profit and client satisfaction. The problem variable that formed the starting point of group model building, and was depicted in the reference mode of behaviour, is one of the target variables. However, usually there are other target variables in addition to the problem variable. It does not make much sense for an organisation to optimise client satisfaction at the expense of everything else, such as employee satisfaction and turnover. The long-term viability of an organisation typically depends on more than one variable. The first step here is to identify variables under the control of the participants in the modelling sessions. For instance, take the model shown in Figure 4.3 which was developed as part of a project aimed at explaining the widening prosecution gap. The final model includes variables that have an impact on the problem variable, such as number of policemen, available detention capacity, and so on. The second step is identifying the target variables. Selecting the most important variables to change is not only a question of choosing the lever with the greatest impact on the original problem. It is likely that policies will have impact on other important variables as well. The model showed, for instance, that increasing the number of crimes reported by the police to the Public prosecution not only led to a rise in prosecuted crimes (as intended) but also swamped the Public prosecution with work (Rouwette et al., 2007). This in turn led the Public prosecution to lower the number of cases presented to a judge and instead offer a financial settlement to the suspect. This is an unintended consequence that participants would like to minimise.

This section described the main steps in group model building, by highlighting important choices and ways to involve participants. As system dynamics has a tradition of facilitated modelling going back to the 1980s, many more tips and resources on how to combine participation and modelling can be found in the literature. If you are interested in practical guidelines on how to set up and guide modelling sessions, the literature on scripts is a useful starting point (Andersen & Richardson, 1997; Hovmand et al., 2012). A script is a repeatable element of process that, if used in a specified context consistently, yields similar outcomes. The total session is broken up into periods of 15 to 20 minutes each, and the activity in each period is carefully planned. Scripts describe in practical terms what the facilitator and recorder do, which reactions can be expected from participants, and which material is created, and how these link to other scripts. Scripts are accessible online via Scriptapedia (https://en.wikibooks.org/wiki/scriptapedia).

4.3 Versions

This section goes into alternatives to the generic group model building procedure described earlier and shown in Table 4.1. We first summarise in brief what is required to build a formal rather than qualitative system dynamics model. Then, we go into a number of approaches that have much in common with group model building but emphasise particular steps in the process or were developed for specific application domains such as environmental studies or communities.

While the procedure outlined in the previous section showed how to involve a decision making team in building qualitative models, participation in constructing a quantified model in many situations has clear benefits. As discussed, developing a full-blown computer simulation model is useful when the problem is external to the decision making team, data are available and there are no major hurdles to quantifying variables. A formal model supports decision making by acting as a cognitive aid, helping decision makers to infer dynamics from structure, something they would not be able to do by themselves. In a personal communication, Vennix formulated this as follows:

> What a computer model brings to the process is one additional participant. This participant does not know more than what you have told him. But he is very consistent: he can tell you exactly what the consequences of your assumptions are.
>
> *Vennix (2005)*

As mentioned, formalising the model also makes it possible to triangulate different data sources, which allows for testing the insights gained in the group process. When transforming a qualitative model into a computer simulation model, each relation in the conceptual model is translated into a mathematical equation. All variables in the model are quantified. Most of the model formalisation work is done backstage as it is quite time consuming, and members of a management team generally are not very interested in this stage of model construction. In this stage, the group is only consulted for crucial model formulations and parameter estimations. Experienced group model builders will start to construct a simple running model as soon as possible and complicate it from there on if required. In the end, the model should of course be able to replicate the reference mode of behaviour (as one of the many validity tests) before it can be sensibly used as a means to simulate the potential effects of strategies and scenarios. When using group model building to construct a quantitative model, the final four steps in the procedure outlined in Table 4.1 change slightly:

- identify causal relations using stocks and flows, and relating stocks, flows, and auxiliaries;
- check feedback loops by simulating the model;
- check validity by testing the formal model;
- identify control and target variables by simulating policy runs and scenario runs.

When building a formal model, instead of a causal loop diagram, a so-called stock and flows model is used. Instead of using only one type of variable, these diagrams separate stocks from flows. Stocks are entities existing at a certain time period, such as inventory, personnel, or water in a reservoir. Flows are entities measured over a time period, for instance, deliveries, recruitments, or inflow of water. Relationships in a stock and flows diagram are separated into physical flows and information flows. Figure 4.6 is a stocks and flow version of the causal loop diagram in Figure 4.1. Information links are depicted with a single and physical flows with a double arrow. 'Delivery delay' is an auxiliary: a variable that is not a stock or flow but is included in the model to make the input for calculations explicit.

The model output is based on the following equations:

- initial inventory = 50
- desired inventory = 100
- delivery delay = 5
- gap = desired inventory − inventory
- orders = gap
- deliveries = orders/delivery delay
- inventory = initial inventory + INT(deliveries)

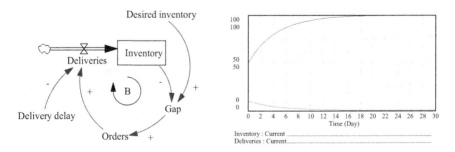

FIGURE 4.6   Example of a stock and flows model and simulation output.

The last equation specifies that the level of inventory at any time is the initial level, plus deliveries up to that time (the integration of the flow variable). As can be seen, the mathematics used in system dynamics modelling is to a large extent 'friendly algebra' (Morecroft, 1992) which will not unfamiliar to decision makers that regularly work with spreadsheets. More complex forms of equations can include delayed and nonlinear effects. When formalising a model by quantifying relations and assigning initial values to variables, the qualitative model is defined more precisely. Formalisation of the model can cause the modeller to backtrack to an earlier phase, if variables or relationships appear to be inconsistent or incompletely defined. The major advantage of a quantitative model over a qualitative model is of course that it can be used to run simulations. Simulation increases understanding of model behaviour and the influence of structure on behavioural patterns. The model can then be tested by changing initial parameter values or changing relationships between variables, and observing the effects on model behaviour. Finally, quantification allows for additional ways to identify control and target variables. Parameters or larger sections of model structure can be changed in order to see their impact on system performance. In this phase, a scenario analysis can be performed by running the model under different conditions for exogenous variables, which clarifies the robustness of (combinations of) solutions.

Given its long tradition of facilitated modelling, it will come as no surprise that different approaches to working with decision makers and other stakeholders have emerged. Andersen et al. (2007) identify the reference group approach, strategic forum, stepwise approach, modelling as learning, strategy dynamics, and Hines' 'standard method'. These approaches differ in terms of the type of model that is built, if and how a preliminary model is used in the process, model size, and finally which phases of model building are supported by direct client involvement. A couple of approaches have been developed with particular application domains in mind. Strategy dynamics applies system dynamics to strategic decision making in private and public organisations (Warren, 2008). Mediated modelling (Van den Belt, 2004) targets environmental issues. Hovmand (2013) adapted facilitated system dynamics modelling specifically to working with communities.

4.4 Applications

The development of facilitated approaches in system dynamics has gone hand in hand with assessment of results. Early research was especially driven by an interest in implementation and resulting impact. Implementation was frequently included as the last phase in modelling and concerns the translation of outcomes to the 'real world'. The ultimate aim of system dynamics is to redesign the system to bring about improvements in system performance. In early work by Roberts (1978) and Weil (1980), it is already evident that implementation is an issue that needs to be considered from the first contact with a client (see also Lee, 1973; Watt, 1977). Some of the titles of these studies are quite clear on the impact of formal modelling without client involvement: 'requiem for large scale models' (Lee, 1973); 'Why won't anyone believe us?' (Watt, 1977). Implementation came to be seen as both pervasive and evasive. Implementation is pervasive as is not so much a separate phase but occurs throughout the process of model construction. Vennix (1996, p. 99) describes it as evasive because it cannot be predicted when and which insights will be produced in modelling. As a result, typically the modeller learns most during the modelling process. It therefore seemed a logical step to involve the client more in model construction ensuring that he or she gets firsthand experience of the insights gained in modelling the problem. If that is not (completely) possible, at least attention needs to be given to communicating results.

In essence, group model building aims to elicit ideas from session participants, confront these with one another and finally integrate these into a shared view of the problem at hand. The main intended outcomes have frequently been formulated as an increase in communication quality (compared to unsupported decision making), insight, consensus, and commitment to recommended actions. Evaluation of group model building frequently takes the form of case studies. The facilitator helps a particular group of participants to construct a model for a particular problem. Case studies typically describe the modelling process and resulting model in detail, while description of implementation and results are often given less attention. Rouwette et al. (2002) compare 107 such case studies. Keeping in mind that case reports are frequently incomplete and may be biased towards successful projects, reported results are generally positive. Increase in insight (learning), consensus as well as implementation of decisions seem to be robust outcomes of group model building. Beyond case studies, recent research has used pretest–posttest measurements to determine changes in attitudes and other antecedents of behaviour (Rouwette et al., 2011; Scott et al., 2015) and looked in more detail at information sharing and patterns of interaction in modelling sessions (McCardle-Keurentjes et al., 2008; Rouwette, 2016). Quantitative assessment of impacts reinforces the view that modelling changes participants' understanding. De Gooyert et al. (2022) conducted a study on eight workshops with a total number of 96 participants. Employing a pretest and posttest measurements of participants' ideas on the central issue modelled (energy transition), they find evidence for cognitive change and consensus formation.

References

Andersen, D. F., & Richardson, G. (1997). Scripts for group model building. *System Dynamics Review*, *13*(2), 107–129.

Andersen, D. F., Vennix, J. A. M., Richardson, G. P., & Rouwette, E. A. J. A. (2007). Group model building: Problem structuring, policy simulation and decision support. *Journal of the Operational Research Society*, 58(5), 691–694.

Barlas, Y. (1996). Formal aspects of model validity and validation in system dynamics models. *System Dynamics Review*, 12(3), 183–210.

Coyle, G. (2000). Qualitative and quantitative modelling in system dynamics: Some research questions. *System Dynamics Review*, 16(3), 225–244.

Coyle, G. (2001). Maps and models in system dynamics: Rejoinder to Homer and Oliva. *System Dynamics Review*, 17(4), 357–363.

De Gooyert, V., Bleijenbergh, I., Korzilius, H., Fokkinga, B., Lansu, M., Raaijmakers, S., Rouwette, E. A. J. A., & Van der Wal, M. (2019). Why we do not always simulate. *SDS Wisdom Blog*. https://sdswisdom.blog/2019/10/02/why-we-do-not-always-simulate/

De Gooyert, V., Rouwette, E. A. J. A., Van Kranenburg, H. L., Freeman, E., & Van Breen, H. (2022). Cognitive change and consensus forming in facilitated modelling: A comparison of experienced and observed outcomes. *European Journal of Operational Research*, 229(2), 589–599. https://doi.org/https://doi.org/10.1016/j.ejor.2021.09.007

Forrester, J. W. (1961). *Industrial dynamics*. Pegasus Communications.

Forrester, J. W. (1975). *Industrial dynamics – after the first decade*. Pegasus Communications.

Forrester, J. W. (1992). Policies, decisions, and information sources for modeling. *European Journal of Operational Research*, 59, 42–63.

Forrester, J. W., & Senge, P. M. (1980). Tests for building confidence in system dynamics models. *TIMS Studies in the Management Sciences*, 14, 209–228.

Homer, J. B., & Oliva, R. (2001). Maps and models in system dynamics: A response to Coyle. *System Dynamics Review*, 17(4), 347–355.

Hovmand, P. (2013). *Community based system dynamics*. Business Media.

Hovmand, P. S., Andersen, D. F., Rouwette, E. A. J. A., Richardson, G. P., Rux, K., & Calhoun, A. (2012). Group model-building 'scripts' as a collaborative planning tool. *Systems Research and Behavioral Science*, 29(2), 179–193.

Lane, D. C. (2015). Validity is a matter of confidence – but not just in system dynamics. *Systems Research and Behavioral Science*, 32(4), 450–458. https://doi.org/10.1002/sres.2337

Lane, D. C. (2022). Fons et origo: Reflections on the 60th anniversary of industrial dynamics. *System Dynamics Review*, 38(3), 292–324. https://doi.org/10.1002/sdr.1717

Lane, D. C., Munro, E., & Husemann, E. (2016). Blending systems thinking approaches for organisational analysis: Reviewing child protection in England. *European Journal of Operational Research*, 251(2), 613–623.

Lee, D. B. (1973). Requiem for large scale models. *Journal of the American Institute of Planners*, 39(1), 163–178.

McCardle-Keurentjes, M. H. F., Rouwette, E. A. J. A., & Vennix, J. A. M. (2008). Effectiveness of group model building in discovering hidden profiles in strategic decision-making. System Dynamics Conference, Athens. www.systemdynamics.org/conferences/2008/proceed/papers/MCCAR357.pdf

Morecroft, J. (1992). Executive knowledge, models and learning. *European Journal of Operational Research*, 59, 9–27.

Richardson, G. P. (1991). *Feedback thought in social science and systems theory.* University of Pennsylvania Press.

Richardson, G. P., & Andersen, D. F. (1995). Teamwork in group model building. *System Dynamics Review, 11*(2), 113–137.

Richardson, G. P., & Pugh, A. L. (1981). *Introduction to system dynamics modelling with DYNAMO.* MIT Press.

Roberts, E. (1978). Strategies for effective implementation of complex corporate models. In E. Roberts (Ed.), *Managerial applications of system dynamics* (pp. 77–85). Productivity Press.

Rouwette, E. A. J. A. (2016). The impact of group model building on behavior. In M. Kunc, J. Malpass, & L. White (Eds.), *Behavioral operational research: Theory, methodology and practice* (pp. 213–241). Palgrave Macmillan. https://repository. ubn.ru.nl/bitstream/handle/2066/178390/178390pos.pdf

Rouwette, E. A. J. A., Korzilius, H., Vennix, J. A. M., & Jacobs, E. (2011). Modeling as persuasion: The impact of group model building on attitudes and behavior. *System Dynamics Review, 27*(1), 1–21. https://doi.org/10.1002/sdr.441

Rouwette, E. A. J. A., Van Hooff, P., Vennix, J. A. M., & Jongebreur, W. (2007). Modeling crime control in the Netherlands: Insights on process. International System Dynamics Conference, Boston, MA.

Rouwette, E. A. J. A., & Vennix, J. A. M. (2007). Team learning on messy problems. In M. London & V. I. Sessa (Eds.), *Work group learning: Understanding, improving & assessing how groups learn in organizations* (pp. 243–284). Lawrence Erlbaum Associates.

Rouwette, E. A. J. A., & Vennix, J. A. M. (2009). Group model building. In R. E. Meyers (Ed.), *Encyclopedia of complexity and systems science* (pp. 4474–4486). Springer Verlag.

Rouwette, E. A. J. A., Vennix, J. A. M., & Van Mullekom, T. (2002). Group model building effectiveness. A review of assessment studies. *System Dynamics Review, 18*(1), 5–45.

Scott, R. J., Cavana, R. Y., & Cameron, D. (2015). Recent evidence on the effectiveness of group model building. *European Journal of Operational Research, 249*(3), 908–918.

Uleman, J. F., Melis, R. R. J. F., Quax, R., Van der Zee, E. A., Thijssen, D., Dresler, M., Van de Rest, O., Van der Velpen, I. F., Adams, H. H. H., Schmand, B., de Kok, I. M. C. M., De Bresser, J., Richard, E., Verbeek, M., Hoekstra, A. G., Rouwette, E. A. J. A., & Olde Rikkert, M. G. M. (2021). Mapping the multicausality of Alzheimer's disease through group model building. *GeroScience, 43*, 829–843.

Van den Belt, M. (2004). *Mediated modeling. A system dynamics approach to environmental consensus building.* Island Press.

Van Nistelrooij, L. P. J., Rouwette, E. A. J. A., Verstijnen, I. M., & Vennix, J. A. M. (2015). The eye of the beholder: A case example of changing clients' perspectives through involvement in the model validation process. *Systems Research and Behavioral Science, 32*, 437–449.

Vennix, J. A. M. (1996). *Group model building. Facilitating team learning using system dynamics.* Wiley.

Vennix, J. A. M., Gubbels, J. W., Post, D., & Poppen, H. J. (1990). A structured approach to knowledge elicitation in conceptual model building. *System Dynamics Review, 6*(2), 31–45.

Warren, K. (2008). *Strategic management dynamics*. Wiley.

Watt, C. H. (1977). Why won't anyone believe us? *Simulation*, *28*, 1–3.

Weil, H. (1980). The evolution of an approach for achieving implemented results from system dynamics projects. In J. Randers (Ed.), *Elements of the system dynamics method*. Pegasus Communications.

Zagonel, A. A., Rohrbaugh, J., Richardson, G. P., & Andersen, D. F. (2004). Using simulation models to address "what if" questions about welfare reform. *Journal of Policy Analysis and Management*, *23*(4), 890–901.

5

APPLICATION

Building the business model of Sioo management education

This chapter describes an application of group model building with Sioo management education. This chapter is written with Jesse Segers. Sioo offers learning trajectories that help to develop skills in change management processes. Clients can choose between open courses and tailor-made in-house courses. While Sioo had seen stable revenues in the previous five years, demand appeared to be shifting from open to tailor-made courses. Sioo's new dean wanted to learn more about changes in the market and how the Sioo business model needed to adapt, if at all. This chapter describes the motivation for starting the project, the two modelling sessions with Sioo employees and external lecturers, the resulting model, and its impact.

5.1   Background and issue

Sioo offers learning trajectories around organisational issues. Founded by seven Dutch universities in 1958, Sioo has established itself as a professional education institute that interweaves theoretical understanding, application in practice, and personal development. In both open and tailor-made in-house courses, participants develop new insights, apply these in their own practice, and reflect on their experiences as part of their learning pathway. Sioo has a permanent core of 17 employees who work from the head office in Utrecht, the Netherlands. Learning pathways are provided in collaboration with more than 200 lecturers who are active in change management in practice, academia or a combination. In March 2018, Jesse Segers started as the new rector of Sioo. Following his appointment, he interviewed 60 clients, employees, and lecturers on their experiences and expectations of Sioo. The interviewees turned out to have largely similar images of Sioo and pointed out that Sioo's working method and structure had not changed for

DOI: 10.4324/9781003404200-7

a long time. A central conclusion from the interviews was that while the organisation seemed stable, developments in the market were less clear. On the one hand, Sioo had a relatively constant total number of clients. On the other hand, a shift seemed to be taking place between learning paths, with open standardised courses shrinking and flexible customer-specific courses growing in the number of clients. Jesse also noted a set of assumptions that seemed to be central to the Sioo mission but in practice led to confusion. One example is the idea that Sioo is a network organisation, in which there is a bidirectional flow of information as well as clients between Sioo and cooperating lecturers. However, in practice, lecturers are hired by Sioo to provide a specific service. Another assumption is that Sioo is a professional organisation, much like a law firm, in which marketing is not needed as it is all about reputation. Nevertheless, competing providers of management courses were active in marketing.

Jesse contacted Etiënne Rouwette by mail in May 2018. They had not met before but Etiënne was one of the lecturers at Sioo, involved in a course on group model building for a number of years already. In his first mail, Jesse emphasised that he did not want to 'reveal' the assumptions identified in interviews to Sioo employees, use them to explain all problems and then 'propose' different assumptions that would allow everyone to move forward from that moment on. He would rather explore as a group which assumptions drove the way of working at Sioo and then see if other assumptions would lead to different outcomes. In a telephone conversation, Etiënne proposed to use group model building to this end. The idea would be to start from a central Sioo performance indicator over time and map the business model that explained this behaviour. In follow-up emails, two options for performance indicators were discussed: the number of participants in Sioo courses and revenues, both if possible separated into open and in-house courses. As course offerings changed regularly, the number of participants fluctuated over time. After looking into available data, it turned out to be time consuming to reconstruct exactly how many people participated in which course. Revenues was therefore chosen as the central indicator. While Etiënne proposed to start from a graph spanning ten years, Jesse argued that going back more than five years would not add much to the analysis as the situation a decade ago was too different from the present. The central goal of the project was formulated as mapping the business model driving Sioo revenues from 2013 to 2018. The term 'business model' was taken to refer to the value created by an organisation for its customers, owners, suppliers, and employees and the resources needed to create this value. This means that in addition to using the language of system dynamics (behaviour over time, variables, relations, and feedback loops), the facilitator also introduced to participants terms connected to business models such as value creation, resources, business growth, (market) constraints, and so on.

In their emails and calls, Jesse and Etiënne also discussed a number of practical topics: how many meetings to plan and when, who and how many participants to invite, who would be involved in facilitation, the location and set-up, deliverables, and the possibility of audio recording the meetings. They agreed to schedule two meetings, each with three hours interaction time (not counting breaks for drinks and meals), on 5 and 21 June 2018. Etiënne suggested that for modelling in a plenary group, between ten and 12 participants were ideal and 15 a rather large group. The decision was made to invite 12 to 15, expecting around 12 in each meeting. Participants were drawn from all functional groups at Sioo, such as course coordinators, financial staff and support, as well as from the group of external teachers. The final decision on who in each of these groups would be invited for the sessions was with Jesse. Jesse would be present in the meetings in the role of participant, meaning after the introductions he would not have more speaking time than others. The facilitation team would be Etiënne Rouwette as a facilitator, master student Imke Gommans as modeller (and co-facilitator when people worked in subgroups), and PhD student Jorge Sousa as observer. Jorge asked to be in the meetings because he wanted to experience group model building firsthand. His role in the sessions would be to take notes and reflect on (intermediate) results. Meetings would be held in the main office in Utrecht with participants seated in a U-shaped setting, facing a projection screen and whiteboard. Imke would be building the model in Vensim software. Deliverables would consist of a workbook after the first meeting and a final report after the last meeting. The workbook was to summarise insights from the initial meeting and include questions to prepare for the next session. Jesse agreed to audio recording the meetings and participants would be asked for their consent. The recording would be a basis not only for the workbook and final report, if specific elements of the discussion could not be reconstructed from notes and memory, but also for potential research into the modelling process and results.

5.2 Process

On the basis of the discussions in the intake as well as final adjustments once the meetings drew closer, the following agenda was developed for the sessions (Table 5.1).

5.2.1 Session 1

A total of 12 Sioo employees and external lecturers participated in the first meeting. Participants were seated in a semi-circle, without tables, with name cards next to them on the floor. They faced the projection screen, with Imke seated behind a table off to the side. The meeting started with an introduction

TABLE 5.1 Group model building agenda, products and procedure

Agenda, products and procedure

Session 1 (5 June 2018, 17–20h)
- 17.00h opening by contact client; introduction participants and facilitators; explanation method and way of working
- 17.15h central issue (1); start construction model (2, 3, 4)
- 19.30h evaluation and next steps (5)
- 20.00h close

After meeting: *workbook*

Session 2 (21 June 2018, 16–20h)
- 16.00h goal, previous session, and further development model (3, 4, 5)
- 17.15h dinner
- 17.45h work in subgroups (3)
- 19.00h analysis and actions; next steps (4, 5, 6)
- 20.00h close

After meeting: *final report*

Procedure group model building
1. identify problem variable and reference mode of behaviour
2. identify variables using nominal group technique
3. identify causal relations
4. check feedback loops
5. check validity
6. identify control and target variables

by Jesse Segers. In brief, he went into the conversations he had after stepping into his new role as dean, and some of the insights gleaned from the round of interviews. Sioo seemed to be in a stable situation, but lately open courses seemed to attract fewer and in-house courses more participants. It therefore seemed useful to explore ideas on the past and future of Sioo with stakeholders. In two sessions, participants would take a closer look at the business model. A round of introductions of participants and members of the facilitation team followed. Etiënne then picked up on the aim of the meetings and the rationale for jointly constructing a model. The term 'business model' was explained using two examples. The first is from the book by Ackermann et al. (2005) and concerns a consultancy firm. Its mission revolves around three elements: building a great firm, attracting exceptional people, and helping clients make improvements in their performance. These elements were captured in a causal loop diagram, to which in the next step resources were added that needed to be in place to make this a reality. Exceptional people are, for instance, attracted by offering high salaries and access to projects with top-level clients. The second example of a business model was a map of the Walt Disney business model in 1957. It shows, for instance, how music, film, and TV material build on one another – with cartoon illustrations. Both examples underline how a business model functions as a system, which means that if we want to explain overall business performance we need to understand how all elements work together. Etiënne then showed the graph of Sioo revenues depicted in Figure 5.1. This was proposed as the central behaviour of interest, keeping in mind the switch in demand from open to in-house courses. The aim of the meetings would be to determine which structure caused the observed behaviour. Participants agreed that this would be a useful aim for the two meetings.

Etiënne emphasised that while the chart focused on the finances of the business, this was only one aspect of a business model. A positive financial result is a necessary condition for the continued existence of a company, but (usually) not the reason for its existence. Its reason for existence is better expressed in the value the organisation creates. The last topic before starting to model was to ask for permission to audio record the sessions. Informed consent forms were passed around and filled out.

The first question for the participants was to think of factors that have to do with Sioo's business model. Factors could relate to the creation of value, the resources needed for value creation, consequences of value creation, or other topics. As indicated, revenue was an important factor, but not the essential part of the business model. Using the nominal group technique, participants took some minutes to note down ideas individually. Proceeding in a round ribbon fashion, each participant in turn mentioned one variable which was then noted down using the modelling software. This created a list of 37 variables visible to all on the central screen.

The next question for the participants was about the central variable in the model. What value does Sioo aim to create for its customers? Participants referred to a recent meeting on Sioo's vision and mission and derived from this the central value to which Sioo wants to contribute: the development of individuals, organisations, and society, or in other words: their learning and development potential. This variable was placed in the centre of the screen. The discussion then turned to what determines value creation and eventually resulted in the submodel in Figure 5.2. Organisational development

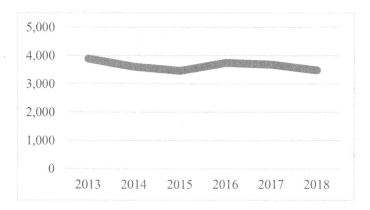

FIGURE 5.1   Sioo revenues (× 1000 euro) 2013–2018.

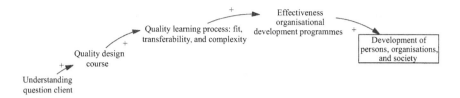

FIGURE 5.2   Submodel from start session 1.

programmes can be effective to different degrees. Programme effectiveness follows from the quality of the learning process, which has three dimensions: (1) fit the client's problem, (2) transferability in the sense that what is learned can be implemented in the learner's practice, and (3) taking into account the complexity of change questions. While drawing these first relations, the facilitator explained what was meant by a plus or minus next to an arrow.

An important prerequisite for a high-quality course is a good design. The design not only focuses on the three aspects of quality but also takes into account the interaction between learners: learners discuss the course content together, give it meaning, and try out things that prepare them for practice. The course environment forms a temporary work system in which behaviour can be practised. Understanding the client's demand is necessary for developing a good design. As described in the previous chapter, each of the relations in the model was first proposed by a particular participant. The facilitator then visualised this suggestion as a new variable and relation in the model. These additions were discussed within the group as a whole and only kept in place if everyone agreed. Note also that there is a choice in how much detail to include in variable names. In the case of quality of the learning process, the three dimensions (fit, transferability, and complexity) are made explicit by including them in the variable name. In discussing quality of course design participants also referred to several separate dimensions, but ultimately the variable name was kept relatively brief. The dimensions of quality course design were described in the text of the workbook and final report but not included in the variable name.

The conversation then turned to two other factors that influence quality of the learning process: teaching staff and the interaction between stakeholders. Next, knowledge development was suggested as a driver for design quality. These submodels can be recognised in the centre and upper left-hand side of Figure 5.3. The facilitator then proposed to switch focus to another part of the model. The reason for this is that experiences and interests differ between participants, which also means some participants are most energised when discussing one aspect of the issue at hand while others favour different aspects. For instance, after a long discussion on the finances driving a business model, non-financial managers might want to change to another topic.

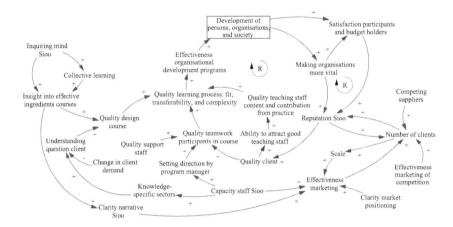

FIGURE 5.3 Model at the end of session 1.

To switch focus, Etiënne asked the participants what would happen if Sioo succeeded in creating added value. What would be the consequences if individuals, organisations, and society developed further? Participants' answers pointed out consequences such as organisations becoming more vital, and increased satisfaction of both clients and those who pay the bill. Again the meaning of terms was discussed in depth. Vitality refers to the potential to meet the organisation's goal in a complex and changing environment. Satisfaction and vitality both drive Sioo's reputation. In turn, an increased reputation allows for selection of clients more in line with Sioo's offering, which raises the quality of interaction in the team of stakeholders involved in developing a course.

Adding the latter relationships closed a number of positive feedback loops, indicated by an 'R' (reinforcing) in the model. At that point in the discussion, the facilitator explained that feedback loops are the 'engine' of a business model and explained how an organisation sustains itself over time. He summarised the core of the loop. According to participants, crucial elements of the Sioo business model are the value it creates in terms of the development of individuals, organisations, and society. This, through a number of channels, shapes Sioo's reputation, determines the type of client attracted and, in conjunction with the knowledge of Sioo staff and a network of lecturers, delivers high-quality learning programmes. Participants agreed to the loop as a whole. These elements are part of positive feedback loops and thus reinforce each other. Starting from an initial increase in any of these elements, they set in motion an upward spiral. On the other hand, if one of the elements initially decreases, this will lead to a downward spiral.

Two further themes emerged in the remainder of the first session. A discussion on attracting clients resulted in the lower part of Figure 5.3. Several participants observed that marketing is difficult, not only because organisational change is a complex topic but also because it is not easy to capture Sioo's way of working in words. "You only get it when you experienced it first-hand". The last theme is capacity of employees. Directing programmes takes a lot of time. The remaining time is divided between marketing and the development of knowledge in specific sectors.

The discussion and resulting model were captured in a workbook and sent to participants. The model was divided into different submodels, each covering a theme as in the previous pages. Care was taken to make the description more than a bland text stating that variable A leads to variable B, which leads to variable C, and so on. Where possible, relations were explained by including examples shared in the meeting that seemed to resonate with the rest of the group. The model description covered about four pages. The total report consisted of 12 pages of running text, including an appendix covering the example of a consultancy business model, the full list of 37 variables generated at the start of the meeting, and the final model resulting at the end. The section on model description was preceded by a brief summary of the aim, participants, and method. These were explained in such a manner that people who did not attend the meeting could understand what was done. The workbook ended with a number of questions to prepare for the next meeting. These addressed, for instance, whether feedback loops worked in the same manner for open as well as in-house courses and 'open ends' in the model (variables with no ingoing or outgoing arrows). One question asked participants to reflect on the business model canvas (Osterwalder & Pigneur, 2010). The canvas has nine dimensions of which four were not yet included in the model: costs, client relations, client segments (beyond the open and in-house courses), and channels. Do these dimensions give rise to additional variables? The last question in the workbook explicitly addressed validity: does this model explain the stability in Sioo revenues? If not, which variables are missing?

5.2.2   Session 2

In the second session 11 participants were present, of which three had not attended the first meeting. The meeting opened by taking participants through the model step by step, using what is called storytelling. This comes down to presenting the model in a series of steps, each building on the previous and adding an additional model layer or submodel. Storytelling started with showing the problem variable (development of persons, organisations, and society), then adding the initial relations around this variable and recapturing the essence of the discussion around these arrows. It then added the next submodel, again summarising the discussion around these variables and relations. Storytelling ended with the full model as developed by the end of the first session. Going through the model in some detail not only served as a reminder to those participants who were present in the first meeting but also gave the three new participants a chance to voice questions and comments.

The plan for the second session reserved one hour for a plenary discussion on further additions to the model. Dinner would be served next, followed by a little over an hour of subgroup discussions. Subgroups were asked to check the overall models for differences between open and in-house courses. The last hour of the meeting would then be spent on checking the final set of feedback loops and the identification of actions.

The discussion on additions to the model started from the questions in the workbook. New variables and relations mainly concerned the part of the model centered on with clients, shown in the lower part of the diagram in Figure 5.4. In addition, several variables were added to the right-hand part of the model specifying the impact of (Dutch) economic developments on company training budgets and eventually on Sioo clients. Here, for the first time, market limitations appear. Next, the plenary group split up into two subgroups. The work in subgroups resulted in a table detailing the differences between open and in-house courses, of which a selection is shown in Table 5.2.

TABLE 5.2 Selected differences between open and in-house courses

	Open courses	*In-house courses*
Basis for approaching Sioo	Reputation Sioo	English website, international offices (the viability of an international ambition is not recognised by all participants)
Acquisition	Multichannel marketing	Approach people in person
Relation	Particularly after course, with participant	Relationship with top management, prior to assignment, long term (not yet included in the model)
Basis for decision client	Reputation Sioo and content (change management knowledge)	Idea Sioo plus relationship plus sector knowledge
Aim and basis for design learning trajectory	Starts from question focused on individual learning, participants must make their own move (personal development)	Starts from purpose organisation, focuses on movement in organisation, together (organisational development)

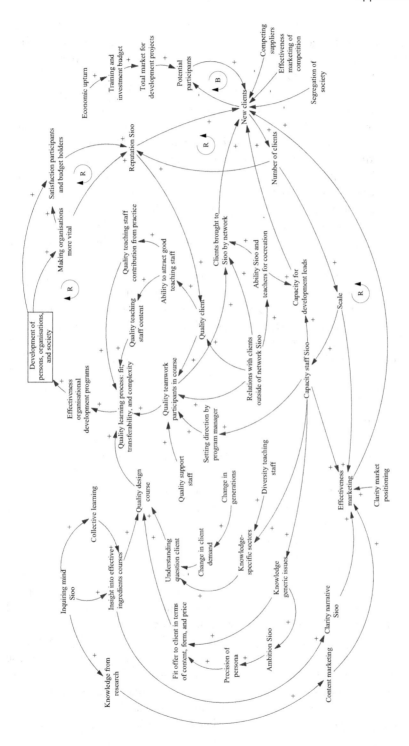

FIGURE 5.4 Final model at the end of session 2.

In the last hour of the session, subgroups presented their results to one another. Where participants deemed this relevant, insights from the subgroups were added to the overall model. The model was then frozen as the last hour was reserved for model analysis and proposing actions. The main implications of the model structure were discussed within the group, focusing on central feedback loops. As shown in Figure 5.4, there are four reinforcing loops. These loops capture Sioo's growth potential. At their core are Sioo's reputation and quality of interaction between stakeholders. Reputation feeds into attracting clients interested in complexity, growing reputation further via a number of paths. Increased quality of interaction between stakeholders increases scale, frees up capacity of staff, which leads to more time to set direction, and further builds quality of interaction. There is only one balancing loop in which new clients reduce the number of potential clients.

Next, to identify actions, participants were asked to indicate where in the model they would focus their efforts in the future. To do this, they could divide an investment budget of 100 euros over model variables. This was not preceded by a plenary discussion of control or target variables, so participants could essentially invest in any part of the model they favoured. The resulting top three investments were as follows: (1) build competence of Sioo and teaching staff for co-creation, (2) increase effectiveness marketing, and (3) identify new opportunities and translate these into client proposals.

5.3 Final product

The modelling process resulted in two products: the workbook described in the previous section and the final report sent to participants after the last meeting. The final report contains 18 pages of text and has a similar setup to the workbook. It is organised in the following sections: background, method, central aim, model structure, comparison open and in-house courses, analysis feedback loops, conclusions, and recommendations. The appendix includes a list of participants, variables resulting from the nominal group technique, and the final model. Jorge's reflection on the final model was part of the section on conclusions. He pointed out that only one negative loop was identified, raising the question if all relevant (market) limitations had been addressed. The discussion and model focused, to a large extent, on service quality, could it be that some parts of the model captured the desired rather than the actual situation? Several important steps in the client choice process were not included: identification of clients, proactively approaching clients, how clients learn about (quality of) Sioo, reasons not to choose Sioo, development of a proposal and determinants of proposal success. These reflections, analysis of the final model, and participants' choices of where to invest were the basis for three recommendations: first, to test the business model further by checking for other negative loops and a comparison against available data on in particular clients, proposals and costs; second, to strengthen co-creation so that open and in-house courses can benefit more from one another; third, to focus more on marketing.

5.4 Implementation and results

The immediate reaction of participants and contact client Jesse to the process and results of the project was positive. The follow-up in the months and years after the project indicates that both the way of working and the substantial recommendations were picked up. The approach to construct a business model using group model building was employed both in a project with an external organisation and in another Sioo project. In September 2021, Jesse invited Etiënne to facilitate a similar project on a management education provider in Belgium. In the aftermath of COVID-19, the three sessions in this project took place online.

Many of the conclusions and recommendations of the project were implemented. In August 2018, a fulltime position was created for a marketeer and a new person was hired. The model was also used as an organising framework to plan and communicate strategy. On 31 January 2019, a strategy meeting was held with all Sioo staff members. Jesse opened the meeting with positive news on Sioo's financial performance. In 2018, Sioo had increased by 13% compared to 2017 and average productivity per person (total revenue/FTE) was higher as well. In looking forward to 2019, Jesse noted that some economists expected the growth of the previous years would cool off. This was not under control of Sioo staff, but the action list was. The new marketing person then presented the actions she had taken since starting in her position and the plans for the new year. These were placed in the visualised business model. Next, all members of staff were invited to place the strategic initiatives they had acted upon in 2018 in the causal map. In this way, the rationale and expected impact of each initiative became clear. It also showed which segments of the model were targeted and which were for the moment ignored. In 2018, several activities had been launched that focused on alumni and targeted the lower right-hand part of the model: effectiveness of marketing, new clients, and reputation. A year later, on 14 January 2020, a strategy meeting was held with the same team. In 2019, revenues had increased 15% compared to 2018. The visualised business model was used again, but this time in a presentation format so without room for direct participation. The feedback from team afterwards was that they liked the presentation, but that it did not stick as it did last year. Co-creating the meeting content would have been better. That said, the right-hand side of the model had received continuous attention in 2019, by investing in ICT to increase marketing effectiveness further and tasking a person with developing leads. Internal sales days to professionalise the process had been held and partner programmes were launched, to both attract clients and increase the number of leads. In addition, in 2019 the focus had broadened to also include the left-hand side of the model. Sioo had reinforced collective learning by starting to publish an edited series of books, coaching meetings with faculty, and a joint development of a vision for learning.

In January 2022, Jesse contacted Etiënne on a project following up on the 2018 business model. Hiring a new person had professionalised the marketing function inside Sioo. Sales, ICT, and back office had also developed further. The overall revenue since 2018 had increased by almost 60%. However, it seemed that many of the pressures in the new business model came together and had their combined effect on the new marketing function. Email exchanges and online conversations resulted in a choice for 'tensions between functional areas in Sioo' as the central variable. Four main functional areas or activities were distinguished: marketing, sales, ICT, and back office. Two meetings were held in the summer of 2022. Core insights were that while marketing had a strategic role in building the Sioo brand, it was also approached by individual course coordinators for urgent short-term initiatives. These included marketing campaigns to help boost the number of participants in particular courses. While this led to tensions and work stress in the marketing department specifically, the organisation as a whole felt pressure from changes in the market. Pressure that was displaced to another part of the system if one of the functional areas got too much work. In the last five years, the complexity and number of client questions, particularly for in-house courses, had markedly increased meaning that sales spent more time per client. As a result, salespeople would rely more on the back office to support upcoming and ongoing programmes. Consequently, they would ask for more help from ICT support, who would have less time to support the marketing function. At the same time the marketing function would get more requests from salespeople for specific open programmes as that business was then somewhat lacking compared to in-house courses, and so on. As in the project in 2018, the end of the last meeting was reserved for identifying actions that could turn this situation around.

References

Ackermann, F., Eden, C., & Brown, I. (2005). *The practice of making strategy. A step-by-step guide*. SAGE.

Osterwalder, A., & Pigneur, Y. (2010). *Business model generation: A handbook for visionaries, game changers, and challengers*. John Wiley & Sons.

6

PARTICIPATORY SCENARIO DEVELOPMENT

Thinking about the future

Will there be a new pandemic? How will Artificial Intelligence develop and which jobs will it affect? Can the worst effects of climate change still be prevented? Answers to these questions have consequences for persons and organisations around the world. In long-term planning, analysing the potential future paths of these trends is known as scenario exploration. In everyday, language 'scenario' refers to a hypothetical sequence of events. Scenarios can, for instance, refer to the plot of a movie or theatre play, to alternative future trajectories of greenhouse gas emissions and their impact, or to possible outcomes of a war. In team decision making, scenario development or scenario planning refers to a set of approaches that aim to construct descriptions of the future environment of an organisation. Often multiple scenarios are developed as it is difficult to predict events or, depending on time horizon and sector, even general trends. The future is inherently uncertain, as becomes clear from this Danish proverb: 'It is difficult to make predictions, especially about the future'. Preparing not just for one but for multiple plausible futures is a practical way to deal with uncertainty. Practitioners in scenario analysis assume that by imagining what the context of an organisation looks like in the future, an organisation is in a better position to determine what is important in the present. While widely known and used for strategy development, scenario planning has received a fair amount of criticism. Because of the bewildering diversity in approaches and guidelines to constructing scenarios, the method has been called a toolbox rather than a tool. In this chapter, we concentrate on one particular school of scenario development which is called intuitive logics. In this school of thought, the qualitative input of team members is leading. The process starts by collecting ideas on trends and developments in the surroundings of an organisation.

DOI: 10.4324/9781003404200-8

Some of these trends are predetermined, meaning that their future behaviour can be predicted with some degree of confidence. Most interesting are those clusters that are uncertain and important as they may develop along alternative paths. These form the basis for a set of alternative, plausible scenarios. A set of scenarios is developed which each describe, in narrative form, what a possible future looks like and how it came to be. The question that then follows logically is 'if the future looks like this, what can we do to prepare?' By analysing what works well across scenarios, in effect using scenarios as a test bed for strategic actions, so-called robust options can be identified. A robust option is a course of action that generates beneficial results, regardless of major developments in the environment. Alternative approaches to scenario building combine input from team members with quantitative data, statistical analysis and simulation. The wide application of scenarios has resulted in a range of published case studies which are summarised in reviews. The tentative conclusion from these reviews is that scenarios may help stakeholders to identify adaptable options, communicate with stakeholders, and increase understanding and acceptance of uncertainty.

6.1 Background

Although the term 'scenario' is much older, the use of scenarios in policy making is often thought to have started in 1942. At the time, a team of American physicists led by Robert Oppenheimer was working on developing the atomic bomb. Before setting off the first man-made nuclear explosion, the team had to assess what the consequences of a nuclear explosion might be. One concern was atmospheric ignition. In a comment on the 2023 movie Oppenheimer, nuclear weapons expert Alex Wellerstein, explains this as follows. What if the nuclear explosion would lead nitrogen and oxygen in the atmosphere to fuse together and release energy? One possibility was this would release enough energy to trigger more nuclear fusion, which would set off a chain reaction and burn up the entire atmosphere. In the movie, Oppenheimer dismisses this concern as 'chances are near zero'. In reality, the team developing the atomic bomb found that the issue was too complex for analytic calculation and reverted to simulations of possible outcomes. These simulations indicated that chances were about one in three million, which apparently was small enough to bet all life on earth on. In the 1950s, developments in computers spurred a wider use of scenarios and simulation. These took the form of Monte Carlo simulations, game theory, and war games. The simulation of social interactions, including conflicts, proved to be a useful tool in defence training and exercise. The RAND corporation brought these three developments together and had a central role in the development of war games (Bradfield et al., 2005). A researcher at RAND, Herman Kahn, is credited with introducing scenarios into non-military decision making (Schwartz, 1997). Around the same time in France a different form of scenarios was developed, which was called La Prospective (Godet, 2000). The La Prospective approach aimed to develop descriptive as well as normative scenarios. Normative descriptions cover, for instance, what France *should* look like in several years' time. Scenarios became more widely known as a method when Kahn published his book *The year 2000: a framework for speculation on the next thirty-three years* in 1967 and Pierre Wack developed scenarios at Shell in 1973. One of the scenarios developed at Shell described an oil shortage, a possibility which was deemed highly unlikely by most managers and experts at the time. Nevertheless, management at Shell decided to prepare for the event that an oil shortage would become reality. When the OPEC eventually decided to lower the production of oil, leading to the oil crisis in 1973, Shell was prepared to react before its competitors.

Considering alternative, plausible futures in planning were, however, a major break with the conventional approach to long-term planning. Traditionally, forecasting future trends was a popular and unquestioned element of developing strategies. Its attraction lay in the fact that by using statistical analysis, a single forecast of the future was formulated, providing a firm foundation for long-term plans. Oppenheimer's use of scenarios and simulation in 1942 resembles this approach. While simulation does not provide a single prediction, it does produce a range of possible outcomes (scenarios) that can be assigned probabilities. However, predicting an event in the realm of physics is one thing, but using the same approach to predict markets or societal trends is another. In the 1970s and 1980s, the assumption that trends could be extrapolated while ignoring discontinuities and shocks, received more and more criticism. Authors such as management scholar Peter Drucker (1973) emphasised the impossibility of making a single-point prediction of the future in the light of discontinuities. Instead planning should be based on alternative future developments. Multiple-scenario development and analysis provided one way of doing that. The oil crisis in 1974 alerted many planners to the possibility and impact of external shocks. In the two years after the oil crisis, the use of scenarios by US companies doubled and later doubled again (Klein & Linneman, 1981). Europe saw a similar increase in the adoption of scenario planning. By the early 1980s about half of the major companies in the US were using some form of scenarios (Bradfield et al., 2005).

Although the experiences at Shell increased the appeal of scenarios as a strategic tool to a business audience, it proved difficult to repeat the process elsewhere. In most organisations, its use was still 'experimental' (Linneman & Klein, 1983). One reason for that was a scarcity of literature on methodology for scenario development. What did seem clear from the example at Shell was that any use of scenarios needed to combine analytical quality with a process to engage stakeholders. 'Even good scenarios are not enough. To be effective, they must involve top and middle managers in understanding the changing business environment more intimately than they would in the traditional planning process' (Wack, 1985, p. 74). Effectiveness here means making an impact on decision making. Wack describes how the project at Shell started with an initial set of scenarios, which were then presented to different groups and departments. Although the scenarios were generally received well, only about one-third of Shell's decision centres acted on the scenario insights. Scenarios were then adapted by highlighting their implications for basic assumptions underlying the worldview of different Shell departments. Exploration and production managers, for instance, were told that concessions and mining rights might be lost. This new approach did have an impact on the thinking and actions of most managers. Wack recounts that it took several years to invalidate existing worldviews and gain acceptance for scenarios as a bridge to new insights. Insights such as these gradually found their way into the literature and were translated into practical methodologies for scenario development. Although the first publication on a methodology for scenario development already appeared in the 1970s (Zentner, 1975), detailed descriptions of the process of developing scenarios were not published until the mid-1980s (Huss & Honton, 1987a, 1987b; Ogilvy & Mantle, 1984). In the 1990s, a range of approaches appeared (Ringland, 1998; Schoemaker, 1993; Schwartz, 1997; Van der Heijden, 1996). Approaches are different in terms of the number of steps and level of detail on which tools and techniques are described, but similarities can be recognised.

At present, the field of scenario analysis has clearly moved beyond the paucity of publications on methodology. We might even say the field has overshot its mark and at present there are too many alternative descriptions of scenario analysis processes. Several authors deplore the lack of a standard and well-tested methodology. Schnaars observes that the literature "offers a plethora of methods for constructing scenarios, some of which are reasonable, many of which are arcane and impractical, most of which have never been fairly tested" (1987, p. 105). Martelli (2001) summarises the situation as a 'methodological chaos'. Chermack et al. (2001) see a drawback in the fact that scenario analysis is rooted in practice and not strongly embedded in theory. This means that key steps in the methodology are not clearly articulated: "The absence of explicit theoretical roots has led to the application of scenario planning as something of a 'club members only' philosophy" (2001, p. 10). Critique from the strategy field concentrates on the qualitative and intuitive nature of scenarios in the intuitive logics school. Porter (1985) regrets that scenarios are based on 'speculation' rather than facts. Mintzberg (1994, p. 248) adds that by describing a range of possible futures 'you might just hit upon the right one'. While this comment seems to confuse the aim of multiple-scenario development with that of forecasting, he also points out that the approach had not yet developed into a mature method. The few successful case studies reported in the literature, with Shell as the most prominent example, do not constitute a solid basis for starting a scenario intervention. In Mintzberg's mind, Wack's (1985) case may stand out as remarkable precisely because many similar cases failed. Failure in this sense means either scenarios were not indicative of possible futures or behaviour of managers was not influenced.

However, since the year 2000, a range of reviews appeared that indicate that this methodological chaos is more apparent than real (Cordova-Pozo & Rouwette, 2023). At the base of many of the criticisms of the scenario planning field is the lack of an agreed-upon definition. Scenarios are alternatively interpreted as descriptions of possible futures versus normative ideals to strive for, as end states versus paths towards the future, and as descriptions of a context over which decision makers have no control versus plans (e.g. disaster management scenarios). However, recent work suggests that there is a synthesised definition that covers most scenario work. The next point of criticism concerns the lack of a standard and well-tested methodology. While there is indeed a confusing diversity of methods and techniques, within the three recognised schools of scenario analysis, the range of methodological choices is more restricted and arguments for choosing between options are clearer. These schools are known as intuitive logics, La prospective, and the probabilistic modified trends school (Amer et al., 2013; Bradfield et al., 2005). Participatory scenario development fits best to the intuitive logics school. In the next section, we outline an approach for stakeholder involvement in scenario construction in the form of a series of steps. The section on alternatives will briefly go into the assumptions and techniques used in the two other schools of thought. The final section will go into evidence for the effectiveness of the approach.

6.2 Procedure, technique, and tools

In this section, we acknowledge the diversity of scenario approaches by first giving an idea of the different interpretations offered by the literature, and then making a motivated choice. We do this first for scenario definitions and then for a procedure for participatory development of scenarios. The process of constructing scenarios described in this chapter focuses on creating qualitatively different contextual scenarios. Definitions that fit with this type of scenarios are the following: focused descriptions of fundamentally different futures presented in coherent script-like or narrative fashion (Schoemaker, 1993, p. 195); the set formed by the description of a future situation and the course of events that enables one to progress from the original situation to the future situation (Godet, 2000, p. 11); an internally consistent view of what the future might turn out to be – not a forecast, but one possible future outcome (Chermack, 2004, p. 305; Porter, 1985, p. 63). The first and last definition focuses on end states: descriptions of the state of the world at some point in the future. The second also includes the course of events leading up to that future state. In the procedure for scenario construction outlined later, the emphasis is on descriptions of the future state. Nevertheless, 'historic' descriptions of how that situation came about add to the plausibility and readability of a scenario and can therefore certainly be part of it. In the first definition, scenarios are script-like or narrative descriptions but we will not limit scenarios to texts here. Scenarios also come in the form of visual depictions, models, simulation output (e.g. graphs over time) with explanations, movies, or other types of media. One study mentions timeline illustrations, colourful drawings, cartoons, oil on canvas paintings, and collages (Oteros-Rozas et al., 2015). Causal diagrams (Chapter 4) can depict the end state or developments leading up to the future. Finally, the last definition refers to internally consistent views. In order for a scenario to be a plausible view of a possible future, it should not include any logical flaws. Spaniol and Rowland (2019) review the literature and come to a synthesised definition, which turns out to cover recent definitions as well (Cordova-Pozo & Rouwette, 2023). Spaniol and Rowland's definition is as follows:

> Scenarios have a temporal property rooted in the future and reference external forces in that context; scenarios should be possible and plausible while taking the proper form of a story or narrative description; and that scenarios exist in sets that are systematically prepared to coexist as meaningful alternatives to one another.
>
> *Spaniol and Rowland (2019, p. 1)*

We use this definition here but allow for a broad interpretation of 'story', as indicated earlier. Note that this excludes some of the alternative views of scenarios described in the previous section. We take scenarios to be descriptions rather than normative ideals, end states as well as paths, capturing organisational contexts rather than plans.

As there is no standard agreed-upon approach for participatory scenario development, later we compare the approaches suggested by some of the most cited authors and institutes in the field. We include the eight-step process proposed by SRI International (Huss & Honton, 1987a, 1987b; Ogilvy & Mantle, 1984), Schoemaker's ten steps (1993), Van der Heijden's process (1996) which introduces the business idea and transactional environment, and Schwartz' eight steps (1997), which are the inspiration for among others Ringland (1998) and Wright and Cairns' (2011) approach that adds two elements to increase impact on participants' thinking: consideration of extreme outcomes and identification of stakeholders.

The left column of Table 6.1 presents our summary of the scenario process in eight steps. Our phases follow the process identified by the majority of methodologies. In some cases, we combined or separated steps to ensure that each was divergent, convergent, or prioritising. The table lays out phases as if the process were sequential, but many authors underline the iterative nature of the process in which cycling back to an earlier phase is common. We made minor changes in the order of steps compared to the original publication. For instance, Schwartz (1997) places the selection of leading indicators and sign-posts in the one before last phase, we moved this to an earlier position. As a last point, note that some key terms are defined differently. Driving forces may, for instance, refer to all contextual developments or only to a selected set of key developments. Van der Heijden (1996) refers to the actor/stake-holder matrix which is at present often referred to as the power–interest grid.

In the remainder of this section, we describe the core concepts and choices in each phase, drawing upon the approaches in Table 6.1 where relevant.

Scenario development starts by identifying an issue or question of concern. The central concern may initially be formulated by an organisation's repre-sentative that seeks contact with a team experienced in scenario methodol-ogy. This concern can be further explored by looking at major uncertainties faced in the past, analysing prior decisions, or identifying the priorities of key stakeholders. SRI proposes to map factors that most directly drive organisa-tional decisions, for instance, market size, price trends or resource availabil-ity (Huss & Honton, 1987b). At the core of scenario analysis is contrasting organisational aims with the future environment (the strategic agenda, Van der Heijden, 1996). To better understand the organisation's aims, Van der Heijden proposes to articulate the business idea. This captures how the organisation's distinctive competencies answer a societal need, which in turn creates competitive advantage. This bears many similarities to the joint devel-opment of a (business) model as described in Chapters 4 and 5. To find out which part of the future environment to focus on, the so-called oracle ques-tion can be used: 'if you could ask an oracle anything about the world in [timeframe scenario], what would you ask?' This first phase should result in an understanding of the question that the scenario project seeks to answer, the relevant timeframe, scope, and decision makers involved.

In Step 2, the aim is to identify trends or developments impacting the organisation. The procedure outlined here works towards scenarios on the contextual environment: that part of the organisation's surroundings that cannot be influenced by what the organisation does (Figure 6.1).

The contextual environment impacts the transactional environment, which is the part of the organisational context with which the organisation has daily interactions (Van der Heijden, 1996, p. 6; 155). The transactional environment includes customers, suppliers, competitors, and employees and is influenced by, and in turn influences, the organisation. The start of scenario construction is identifying which trends shape the contextual environment. These trends can be categorised using the SEPTE acronym, for social, eco-nomic, political, technological, and ecological developments. (Other versions of this acronym are also used, such as PESTEL which includes legal develop-ments.) The SEPTE acronym is used as a prompt for participants, helping them to generate a wide range of trends and developments. Using divergent methods such as nominal group technique or electronic brainstorming typi-cally generates dozens of trends within minutes.

TABLE 6.1 Alternative procedures for participatory scenario development (intuitive logics school)

	SRI (Huss and Honton, 1987b)	Schoemaker (1993)	Van der Heijden (1996)	Schwartz (1997)	Wright and Cairns (2011)
1. Formulate starting issue or question	Analyse decisions and strategic concerns; Identify key decision factors	Identify issue; Identify major stakeholders or actors	Articulate strategic agenda; Develop business idea (SWOT)	Identify focal issue or decision	Set agenda
2. Identify trends (SEPTE)	Identify key environmental forces	List current trends or predetermined elements	List key trends (SEPTE), develop database	Identify key forces in local environment	Determine driving forces
3. Cluster trends			Cluster data	Identify driving forces	Cluster driving forces; Define cluster outcomes
4. Score clusters on uncertainty and impact	Analyse environmental forces	Identify uncertainties	Rank by unpredictability and impact on strategic agenda	Rank by importance and uncertainty	Develop impact/uncertainty matrix
5. Determine driving forces, elements, policies, and indicators			Identify driving forces, using inductive or deductive structuring	Select leading indicators and signposts	
6. Translate into scenarios and write texts	Define scenario logics; Elaborate scenarios	Start from two scenarios and work towards consistent set; Ensure scenario consistency, if needed by formalisation	Scenario development	Select scenario logics; Flesh out scenarios	Frame, scope, and develop scenarios; Include extreme outcomes
7. Determine impact on transactional environment	Analyse implications for key decision factors	Identify behaviour stakeholders in scenario	Power–interest grid; Competitive positioning	Determine implications	Identify stakeholders
8. Determine robust options	Analyse implications for decisions and strategies	Formulate decision scenarios	Wind tunnelling in scenario/option matrix; Option planning; Stakeholder–option matrix		

Notes: An early version of this procedure is presented by Van Mullekom and Vennix (2004).

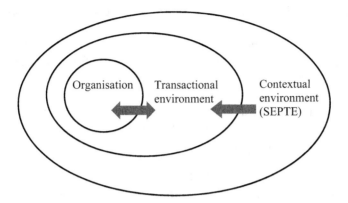

FIGURE 6.1 Transactional and contextual environments.

Source: Adapted from Van der Heijden (1996, p. 155)

In Step 3, trends are clustered into themes. These are not any of the SEPTE categories but new topics that emerge in the discussion.

Step 4 takes the clusters of contextual developments and scores them on importance and uncertainty. Given that scenarios aim to help in exploring possible futures, it is especially important to know which of the contextual developments will have a major impact on the organisation. In addition, if it was known which direction the development would take, we would be back in the forecasting mode and planning would be relatively unproblematic. For instance, as our understanding of the impact of climate change is growing, so does the certainty around its effects in the coming years. As a result, many countries are now implementing adaptive measures to reduce the impact of flooding or heatwaves. In contrast, the possibility or timing of another pandemic is much less certain. This means planning on protective medical gear, or Intensive Care capacity needs to 'fit' to two very different situations: a world in which demand for medical care is much like it is now, as well as a pandemic.

In Step 5, four sets of variables are identified: driving forces, elements, policies, and indicators. An organisation uses indicators to know if it is still achieving its aims. Performance indicators such as profit or market share can be found in the transactional environment, as they are not in complete control of the organisation but are the result of interaction with its environment. Another term for this is signposts: trends and events that need to be monitored to see if the organisation is going in the right direction (Schwartz, 1997). To keep its course or reach its goal, an organisation uses policies or strategies. It may, for instance, lower price (policy) to achieve a higher market share (indicator). For scenario planning, in particular, those policies are relevant that represent major commitments and cannot be easily reversed. Driving forces are those contextual developments that are both important and uncertain. The number of driving forces selected determines how many alternative scenarios are developed. Selecting two driving forces leads to four extreme scenarios, as in Figure 6.2.

However, selecting the key driving forces is not just a technical step and is not always a straightforward process. The driving forces set the scene for the scenarios, which means they should also be contrasting and capture the attention of the intended audience. For instance, electing economic growth and technological innovation as two axes might be problematic. For a starter, is the scenario imaginable in which the economy stagnates but innovation soars? Several inductive and deductive approaches may help to select driving forces and scenarios (Van der Heijden, 1996). An example of inductive scenario selection is the following. In 1991, Adam Kahane facilitated a scenario workshop with representatives of South Africa's constituencies (Van der Heijden, 1996, p. 199). These included ANC officials, trade unionists, activists, and corporate executives. Given the tensions and conflicts between these groups, Kahane did not think there would be any agreement on the desired state of the country in the future. Instead, the group was asked to discuss what might happen. In subgroups, participants were asked to come up with stories of what might happen to South Africa between now and 20 years. In the plenary discussion that followed, scenarios were presented and the audience was only allowed to ask two questions: 'why does that happen?' and 'what happens next?' Some of the scenarios developed in the subgroups were rather wild, such as one in which the Chinese government would help a South African communist liberation movement by supplying arms. When other participants asked 'why would this happen?' there was no clear answer and the scenario was dropped from further consideration. By using this process, the initial set of 30 scenarios was brought down to just four.

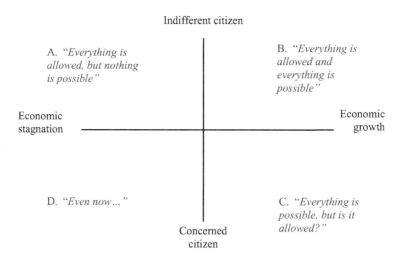

FIGURE 6.2 Example scenario axes.

Step 6 is to write scenario texts. Figure 6.2 shows driving forces selected in a project on public safety for the Dutch Ministry of the Interior. In the contextual environment of the Ministry, economic developments and the degree to which the Dutch citizen was involved in society were found to be the most important and uncertain developments. The four scenarios, of which the names are indicated in the figure, were then written. In scenario writing, it is important that each of the scenarios is equally plausible to a reader. One way of establishing this is to make sure all scenarios cover the same topics. In the example, this meant, for instance, that all scenarios needed to say something about immigration. In one scenario, immigration may be low and in another high. In addition, there may be qualitative differences in how immigration would play out in scenarios, for instance, when in one scenario immigrants are mostly war refugees, while in another scenario immigrants primarily flee the bad economic situation in their homeland. Other topics, such as demographic developments in the Netherlands, were rated as certain and so have the same value in all scenarios. These factors are also called predetermineds. For instance, all scenarios would assume the same size of the Dutch population. The uncertain and certain factors that need to be covered in all scenarios are called scenario elements. Scenarios need to be written in such a way that there is a clear storyline and logical flow of argument. Scenarios need to be internally consistent and plausible (Schoemaker, 1993). Schoemaker proposes to work from two opposing scenarios or formalise scenarios to increase consistency. Wright and Cairns (2011) progressively make scenarios more concrete by going through framing, scoping, and full development. An important consideration in the writing phase is whether the scenarios connect to the intended audience. Ultimately scenarios need to be not only consistent and plausible but also original yet credible and relevant (Amer et al., 2013). Does the scenario challenge managers? Can managers place themselves in the scenario, is it important to their core concerns? Wright and Cairns suggest to consider extreme outcomes to grasp the reader's attention. Going back to the example earlier in the paper, for Shell managers the nationalisation of mining across the globe was one such extreme outcome.

Step 7 is about laying out the consequences of each scenario in more detail. Here, the scenarios – that play out in the contextual environment – are brought one step closer to the organisation by specifying their impact on the transactional environment. This can be accomplished by identifying stakeholders and their behaviour in each alternative scenario. The power–interest grid is an excellent way of identifying stakeholders and the degree of their influence over developments. An example will be given in Chapter 7. Performance indicators are also located in the transactional environment, as they are the result of the interplay between organisational decisions, clients, and competitors. Understanding the behaviour of stakeholders helps to get a better idea of changes in performance scores. This connects to the idea of SRI, which is to go back in this step to the factors that most directly drive organisational decisions, such as with market developments and resource availability (Huss & Honton, 1987b).

Step 8 is about comparing policies and scenarios. Here, the alignment between the organisation and its surroundings is determined. The different but equally plausible scenarios are used as a testing bed for policy options. This may be done in two ways. In some cases, the organisation already has a strategic plan which it would like to pursue. This plan can then be contrasted with the scenarios to see what results it would lead to in each future. If results in all scenarios are positive, the plan would be robust for the developments captured by the scenarios. If in one or a few scenarios results are negative, the plan may be adapted. If changes in the plan are not possible, at least an early warning system may be developed so that the organisation knows beforehand if the environment threatens to go in the direction described in the 'difficult' scenario. In other cases, an organisation does not already have a strategic plan. In those circumstances, the scenarios can be used in a divergent activity and options can be identified that might generate good outcomes in a particular scenario. Again, the aim is to define options that work well in all scenarios. The literature describes this phase as analysing implications decisions and strategies (Huss & Honton, 1987b) or as formulating decision scenarios (Schoemaker, 1993). Van der Heijden (1996) uses the metaphor of a wind tunnel. Similar to testing a plane design by placing a model plane in a wind tunnel, a business idea can be tested against alternative scenarios. The question to be answered is then if the business idea without any changes can survive in a particular scenario or, alternatively, if changes are needed. Other authors do not propose to test the business model as a whole but look at particular policies. The impact of policies in each scenario is determined by the score on performance indicators defined in an earlier phase. Those policies that work out well in all scenarios are called robust options. Option planning and a stakeholder–options matrix (Van der Heijden, 1996) help to specify options further.

6.3 Versions

The approach outlined earlier is particular with regard to the school of thought it draws on, its orientation, and scope. It mainly draws on participant insights. This section briefly addresses alternatives to these choices, in particular, how participant insights (a qualitative dataset) can be complemented by quantitative data.

The approach outlined in the previous section, as mentioned, fits within the intuitive logics school of scenario planning. It aims to construct contextual rather than policy scenarios, and explorative rather than goal-setting (normative) scenarios. The La Prospective school of scenario planning (Godet, 2000) also constructs normative scenarios and may use participation in the process. In terms of scope, the explanation and examples for each step highlighted the development of scenarios for a single organisation. Other types of scenarios concern a sector or several sectors of the economy, or a societal challenge. Global scenarios are used, for instance, to explore climate change. Climate scenarios developed by the Intergovernmental Panel on Climate Change (IPCC) illustrate a number of key considerations in the use of large-scope scenarios. IPCC develops narrative and model-based (quantitative) climate scenarios (IPCC, 2023) with the ultimate aim to provide scientific information to support climate policies. The panel's definition of scenarios will by now seem familiar, but does place particular emphasis on consistency:

> Scenarios provide plausible descriptions of how the future may develop. Based on a coherent and internally consistent set of assumptions about key driving forces (e.g., rate of technological change, prices) and relationships, they . . . provide a view of the implications of developments and actions.
>
> *(IPCC, 2023, p. iv)*

These scenarios are constructed by researchers with expertise in domain areas and modelling with a variety of users in mind. For this topic, user participation in scenario construction is impossible and the foundation in science precludes building extreme scenarios. (Although we could say that these scenarios include extreme events that are likely to draw the user's attention, cf. Wright & Cairns, 2011.) Therefore, it is not a given that scenarios will affect decision makers and the general public. The report notes that communication of results is difficult as they are phrased in academic language and because of the large differences between target audiences (e.g. politicians, board members, consumers). One suggestion the report offers is to use 'storylines to complement graphs, tables, and to illustrate how a scenario evolves over time' (IPCC, 2023, p. 24). It seems fair to say that the goal of developing consistent scenarios anchored on the latest scientific knowledge creates a challenge when it comes to impacting decision making.

Naturally, there is a great contrast between participative development of scenarios for a single organisation on the one hand, and integrating scientific knowledge into global scenarios on the other hand. Many applications aim to combine a foundation in available evidence with stakeholder participation of some kind. For supporting team decision making, alternative approaches that complement the qualitative analysis of participant input are most relevant. The third school of scenario analysis, the probabilistic modified trends school, takes a quantitative approach and builds on traditional forecasting methods (Börjeson et al., 2006; Bradfield et al., 2005). This approach combines extrapolation of historic time series with a consideration of the impact of unprecedented future events. Expert judgment is combined with statistics or simulation modelling. The probabilistic modified trends school uses two distinct methods: trend-impact analysis and cross-impact analysis

(Cordova-Pozo & Rouwette, 2023). The first method starts by generating a list of events that could lead to deviations from extrapolated trends, after which experts estimate the probability of these events and their expected impact. Cross-impact analysis follows a similar approach but uses a more elaborate process to determine probabilities of future events. Experts do not directly estimate probabilities but instead determine the likelihood of future events given that specific previous events have or have not occurred.

In considering which approach is most useful, a major factor is how far we are looking ahead (Van der Heijden, 1996, p. 92). In the short term, predictability is high and forecasting can provide a useful input to decision making. Looking further ahead, some variables are predictable while around others there is substantial uncertainty. Here, scenarios based on intuitive logics or probabilistic modified trends are most useful. In the very long term (almost) everything is uncertain. In this situation of so-called deep uncertainty, there are conflicting opinions or lack of knowledge on the relation between elements of the situation and the probabilities around changes in key elements and/or values (Marchau et al., 2019). Approaches such as robust decision making and adaptive planning (www.deepuncertainty.org) are valuable here.

6.4 Applications

As mentioned, the use of scenarios for corporate strategic planning soared in the mid-1970s (Linneman & Klein, 1983). In terms of publications, attention grew considerably in the period 1990–2005 (Varum & Melo, 2010). Data on publications until 2017 indicate the upward trend continued after that (Oliveira et al., 2018). A 2023 survey of management tools by Bain & Company places scenarios in the top five strategy support tools in terms of use and satisfaction (www.bain.com). This position has not changed much over the 30 years that this survey has been in use. Cordova-Pozo and Rouwette (2023) conclude that an increasing number of organisations are employing some form of scenarios, in a variety of disciplines (e.g. management, social systems, education, health, and climate adaptation).

Decision making teams are expected to benefit from using scenarios in a number of ways. Varum and Melo (2010) group these into three main expected impacts. By providing an opportunity to envision plausible future states, scenarios can help to generate strategies that reduce risks, build on opportunities, and avoid threats. They help to pre-experience the future, frame emergent ideas, and develop and communicate strategies. Scenarios are also often credited for creating individual and organisational learning (Varum & Melo, 2010). Nevertheless, only few studies evaluate whether these results actually materialise. Out of the 13 reviews analysed by Cordova-Pozo and Rouwette (2023), only four report on evaluation studies. Evaluations that are available are typically single or multiple case studies, and a small number is

experimental. A relevant example of a single-case study is reported by Hodgkinson and Wright (2002) and describes how scenarios pictured a future that
was seen as too challenging to the organisation concerned. This raises the
point of the distance of scenario narratives to the decision maker's everyday
reality. As we saw, extreme events can grasp attention (Wack, 1985; Wright &
Cairns, 2011) but apparently a too challenging scenario can backfire. On the
other hand, if the scenario narrative is too close to current reality, the reader
may not pay attention. Oteros-Rozas et al. (2015) analysed 23 participatory
scenario planning case studies conducted by the authors in a wide range of
social–ecological settings and concluded that these result in building common
understanding and fostering learning about future planning. They point to
three beneficial outcomes of participatory scenario construction, in line with
Varum and Melo (2010). First, Oteros-Rozas et al. find that scenarios help to
generate policy options and increase the legitimacy and acceptance of policy
options across stakeholders. Second, scenario planning creates awareness, an
increased need for long-term planning, and enables collective reflection and
discussion. In this way, a shared understanding is built and stakeholders are
mobilised into action. Third, multiple learning outcomes between stakeholders are enhanced by increasing dialogue and resolving conflicts.

The variety of approaches to scenario development makes it difficult to
pinpoint why effects materialise. Although success stories of scenario applications are published and widely known, it still remains difficult to establish how results are actually achieved (Hodgkinson, 2004; Mintzberg, 1994).
Recent studies have contributed to clarity on central concepts and phases in
scenario construction, which puts others in a better position to repeat the
procedure and hopefully the outcomes. Using case studies, it is difficult to
disentangle the impact of elements of the scenario approach from changes in
the context of the team or organisation. Experiments are better equipped to
discover the path between intervention elements and impacts on participants.
Concerning scenario planning, two experiments are especially noteworthy.
Schoemaker (1993) conducts four experimental studies on the role of biases
in scenario planning. He finds that scenarios are perceived to be more believ-
able if they are more detailed and cohesive (Schoemaker, 1993). This is para-
doxical, as more detail will make a scenario less likely. A scenario in which
internet sales decline and Brexit is reversed, is more unlikely than a scenario
in which only internet sales decline. In part this is due to another bias, called
the conjunction fallacy. People fall for this bias whenever they consider that
the chance that A and B will happen is higher than either A or B happening. Using classroom experiments, Schoemaker (1993) finds that scenarios
exploit one bias (the conjunction bias) to counteract another bias (availability). His main conclusion is that after working with scenarios, participants
accept a wider range of uncertainty (indicated by an increase in subjective
confidence ranges) which lowers overconfidence and tunnel vision. Another

experiment (Gong et al., 2017) compares scenarios against forecasts. Participants work with a decision support tool in either a scenario or forecast condition. Compared to those in the forecast condition, participants in the scenario condition more often chose the strategies that performed well over the full range of uncertainties (robust options). This difference was not due to the exploration of options, as participants in both conditions explored options in a similar manner. The scenario group, however, paid more attention to worst-case outcomes.

In conclusion, multiple-scenario construction is a popular approach for developing strategy. While the approach has been criticised for its lack of clarity, central concepts and phases in the scenario methodology are becoming more clear. There is some evidence that considering plausible, alternative future supports the identification of robust options and helps to discuss and reflect on plans for the long term. Working with scenarios encourages learning, in the sense that participants accept a wider range of uncertainty. For that to happen, scenarios need to be carefully balanced and strike a middle ground between originality and credibility. If a scenario is too close to current reality, users may not pay attention. A too-extreme scenario might lack credibility, be too challenging for the audience, and be rejected.

References

Amer, M., Daim, T. U., & Jetter, A. (2013). A review of scenario planning. *Futures*, *46*, 23–40.

Börjeson, L., Höjer, M., Dreborg, K.-H., Ekvall, T., & Finnveden, G. (2006). Scenario types and techniques: Towards a user's guide. *Futures*, *38*(7), 723–739.

Bradfield, R., Wright, G., Burt, G., Cairns, G., & Van der Heijden, K. (2005). The origins and evolution of scenario techniques in long range business planning. *Futures*, *37*(8), 795–812.

Chermack, T. J. (2004). A theoretical model of scenario planning. *Human Resource Development Review*, *3*(4), 301–325.

Chermack, T. J., Lynham, S. A., & Ruona, W. E. A. (2001). A review of scenario planning literature. *Futures Research Quarterly*, *17*(2).

Cordova-Pozo, K., & Rouwette, E. A. J. A. (2023). Types of scenario planning and their effectiveness: A review of reviews. *Futures*, *149*. https://doi.org/10.1016/j.futures.2023.103153

Drucker, P. F. (1973). *Management: Tasks, responsibilities, practices*. Harper & Row.

Godet, M. (2000). The art of scenarios and strategic planning: Tools and pitfalls. *Technological Forecasting and Social Change*, *65*, 3–22.

Gong, M., Lempert, R., Parker, A., Mayer, L. A., Fischbach, J., Sisco, M., Mao, Z., Krantz, D. H., & Kunreuther, H. (2017). Testing the scenario hypothesis: An experimental comparison of scenarios and forecasts for decision support in a complex decision environment. *Environmental Modelling & Software*, *91*, 135–155.

Hodgkinson, G. P. (2004). *Towards a (pragmatic) science of strategic intervention: The case of scenario planning*. Advanced Institute of Management Research.

Hodgkinson, G. P., & Wright, G. (2002). Confronting strategic inertia in a top management team: Learning from failure. *Organization Studies*, *23*, 949–977.

Huss, W. R., & Honton, E. J. (1987a). Alternative methods for developing business scenarios. *Technological Forecasting and Social Change*, *31*(3), 219–238.

Huss, W. R., & Honton, E. J. (1987b). Scenario planning – what style should you use? *Long Range Planning, 20*(4), 21–29.

IPCC. (2023). *Workshop report of the Intergovernmental Panel on Climate Change workshop on the use of scenarios in the sixth assessment report and subsequent assessments.* Working Group III Technical Support Unit.

Klein, H. E., & Linneman, R. E. (1981). The use of scenarios in corporate planning – eight case histories. *Long Range Planning, 14*(5), 69–77.

Linneman, R. E., & Klein, H. E. (1983). The use of multiple scenarios by United States industrial companies – a comparison study, 1977–1981. *Long Range Planning, 16*(6), 94–101. https://doi.org/10.1016/0024-6301(83)90013-4

Marchau, V. A. W. J., Walker, W. E., Bloemen, P. J. T. M., & Popper, S. W. (2019). *Decision making under deep uncertainty: From theory to practice.* Springer Nature.

Martelli, A. (2001). Scenario building and scenario planning: State of the art and prospects of evolution. *Futures Research Quarterly, 17*(2), 57–74.

Mintzberg, H. (1994). *The rise and fall of strategic planning.* Prentice-Hall.

Ogilvy, J. A., & Mantle, T. (1984). *How to construct and use scenarios.* SRI International.

Oliveira, A. S., de Barros, M. D., de Carvalho Pereira, F., Gomes, C. F. S., & da Costa, H. G. (2018). Prospective scenarios: A literature review on the Scopus database. *Futures, 100*, 20–33.

Oteros-Rozas, E., Martin-Lopez, B., Daw, T. M., Bohensky, E. L., Butler, J. R. A., Hill, R., Martin-Ortega, J., Quinlan, A., Ravera, F., Ruiz-Mallen, I., Thyresson, M., Mistry, J., Palomo, I., Peterson, G. D., Plieninger, T., Waylen, K. A., Beach, D. M., Bohnet, I. C., Hamann, M., Hanspach, J., Hubacek, K., Lavorel, S., & Vilardy, S. P. (2015). Participatory scenario planning in place-based social-ecological research: Insights and experiences from 23 case studies. *Ecology and Society, 20*(4), 66, Article 32. https://doi.org/10.5751/es-07985-200432

Porter, M. E. (1985). *Competitive advantage: Creating and sustaining superior performance.* Free Press.

Ringland, G. (1998). *Scenario planning: Managing for the future.* Wiley.

Schoemaker, P. J. H. (1993). Multiple scenario development: Its conceptual and behavioral foundation. *Strategic Management Journal, 14*, 193–213.

Schnaars, S. P. (1987). How to develop and use scenarios. *Long range planning, 20*(1), 105–114.

Schwartz, P. (1997). *The art of the long view.* Doubleday.

Spaniol, M. J., & Rowland, N. J. (2019). Defining scenario. *Futures & Foresight Science, 1*(1), e3. https://onlinelibrary.wiley.com/doi/full/10.1002/ffo2.3

Van der Heijden, K. (1996). *Scenarios: The art of strategic conversation.* John Wiley.

Van Mullekom, T., & Vennix, J. A. M. (2004). Using groupware to build a scenario-based early warning system. In *Information and Communications Technology for Competitive Intelligence*, 269–285. IGI Global.

Varum, C. A., & Melo, C. (2010). Directions in scenario planning literature–a review of the past decades. *Futures, 42*(4), 355–369.

Wack, P. (1985, November-December). Scenarios: Shooting the rapids. *Harvard Business Review*, 139–150.

Wright, G., & Cairns, G. (2011). *Scenario thinking: Practical approaches to the future.* Palgrave Macmillan.

Zentner, R. D. (1975). Scenarios, a new tool for corporate planners. *Chemical and Engineering News, 53*, 22–34.

7

APPLICATION

Understanding possible futures
of Nijmegen municipality

This chapter describes an application of participatory scenario development with Nijmegen municipality. At the time of the project, Nijmegen was facing a number of major choices in housing and spatial planning. Each of the possible options represented major investments, would take years to realise, and would continue to shape the city for the coming decades. To bring a broad range of expertise to bear on these decisions and ensure that policies would work in the light of future uncertainty, a participatory scenario planning project was initiated. A total of 31 city representatives participated in five sessions, constructing scenarios and wind tunnelling policy measures. Below, we describe the motivation for starting the project, the two modelling sessions with Sioo employees and external lecturers, the resulting model, and its impact.

7.1 Background and issue

In March 2015, Jos Sprangers, director Spatial domain, and Tom Merkx, director Administrative Support and Advice of Nijmegen municipality, sought contact with Radboud University. In his previous position at the Ministry of Infrastructure, Jos had experienced the use of scenarios in strategic planning (Van der Steen et al., 2011). In particular, the confrontation of proposed policies with external, uncertain developments appealed to him. In his current job, one of the pressing issues was the planned construction of 10,000 houses near to the Waal River, in the Waalfront and Waalsprong districts. In planning these and other construction projects, land exploitation plans (how many dwellings to build, in which price class) tended to be based

DOI: 10.4324/9781003404200-9

on a narrow range of predictions about the growth of Nijmegen's population. While demographic changes were assumed to be relatively predictable, in the longer term these predictions were actually very uncertain. Besides demographics, other (uncertain) developments would influence future construction projects, such as the development of retail and catering in the city centre, ICT and its use in all kinds of activities (such as living, working, recreation, and education) and, related to this, the development of urban mobility and the economy in the region. Beyond spatial planning, Nijmegen municipality is responsible for a range of domains such as among others mobility, social cohesion, sustainability, and knowledge valorisation. An exploration of certain and uncertain environmental developments was deemed to be desirable. This would help to clarify which challenges the municipality would face in the coming decades and whether the current plans were sufficiently robust to deal with them.

The goal and planning of the project were discussed in a meeting between Jos Sprangers, Tom Merkx, Karin Heiligers (senior advisor on strategy), Vincent Marchau and Etiënne Rouwette (Radboud University). The project aim was formulated as follows: is Nijmegen municipality developing the right things for 2035? The project was to have two phases. The first, planned before summer, aimed to create awareness of the (uncertain) future. This entailed the construction of alternative contextual scenarios. The goal of the second phase, after summer, was to make policies future-proof. For this part, stakeholders outside of the municipality would be invited to a process of adaptive planning.

A total of 31 people participated in the meetings. Principals were Tom Merkx and Jos Sprangers. The meetings were facilitated by Etiënne Rouwette and Vincent Marchau, supported by Brigit Fokkinga, Monic Lansu, and Martijn van Latum (Radboud University). The next section discusses the process followed during the five meetings and the partial results to which the sessions led. Each meeting is briefly evaluated.

7.2 Process

It turned out to be more difficult than expected to bring over 30 people together for the sessions. This led to a decision to abandon the idea to organise a separate second phase of adaptive planning. Instead mapping the behaviour of stakeholders and wind tunnelling of policies was planned for sessions 4 and 5, after summer. The agenda that was developed for the sessions is shown in Table 7.1. Each meeting was 3.5 hours including breaks. Meetings took place in the group decision room on the Radboud University campus. Electronic meeting support software (MeetingSphere, now Xleap) was used to gather, cluster, and prioritise ideas. All meetings were audio recorded.

TABLE 7.1 Participatory scenario development agenda, products and procedure

Agenda, products and procedure

Session 1 (22 May 2015)
- Mapping the contextual environment of Nijmegen municipality: which developments and trends in the social, economic, political, technological, and ecological (SEPTE) domain play a role between now and 2035? (1, 2)
- Clustering developments (3)

Session 2 (12 June 2015)
- Scoring developments on uncertainty and importance (4)
- Selection of two driving forces as a basis for four scenarios (5)

Session 3 (3 July 2015)
- Development of four alternative scenarios in text, in four subgroups (6)

Session 4 (15 September 2015)
- Feedback on scenarios and further development (6)
- Mapping the transactional environment: which stakeholders are important to Nijmegen municipality? (7)
- Assessment of stakeholder behaviour in each scenario (7)

Session 5 (16 October 2015)
- Wind tunnelling: how do important policies score in each scenario? (8)
- Determination of robust and non-robust policies (8)

After meeting 1 to 4: *workbook*
After meeting 5: *final report*

Procedure participatory scenario development
1. formulate starting issue or question
2. identify trends (SEPTE)
3. cluster trends
4. score clusters on uncertainty and impact
5. determine driving forces, elements, policies, and indicators
6. translate into scenarios and write texts
7. determine impact on transactional environment
8. determine robust options

7.2.1 Session 1

The first session project began with a round of introductions by participants and facilitators. The central question of the project was explained: is Nijmegen municipality developing the right things for 2035? Participants completed a short questionnaire on the topics they considered most important for the future of the municipality of Nijmegen, and what they would like to know about the environment of the municipality of Nijmegen in 2035. A short presentation highlighted the benefits of constructing contextual scenarios with municipality staff and the steps in doing so. The main part of the first meeting was an electronic brainstorming session. Participants mapped out the municipality's contextual environment. The facilitator used the SEPTE categories (social, economic, political, technological, and environmental developments) as a prompt for participants, encouraging them to think of a broad range of developments. After the brainstorm had lasted a few minutes, participants were shown so-called trend cards. Trend cards are pictures of possible trends or developments. The trend cards used in this meeting were developed by the Dutch Ministry of Infrastructure. Participants generated over 300 ideas. In the next step, they grouped the ideas into 16 clusters. In a follow-up meeting with a subset of participants, the material was further condensed into the following ten clusters:

1. Demographic changes (demographics, migration)
2. Labour market (flexible labour/work demand/supply jobs, demand- vs. supply-driven education, mix leisure/work/care)
3. Mobility (e.g. intelligent transport systems)
4. Climate (e.g. water levels/flooding)
5. Health (e.g. population health, food, leisure/work/care mix)
6. Energy (e.g. decentralised/self-sufficient/circular generation of energy, including self-sufficient/local production of food)
7. Role of government (city government and city administration vs. province, state, Europe)
8. Economic development (e.g. macro-economy, sharing economy, buying behaviour)
9. Living environments (e.g. working follows living, living follows facilities)
10. Technological development

Over the course of the meeting, participants' comments seemed to indicate that they were enthusiastic about the methodology and saw the relevance of the proposed approach. The ideas generated would form the basis for the scenarios to be created and should therefore neither be too close nor too far away from the participants' current world. In the former case, scenarios would be unchallenging; in the latter, they would be incomprehensible to employees who are not present in the session, or too threatening. The more than 300 ideas generated by the brainstorming seem to strike a good balance between these two extremes. A final criterion for assessing the ideas is whether they covered the full space of developments. It is notable that the brainstorming included only limited discussion of safety: only two out of more than 300 developments touched on safety. The question is whether this is a good reflection of the role safety will play in the future of the municipality of Nijmegen.

7.2.2 Session 2

To remind participants of where they were in the scenario construction process, this and every subsequent meeting was started with an overview of the major steps in the entire project, an indication of where they were at that moment and a summary of previous results.

The clustering after the first meeting was discussed and adjusted by a small committee. While this approach saved session time that could then be spent on other topics, it brought with it the danger that the other participants would not recognise the new clusters. This potential drawback did not seem to be an issue in this session: after explaining why the clustering was adapted 'en petit comité' and explaining the new clusters, a brief discussion followed and participants readily accepted the results.

Getting from possible developments to alternative futures required a next step: scoring developments on importance and certainty. After all, not all developments were equally important to Nijmegen municipality. In addition, some developments can be extended into the future with reasonable certainty, and others are much less predictable. The uncertain developments are particularly interesting: they indicate a bandwidth that an organisation needs to take into account. In MeetingSphere, participants gave each cluster a score on importance and uncertainty. A development that turned out to be very important and uncertain was social cohesion or solidarity. In other words, it is difficult to indicate whether in 2035 society will be more individualistic or more inclusive. A second important and uncertain development concerns knowledge institutions in Nijmegen. Will HAN and Radboud University be much larger in 2035 than they are now or will they have left the region? These two developments formed the so-called driving forces, because they determined the state of the world in 2035. The combination of driving forces led to four scenarios (see Figure 7.1).

At the start of the voting process, there was some confusion about the criterion 'uncertainty' as it was phrased negatively. The step of choosing the two most important and uncertain developments, the driving forces, inspired a long discussion. In this step, as in clustering, it often seems as if the richness of the material should be reduced to a few overarching concepts. The facilitators indicated that the remaining clusters and the ideas in them would not be lost and could be included in the scenario texts. In the next step, participants then made a first sketch of scenarios. In subgroups, they wrote a newspaper article and provided it with a catchy title. The following newspaper article was written for Scenario A.

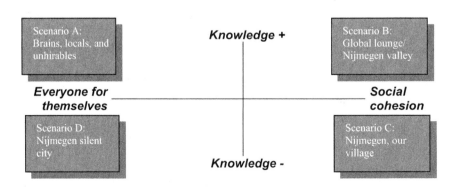

FIGURE 7.1 Driving forces and scenarios.

Mayor Jetten receives 60,000th student at Nijmegen train station

Dieter (22) from Munich would have liked to study in Tilburg but ended up in Nijmegen because of the major university merger. He now lives on the campus in Dukenburg, where the last resident passed away three years ago. Mayor Jetten solemnly handed him the access pass to the new campus. The mayor: "Dukenburg has become a beautiful campus. A golden opportunity for the city. By truly opting for completely restructuring the Centre and East into student rooms and relocating other residents to the Beuningen district, the nuisance caused by lodgers has now been minimised. Something we as the D66/VVD coalition are proud of! The city centre is now one large entertainment centre for the large group of knowledge workers and students, served by the people from Beuningen who commute daily by light rail to the centre." The mayor continued: 'Our community centres have thankfully been repurposed as student union houses. But I must now excuse myself, I must go and open the third casino on Veur Lent'.

Creating the newspaper articles in subgroups eventually went smoothly, and the presentations were enthusiastically received. With this, the intended end result seemed to have become more clear to participants.

7.2.3   Session 3

The meeting again started with a summary of the results so far, explanation of the roadmap for the project as a whole and where the current meeting fit in. An example of a scenario text from another project was presented. The reason why this was a successful scenario was because it met the four quality criteria for scenarios: consistency, plausibility, originality as well as credibility, and relevance. Participants were asked to add to the newspaper reports written in the previous meeting and work towards a text that met the four criteria. In doing so, it was also important to avoid creating positive and negative or desirable and undesirable scenarios. All four worlds should be equally probable for the reader, and if a world is considered very negative, there is a risk that a reader will not want to dive into it or even reject the whole story. In four subgroups, participants wrote a text for each of the scenarios. Table 7.2 a, b gives a brief summary.

At the end of the meeting, the texts had advanced substantially but were not yet finished. Over the summer, the four subgroups continued working. Each subgroup had a leader who coordinated the work. Participants agreed to send in scenario texts that would meet the quality criteria before the fourth meeting.

7.2.4   Session 4

The start of fourth meeting was a final round of comments on the scenario texts. The comments were further processed by the subgroups. The session

TABLE 7.2A Excerpt from scenarios A and B

	Scenario A: Knowledge+/ Individual Brains, locals, and unhirables	Scenario B: Knowledge+/ Collective Global lounge/Nijmegen valley
Demographic development	210,000 inhabitants, mostly scientific nomads, relatively many 20–40-year-olds	210,000 inhabitants, international knowledge workers who stay in Nijmegen after their studies, migrants, and refugees
Labour market	Three-way split: international knowledge workers with top wages, local service providers/ professionals, (unemployed) outsiders including independents and creatives	Flexibilisation, many self-employed who keep work via online reputation, entrepreneurs, developers, creatives and scientists meet in global lounges, 40% do not speak Dutch, labour is 24/7, separation of adaptables and non-adaptables
Mobility	Car trains, emission-free transport, RUHAN at Tolhuis/Zwanenveld, Dukenburg new Nijmegen CS	Scale leap in mobility, expansion of public transport, with focus on fast, sustainable and clean, fewer and more shared cars, more fast cycling
Climate	Extreme weather and mounds in lower town, heat dissipation big problem	Extreme weather but Nijmegen is water safe, enough greenery and water storage and drainage

TABLE 7.2B Excerpt from scenarios C and D

	Scenario C: Knowledge-/ Collective Nijmegen, our village	Scenario D: Knowledge-/ Individual Nijmegen silent city
Demographic development	From 2025, RU and HAN leave, in 2035, 135,000 inhabitants, fewer students and places to go out, relatively many elderly people, arrival of refugees, some highly educated and some traumatised and not integrated	110,000 inhabitants, ageing, small town, highly educated people leave Nijmegen and no new influx of young students, arrival of refugees, integration is difficult: no money for counselling, native Nijmegen citizens do not contribute

	Scenario C: Knowledge-/ Collective Nijmegen, our village	Scenario D: Knowledge-/ Individual Nijmegen silent city
Labour market	Loss of employment due to disappearance of university, more work in recreation: walking, water, history, more work in healthcare	Middle class disappeared, academics gone, professionals and healthcare workers in great demand, return of production work due to low wages
Mobility	The city is internally focused, no major traffic flows, not connected to high-speed train network, but shared cars and community bus	After 2020 no more investments in infrastructure, public transport severely limited, roads poorly maintained, fossil car use limited, cycling popular
Climate	Released space used for solar panels, knowledge side channel is monetised	Extreme seasons and parts of Nijmegen (West, Dukenburg) flooded for third time and expected to become uninhabitable, houses affected

then continued on the transactional environment: that part of the environment with which the municipality cooperates and conducts transactions. To start thinking about the transactional environment, participants indicated which groups Nijmegen municipality particularly cooperates with. These stakeholders were ordered by power (to what extent can they influence the municipality) and interest (how much do they care about the direction the municipality takes). Figure 7.2 provides an overview of stakeholders.

This classification led to four clusters of stakeholders. At the top right are the parties that score high on both power and interest. These are the 'players' who set the playing field: school sector organisations, large companies, housing associations, provinces, and knowledge institutes. At the bottom right are the 'context setters': they also have a lot of power but have less interest. Here, we find (social) media, large transport companies, the national government, investors, utilities, and health insurers. In the opposite corner, top left, are the 'subjects' with little power but a lot of importance. These are citizens and their platforms, welfare and care institutions, SMEs, associations, events and nature clubs, and surrounding municipalities. Finally, there are parties with little power and little interest: the 'crowd'. These are the combined creative institutions, youth, EU, and religious organisations. As an example of stakeholders' preferences in each scenario in 2035, consider the following.

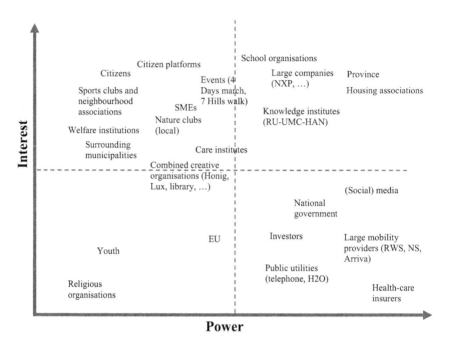

FIGURE 7.2 Power-interest grid of Nijmegen municipality stakeholders.

Large companies

A. Global growth and global revenues. Focus on Nijmegen as a place where these objectives are partly realised. There is a positive business climate, room for entrepreneurship and ample human capital. International profile.
B. See scenario A.
C. Large companies are no longer present in Nijmegen and do not consider establishing themselves. They are therefore no longer stakeholders.
D. Large companies no longer exist and do not consider relocating. Are therefore no longer stakeholders.

Citizens

A. Citizens stay in Nijmegen, prioritise their own comfort and interests. On the basis of their diversity, and operating from the principle of 'what's in it for me', they seek out like-minded people from their own group. The vulnerable and unhirables come to the government asking for help.
B. There is great cohesion among citizens regardless of their wealth and educational differences. Citizens do appreciate maintaining this cohesion, so the municipality is asked to help shape consultation platforms and support.

C. The city's DNA is changing, the population is ageing, citizens are more forced to arrange things by themselves and to help each other, to act together. Dependence on one another is increasing.

D. The city's DNA is changing; the motto is now every person for themselves and, the Diocese for us all. Self-interest prevails and people no longer care for interaction with their neighbour, neighbourhood, or city. Environment or sustainability are no longer an issue, unless they provide cheaper options. The government or to regulate it all, including healthcare. For traditional tasks, the government is overburdened. It cannot deliver as there is no money, no manpower.

Identifying stakeholders, describing their behaviour and wishes towards the municipality gave a lot of new information. This brought the scenarios to life for participants. Some of this information would be used in the further elaboration of the scenario texts.

7.2.5   Session 5

Prior to the fifth and final meeting, a list of Nijmegen municipality policy measures and the objectives the measures aimed to achieve was drawn up. Based on a comparison of the documents City Vision Nijmegen 2020 and City Budget 2015–2018 and the political agenda, the facilitators made an initial selection. These were then discussed in a smaller committee. Ultimately, the municipality's tasks and responsibilities were grouped in six themes: caring city, living and growing city, city that works and learns, sustainable city, vibrant city centre, and city in the region. For each theme, a number of policies and objectives were chosen. This was a difficult process as in some cases policies and objectives turned out to be very close to each other. It was a challenge to describe them unambiguously. Judging from the participants' comments, the description used in the session seemed clear.

In this meeting, participants again worked in four subgroups. For each policy, the subgroup was asked to indicate how well or badly it performed in their scenario with a rating from 0 to 10. This means that participants summarised all the effects of a policy into one overall rating. This approach was chosen because scoring all measures on each objective would take too much time. Participants were asked to give their scores individually first and then compare them within their subgroups. In the end, each subgroup integrated their scores into one subgroup score per policy and provided a short explanation for their score.

Table 7.3 shows the objectives and policies for each theme. Each theme also has a do-nothing option (in italics). In the meeting, subgroups also processed the comments on the scenarios raised in the previous session. The final scenarios were described in five to seven pages. The highlights of Scenario A were the following.

TABLE 7.3 Goals, (specific) objectives, and policies for wind tunnelling

What do we want to achieve (goal)	(Specific) objectives	Policies
Caring city (solidarity, together, robust)	• Inclusive society • Cooperation instead of competition between care institutes, linked up with social environment	1. Stimulating informal care, use of volunteers 2. Organise care services/ neighbourhood teams *What if we do not invest in care?*
Residential and growth city (being able to live comfortably)	• Sufficient housing for groups we want in Nijmegen • Sufficient affordable rental housing • Allowing the elderly to live in their own neighbourhood (life-course-proof housing) • Sufficient space for companies (including freelancers and new jobs) • Water safety • Sufficient (sustainable) accessibility	3. Build only in Waalfront and Waalsprong (no, unless policy) (4,000 dwellings until 2020, 10,000 building assignments) 4. No more investments in student housing 5. High-quality public transport, influencing behaviour: out of car, tram, public transport connection with Germany 6. Lifetime proof living *What if we do not invest in housing?*

Scenario A brains, locals, and unhirables

In the knowledge city of Nijmegen, individualism reigns supreme; there is little social cohesion. The city's population has grown to 210,000. Including surrounding villages, the municipality of Nijmegen has 457,000 inhabitants. The university attracts many students and scientists, but their stay here is too brief to care about integration and their fellow human beings. They are also too busy trying to keep their seat on the international scientific job carousel. The group of 20–40-year-olds dominates. Smart software has made the middle class redundant in this knowledge economy. Apart from knowledge workers, the workforce consists mainly of self-employed service providers. Unemployment is high and social security meagre. The gap between knowledge workers and outsiders is deep. Some of the marginalised maintain themselves in a subculture and a flourishing parallel creativity economy, an underestimated pillar of Nijmegen's attractiveness as a city to live in. The local government outsources to the market and directs a network of seconded specialists from a very small organisation.

Table 7.4 shows how each policy scores in the scenarios. The do-nothing option was formulated positively so that scoring became easier. The final scores were converted into a colour: green for a score of 8 or higher (the white cells in Table 7.4). Orange indicates a score from 4 to 7 (light grey cells); red refers to a score of 0 to 3 (dark grey cells).

What is the result of wind tunnelling policies planned by the city of Nijmegen? What first stood out was the large number of measures that were robust: 12 of the 26 policies score green or orange in every scenario. One measure that was clearly not robust was building 10,000 houses in the Waalfront and Waalsprong. This measure scored red in all scenarios. A number of other infrastructural measures score red in two scenarios: constructing transport hubs, not investing in student housing, spatial development, campus development, investing in the heat network, and sustainability. One measure within Care City, stimulating informal care, also scored red in two scenarios.

What did these scores mean for the municipality of Nijmegen? The measures that scored well in each scenario were robust for the contextual developments described in the scenarios. These measures therefore did not need to be adjusted. For measures that scored red in one or two scenarios, possible adjustments could be explored. If adjustment at present were not possible, another option was to develop a backup plan and monitor how the environment developed. If monitoring revealed that the scenario in which the measure does not work approaches, the backup plan could be implemented. A measure that did not score well in any scenario should better not be implemented in its current form.

At the end of the session, one participant commented that it was quite a shock to see that 10,000 additional homes did not work out well in any of the scenarios. Nevertheless, the results were discussed and acknowledged in the meeting. In a separate meeting with other departments of Nijmegen municipality in December 2015, results were also shared and recognised.

7.3   Final product

Participants in the scenario project received a workbook after each session and a final report at the end. The intermediate reports were generated by Meeting-Sphere and contained the ideas generated by participants and – when used – clusters or votes. Intermediate versions of scenario texts were also shared. The final report was 67 pages, including 45 pages of appendices. The main text included an introduction specifying the aim, method, and participants, the procedure with an agenda for each session, and a description of each meeting. By request of the contact persons, after outlining the process and results of each meeting, there was a short evaluation of process results and insights obtained. Results of a short questionnaire on future developments were also included (see the next section). Conclusions highlighted the two driving forces and the results of wind tunnelling 26 municipal policies. For

TABLE 7.4 Excerpt results wind tunnelling

Goals	Policies	Scenario A: Brains, locals and unhirables	Scenario B: Global lounge/Nijmegen valley	Scenario C: Nijmegen, our village	Scenario D: Nijmegen silent city
Caring city	1. Stimulating informal care, use of volunteers			░	░
	2. Organise care services/neighbourhood teams	░	░		
	We invest in a caring city				
Residential and growth city	3. Build only in Waalfront and Waalsprong (no, unless policy) (4,000 dwellings until 2020, 10,000 building assignments)	░	░	░	░
	4. No more investments in student housing	░	░		
	5. High-quality public transport, influencing behaviour: out of car, tram, public transport connection with Germany			░	░
	6. Lifetime proof living	░	░	░	░
	7. Extra: connection points public transport			░	░
	We invest in spatial development		░	░	░

policies that were not robust, the recommendation was to develop a moni-toring and backup plan. The reader was reminded that the participants – all working with the municipality – were the only source of information for these conclusions. Results could be validated by comparing them against the opinions of a broader representation of stakeholders and other data sources. The appendix included the following: (1) the 300 ideas on trends and devel-opments gathered in the first meeting, placed in clusters; (2) for each of the ten clusters of trends, a definition, the current way of thinking and how it was included in scenarios; (3) a newspaper article for each scenario; (4) a list of stakeholders and for each scenario their preferences in 2035; (5) final sce-nario texts; and (6) the results of a comparison between pretest and posttest questionnaires on future developments.

7.4 Implementation and results

The project started with the question 'is Nijmegen municipality developing the right things for 2035?' The meetings provided more clarity on which measures should and should not be further examined and possibly adjusted. Participants established that some measures did not work out well in several scenarios and were willing to look into them further. Thus, the goal of making the munici-pality more aware of the uncertain future seems to have been achieved.

In addition, there are some indications that during the project partici-pants adjusted their views on the future of the Nijmegen municipality. Before and after the project participants were asked to answer the following ques-tion: 'Which three topics do you see as most important for the future of the municipality of Nijmegen?' A total of 23 participants provided answers at the beginning of the first session and 11 at the end of the last session. The topics mentioned were clustered. The limited number of answers gives some indication of collective and individual changes in perception of the contex-tual environment. There are five clusters of topics (demography, economy, coherence society, governance, spatial, and transport) that were expected to change in importance, and for three clusters the expectation is supported. In other words, there is a limited change in importance attached to contextual trends. There is also some evidence for individual change. Nine people com-plete both a pre- and post-measurement, allowing 25 combinations of topics to be compared. Of these, 14 changed, or 56%.

The description of the sessions in the previous section indicated that results were accepted and shared with other departments of Nijmegen municipal-ity in a meeting in December 2015. That acceptance of results is not self-evident is shown by an unsuccessful application of scenarios by Hodgkinson and Wright (2002). In their case, the scenarios made it clear that there were great dangers in continuing with the existing strategy. Some participants responded by withdrawing from the project and distancing themselves from the scenarios. They remained committed to the existing strategy and shrugged off responsibility for any negative consequences. The scenarios developed with Nijmegen municipality and wind tunnelling of policies seemed to have avoided this pitfall. While it was something of a shock to see that 10,000 additional homes did not work out well in any of the scenarios, in other respects results were not perceived as too challenging.

Whether the scenarios and results of wind tunnelling were too close to current reality remains an open question. Results on the level of the organisation were discussed with contact person Tom Merkx in August 2023. In line with the above, he underlined some of the surprising insights that were gained in the scenario sessions. Nevertheless, he also noted that once the results had been taken in, the organisation after some time went back to business as usual. Ironically, an unexpected and major new development – COVID-19 – is one factor in this. In summary, while the scenario project raised awareness of uncertainties and has to a limited extent changed thinking, it did not lead to a major change in direction of the organisation or change in the planning process.

References

Hodgkinson, G. P., & Wright, G. (2002). Confronting strategic inertia in a top management team: Learning from failure. *Organization Studies, 23*, 949–977.

Van der Steen, M., Van Twist, M., van der Vlist, M., & Demkes, R. (2011). Integrating futures studies with organizational development: Design options for the scenario project 'RWS2020'. *Futures, 43*(3), 337–347.

8

GROUP CAUSAL MAPPING

Clarifying issues, understanding purpose and developing options

In this chapter, we again describe an intervention approach that covers more than one task in team decision making. Group causal mapping covers divergence, convergence as well as prioritisation. The model constructed is a *map* that captures issues *as a hierarchical chain of networked argumentation* representing team members' interpretations of the situation of concern. As the discussion progresses, team members connect issues to perceived consequences and higher level goals (laddering up), and also to their perceived causes and suggested options or solutions (laddering down). Analysis of the map can reveal issues that are central to the argument, purpose as a system of interconnected goals, and options deemed to be effective (i.e. potent) in achieving the goals. Group causal mapping can be implemented with or without computer-supported technology. Here we will focus on the manual version of the approach, but readers interested in computer-supported group causal mapping are advised to consult the relevant literature (e.g. Ackermann & Eden, 2011; Bryson et al., 2004).

8.1 Background

An early version of group causal mapping, known as Strategic Options Development and Analysis (SODA), was developed in the 1980s as part of an action research programme led by management scientist Colin Eden that started at Bath University (Eden & Ackermann, 2018; Eden et al., 1983). Central to this intervention approach is the idea that individuals differ in their perception and interpretation of one and the same situation because they use different mental constructs to make sense of that situation. These constructs are organised as a hierarchical system: beliefs and values are constructs at the top of the hierarchy – what drives an individual's behaviour – with those further

DOI: 10.4324/9781003404200-10

down the hierarchy representing either issues affecting these beliefs and values or explanations and alternative courses of action (Kelly, 1955). This often creates a challenge for coordinated action, because different interpretations lead people to take different courses of action. Thus, when individuals need to work together to accomplish goals within or across organisations, much of what happens comes down to negotiating and renegotiating between different interpretations and courses of action.

Failure to reconcile different interpretations through negotiation often leads to poor ownership and implementation (Nutt, 2002). Eden argues that the process of negotiation is both social and psychological. Specifically, effective behavioural change leading to commitment to a decision is often the result of individuals socially negotiating a new order – that is, a new situation – *and* creating a new negotiated order – that is, new relationships between individuals (Eden, 1992; Eden & Ackermann, 1998, 2010).

While originally developed with a focus on supporting decision making in complex problem situations, in later years SODA developed into a comprehensive strategy making methodology called Journey Making (Ackermann & Eden, 2010, 2011). In this book, we focus on SODA rather than Journey Making but will use the term group causal mapping instead. The approach works by capturing individual interpretations of a situation of concern through a *cognitive mapping technique* or a *group causal mapping technique*: the former is used when the elicitation process is conducted with an individual in an interview setting; the latter is used with a team in a workshop setting. These techniques allow views to be represented as individual *cognitive maps* or a *group causal map* that capture how people construe a given situation by showing the interrelated issues, goals, and possible options or solutions they associate with that situation. Maps are models that depict means–ends relations and show how certain options are perceived to help to resolve some issues, which in turn might help to achieve particular goals. Creating and discussing these maps in a facilitated environment is thought to help a team arrive at a negotiated agreement on how to improve the situation of concern. In other words, a facilitated modelling approach (Franco & Montibeller, 2010) is used to influence the psychological and social negotiation processes needed to create the required levels of shared understanding and commitment to a proposed course of action (Eden & Ackermann, 2010).

8.2 Procedure, technique, and tools

The process of building a group causal map using manual technology will be broadly described in this section. The basic set up for a group causal mapping session comprises a board (e.g. whiteboard, wall, or similar) on which the map will be built, and around which team members are seated forming a horseshoe shape. The facilitator guides the team through the mapping process,

TABLE 8.1 Elements of group causal mapping

Procedure
 1. Introduce topic
 2. Gather issues
 3. Develop clusters
 4. Develop means-ends structure of clusters
 5. Identify central issues
 6. Rate central issues
 7. Develop goals system
 8. Identify potent loops and options
 9. Develop solutions
10. Prioritise solutions and agree on actions

Activity/technique:
• Group causal mapping technique, rating and resource allocation techniques

Tool:
• Board, coloured sticky notes, sticky dots, pens, map, map analysis results
• Optional: group decision support system such as *Decision Explore Connect* or *Strategyfinder*

---

helping team members to articulate and jointly explore their interpretations of the situation of concern, and agree on the way forward. Table 8.1 summarises the main elements of group causal mapping.

The process starts with a question or prompt given to the team such as "what are the key issues that we must address in order to achieve Z within timeframe Y?" or "what can we do about problem X within timeframe Y?". Team members are asked to note down their answers individually, in the form of brief issue statements that must include a verb and are no longer than 6–8 words. Examples are '*strengthen* the skills of sales and marketing staff' and '*increase* students' attention societal impact issues'. The starting question invites team members to voice issues and concerns about the situation of concern, and is intended to help them share their interpretations about the situation and what should be done about it. Team members write their answers on large sticky notes,[1] and they can write as many as they wish. The facilitator gathers the answers in a round-robin fashion and places each issue statement on the board. Often, however, team members are encouraged to place their answers on the board without the facilitator's intervention. Answers are placed on the board using all the available two-dimensional space rather than displayed as lists.

As the elicitation proceeds, issues that the facilitator thinks are related are placed close together in tentative clusters. Superordinate issues are noted at the top and subordinate issues at the bottom of each cluster. After all issue statements are brought to the board, the facilitator then asks team members to first validate the tentative clusters produced, make any necessary changes, and then relate the issues, within and across the clusters, to one another in a means-ends fashion.

At this point, the divergent way of working stops and convergence starts. This means that instead of following the wording as suggested by an individual team member (divergence), now the whole team have to agree to either drawing a link between issues or changing the wording of the issues themselves (convergence). Thus, in this convergent phase, whenever a link or re-wording is suggested by a team member the facilitator checks with the other members whether they agree before adding the link to or change the wording of an issue statement. This process transforms the displayed material into an emerging group causal map, in which the vertical dimension shows how facts or options at the bottom relate to issues in the middle and then to goals at the top of the map. In this way, the map represents a visual model that shows how facts or options help to explain or resolve issues, respectively, and how issues stand in the way of achieving goals. The result is a hierarchical chain network of argumentation. An excerpt from a map developed by a team that got together to discuss issues concerning academic partnerships in the higher education sector is shown in Figure 8.1.

Another convergent activity involves the identification of priority issues. Typically, the facilitator asks: "since we cannot work on all of these issues at once, we need to identify where we want to spend our time and energy first". Then the facilitator does a visual check to identify issues that have a high number of in-arrows and out-arrows. These issues represent 'busy nodes' that are central to the structure of the map, and thus the facilitator categorises them as *central*. Next, the facilitator asks team members to rate the identified central issues in terms of their relative significance to resolve the situation of concern.

Practical applications indicate a number of traps teams may fall for during the mapping process. For example, some team members' contributions may be

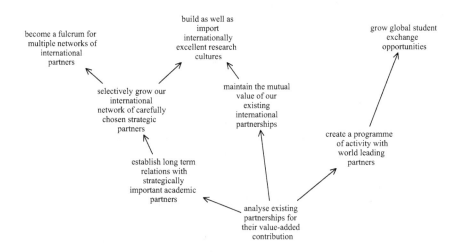

FIGURE 8.1 Excerpt from a group causal map.

written in the form of questions, and these have to be reformulated as propo-
sitions that include a verb so that the action orientation of the contribution
becomes clear. Some members may also phrase their concerns using modal
verbs such as 'need', 'should', or 'ought', which indicate covert individual aspirations that form the basis for proposing and prioritising particular actions.
For instance, a contribution such as "need to increase service customization"
may be seen as a means to "maintain high levels of customer satisfaction"
(an explicit or implicit aspiration), and the use of the word 'need' is already
suggesting a sense of priority for action. In this case, team members would be
asked to avoid taking out the word 'need' and instead phrase the statement
as, for example, "increase service customization". That way, the statement
becomes just a candidate proposal for action that could be discussed later in
the process and made a priority if deemed appropriate at that stage.

A common trap is to leave issues unconnected to the rest of the model. In
this case, the facilitator will ask the team to identify these 'orphans' and link
them to other issues. Another common trap relates to the direction of the
link between two issues, which can be mistaken by the team. For example,
a team member may link the issue "achieve a better image in the market" to
the issue "better use of social media in marketing". This argument starts from
an aspiration or goal and then goes on to propose an action. The logic of
cognitive and group causal maps is exactly the reverse: actions contribute to
achieving goals or means-statements lead to ends-statements. Team members
are therefore asked to link the proposed means of "better use of social media
in marketing" to the desired end of "achieve a better image in the market".

Sometimes team members include a causal relation when they phrase their
issue statements, as in "recruit people with relevant skills and expertise in
order to achieve our strategic vision". In this case, the phrase "in order to"
implies a causal relationship between "recruit people with relevant skills
and expertise" and "achieve our strategic vision", and so these two elements
should be considered separate but linked issue statements. Similarly, transition words such as 'because', 'therefore', 'in order to', 'due to', 'may lead to',
'as a result of', 'through', and 'caused by' should warn the facilitator that
causal relations are implied and issue statements need to be split into two.

Additional traps emerge when relations between issues imply a feedback
mechanism. As shown in Figure 8.2, in maps causality typically 'flows from
bottom to top'. However, some issue statements in the map can be part of
feedback loops, as in the case of the two issues located on the left-hand side
of the map.

The trap to avoid here is to draw a feedback loop between just two issues,
in which A influences B and vice versa. Instead, the facilitator asks team
members why there is a relation back from B to A and adds that to the map.
In the example earlier, there is a direct impact of improving position in global
league tables on attracting high calibre faculty, but the relation in the other

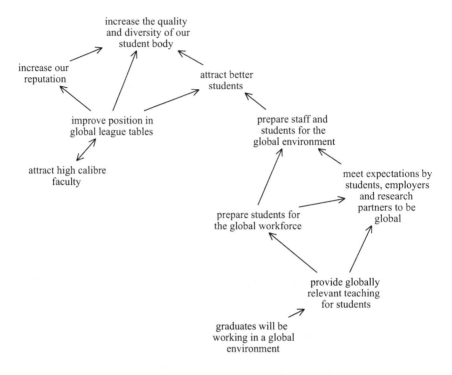

FIGURE 8.2 Excerpt of a group causal map with a feedback loop.

direction is perhaps less clear. Indeed, the impact is indirect: attracting high calibre faculty improves the capacity and capability to conduct world leading and internationally recognised research, which in turn enables to carry out research that addresses the global challenges, which increases the reach of research impact and thus improves citations, which then improves position in the global league tables. This line of argumentation is shown in Figure 8.3.

As team members keep adding concepts and relations, the map may grow to become quite large. Ackermann and Eden (2001) report that maps often consist of more than 800 nodes. In this case, noting concepts within the space of whiteboard is not feasible. Instead, a wall surface covered with flipcharts can be used, and team members' statements can be placed directly on the flipchart-covered wall. Figure 8.4 shows a very large causal map that resulted after spending substantial time on linking.

The last part of the mapping session is the development and prioritisation of solutions, and agreement on actions. For this the facilitator first has to do two different visual checks. In the first one, the facilitator has to identify issues that impact on many goals and categorises them as *potent options*; in the second one the facilitator identifies bundles of issues that represent a feedback loop (i.e. a vicious, virtuous or balancing cycle) and impact on many

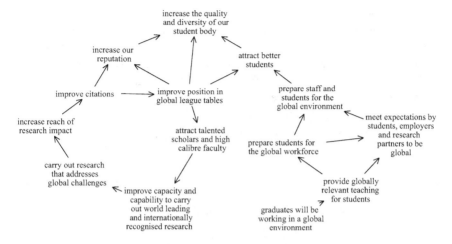

FIGURE 8.3   Excerpt of a group causal map with the feedback loop explained.

FIGURE 8.4   Large group causal map displayed on a flipchart-covered wall

Source: Eden & Ackermann (2010, p. 248).

goals, and categorises them as potent loops. The facilitator then asks team members to first propose solutions to tackle the *potent loops* (e.g. solutions to eliminate or alleviate a vicious cycle, transform a vicious cycle into a virtuous cycle). Next, the facilitator asks team members to propose solutions to deliver the potent options. Finally, using a simple resource allocation scheme, the facilitator asks team members to state their preferences concerning which solutions are both *impactful* and *practical* by giving them a limited number of resources (e.g. blue sticky dots for impact, green sticky dots for practicality) to allocate. After all team members have allocated their resources, the facilitator summarises results with the whole team, and proposes that solutions with a high number of resources allocated and good consensus become agreed actions. A logical end point is to produce an overview map showing all the solutions, potent loops, potent options and goals together, and representing a summary of the team's agreements.

8.3   Versions

As noted at the start of this chapter, a group causal mapping intervention may be supported with computer-supported technology. In general, group causal maps can be created by using a group decision support system (GDSS) with map building and analysis capabilities.[2] When using a GDSS, team members have each access to a laptop, tablet or phone, and thus the map will appear on a digital screen as it is being built. In the divergence phase, team members can add issues anonymously. After a first round of discussing the issues and emergent clusters, team members can then also add links using their mobile devices. This typically creates a profusion of links very fast. A GDSS offers a range of analytical routines to help find central issues, goals, feedback loops and potent options.

Both the manual- and computer-supported versions of group causal mapping can be used to support not only team decision making but also strategic management (Ackermann & Eden 2011; Bryson et al., 2014; Eden & Ackermann, 1998). For example, Eden and Ackermann (2000) show how mapping can help to identify an organisation's distinctive competencies. These are the basis for a business model or, in the case of a public organisation, a livelihood scheme. Constructing a business model in this way helps to craft a mission statement that is anchored in the organisation's day-to-day work and represents its identity better than a top-down developed statement. Group causal mapping has also been used for the elicitation of systemic risks (Ackermann et al., 2014) and the analysis of disruption and delays in large complex projects (Eden et al., 2000).

8.4   Applications

Applications of group causal mapping to real-life problems in both isolation and combination with other intervention approaches are reported in various reviews (Abuabara & Paucar-Caceres, 2021; Howick & Ackermann, 2011; Mingers & Rosenhead, 2004). The large number of case studies shows that the approach is used across different countries and in multi-national organisations such as Shell, British Airways as well as public-sector bodies such as the UK Department of Health. In these applications, group causal mapping supports the negotiation process resulting in a consensus view on the problem situation (Eden & Ackermann, 2004; Hjortsø, 2004; Paroutis et al., 2015).

Notes

1. For example, oval Post-it™ notes or similar.
2. Decision Explorer Connect is a GDSS available from Banxia Software Ltd. (www. banxia.com). Strategyfinder is a GDSS developed for building group causal maps with virtual teams, and is available from Formfinder Software GmbH (www. strategyfinder.com).

References

Abuabara, L., & Paucar-Caceres, A. (2021). Surveying applications of Strategic Options Development and Analysis (SODA) from 1989 to 2018. *European Journal of Operational Research*, 292(3), 1051–1065. https://doi.org/10.1016/j. ejor.2020.11.032

Ackermann, F., & Eden, C. (2001). Contrasting single user and networked group decision support systems for strategy making. *Group Decision and Negotiation*, 10(1), 47–66.

Ackermann, F., & Eden, C. (2010). Strategic options development and analysis. In M. Reynolds & S. Holwell (Eds.), *Systems approaches to managing change: A practical guide* (pp. 135–190). Springer.

Ackermann, F., & Eden, C. (2011). *Making strategy: Mapping out strategic success.* SAGE.

Ackermann, F., Howick, S., Quigley, J., Walls, L., & Houghton, T. (2014). Systemic risk elicitation: Using causal maps to engage stakeholders and build a comprehensive view of risks. *European Journal of Operational Research*, 238(1), 290–299.

Bryson, J. M., Ackermann, F., & Eden, C. (2014). *Visual strategy: Strategy mapping for public and nonprofit organizations.* John Wiley & Son.

Bryson, J. M., Ackermann, F., Eden, C., & Finn, C. B. (2004). *Visible thinking: Unlocking causal mapping for practical business results.* Wiley.

Eden, C. (1992). A framework for thinking about group decision support systems (GDSS). *Group Decision and Negotiation*, 1, 199–218.

Eden, C., & Ackermann, F. (1998). *Making strategy. The journey of strategic management.* SAGE.

Eden, C., & Ackermann, F. (2000). Mapping distinctive competencies: A systemic approach. *Journal of the Operational Research Society*, 51(1), 12–20.

Eden, C., & Ackermann, F. (2004). Cognitive mapping expert views for policy analysis in the public sector. *European Journal of Operational Research*, 152, 615–630.

Eden, C., & Ackermann, F. (2010). Decision making in groups: Theory and practice. In P. C. Nutt & D. C. Wilson (Eds.), *Handbook of decision making* (pp. 231–272). Wiley-Blackwell.

Eden, C., & Ackermann, F. (2018). Theory into practice, practice to theory: Action research in method development. *European Journal of Operational Research*, *271*(3), 1145–1155.

Eden, C., Jones, S., & Sims, D. (1983). *Messing about in problems: An informal structured approach to their identification and management*. Pergamon.

Eden, C., Williams, T., Ackermann, F., & Howick, S. (2000). The role of feedback dynamics in disruption and delay: On the nature of disruption and delay (D&D) in major projects. *Journal of the Operational Research Society*, *51*(3), 291–300.

Franco, L. A., & Montibeller, G. (2010). Facilitated modelling in operational research. *European Journal of Operational Research*, *205*(3), 489–500.

Hjortsø, C. N. (2004). Enhancing public participation in natural resource management using Soft OR—an application of strategic option development and analysis in tactical forest planning. *European Journal of Operational Research*, *152*(3), 667–683. https://doi.org/10.1016/S0377-2217(03)00065-1

Howick, S., & Ackermann, F. (2011). Mixing OR methods in practice: Past, present and future directions. *European Journal of Operational Research*, *215*(3), 503–511.

Kelly, G. (1955). *The psychology of personal constructs. A theory of personality*. Norton.

Mingers, J., & Rosenhead, J. (2004). Problem structuring methods in action. *European Journal of Operational Research*, *152*, 530–554.

Nutt, P. (2002). *Why decisions fail. Avoiding the blunders and traps that lead to debacles*. Berrett-Koehler.

Paroutis, S., Franco, L. A., & Papadopoulos, T. (2015). Visual interactions with strategy tools: Producing strategic knowledge in workshops. *British Journal of Management*, *26*(S1), S48–S66. https://doi.org/10.1111/1467-8551.12081

9

APPLICATION

Prioritising projects to tackle teenage pregnancies in a multi-cultural neighbourhood (part I)

This chapter describes an application of group causal mapping with the London Borough of Newham's strategy group tasked with reducing teenage pregnancies. Group causal mapping constituted the first part of a mixed-method intervention, although not all the steps were carried out. The second part of the intervention, decision conferencing, is described in Chapter 11. This chapter draws on the work by Ewan Lord and L. Alberto Franco (Franco, 2013; Franco & Lord, 2011; Lord, 2009), who acted as facilitators in the case. In 1999, a report by the UK government's Social Exclusion Unit highlighted the severity of the problem of teenage pregnancy in the UK (SEU, 1999). Up to 2005, the teenage pregnancy rate in the UK remained similar to that in the 1970s, while in most of Western Europe it halved. In response, the UK government set demanding targets to be achieved by 2010. The direct client in this case is the team tasked with making the strategic decisions to achieve the 2010 target, the Teenage Pregnancy Strategy Committee (TPSC). Around 2006, the TPSC realised that although ongoing projects had reduced the teenage pregnancy rate, it had not done so at a pace sufficient to achieve the TPSC targets by 2010. As a result, the TPSC recognised it needed to explore more effective and efficient ways to achieve its targets. Later, we describe the motivation for starting the project, the cognitive mapping interviews, the group causal mapping session, resulting model, and its impact.

9.1 Background and issue

In 1997, the New Labour government in the UK coined the term 'joined-up government' to capture its approach to public-sector reform. The term encompassed a wide range of activities and developments intended to improve

DOI: 10.4324/9781003404200-11

services for particular social groups or populations, including substantial cross-organisational work to tackle complex social and economic issues. One such issue concerns the impact on welfare systems and society as a whole caused by people becoming disconnected from schooling and further education, and hence the labour market. Drug-taking, crime, family breakdown, and teenage pregnancy are often cited as possible explanations for this phenomenon. With regard to the latter, teenage pregnancy rates in the UK in the early 2000s were twice as high as in most Western European countries. Tackling teenage pregnancy was a priority for the government and, in 2002, all local authorities in England were required to set up a Teenage Pregnancy Strategy Group (TPSG).

The client of the intervention described later was one such group working for Newham, a borough that encompasses a large area in East London with inhabitants of diverse ethnic and religious backgrounds. Newham had been experiencing significant issues of social deprivation and poverty. The area also has a disproportionately young and needy population and a much higher rate of pregnancy among teenagers than in other London boroughs. Indeed, the borough has one of the highest teenage pregnancy rates in the country. In 2003, the number of conceptions for teenagers within the 15–17-year-old range was about 55 per thousand, and the borough was under high pressure to bring this number down to below 30 per thousand by 2010. The team tasked with making the strategic decisions to achieve this target, the Teenage Pregnancy Strategy Committee (TPSC), was made up of representatives from the borough's council, the National Health Service, the education authorities, and other stakeholders such as the voluntary sector which included young parents' representatives. Its budget was made up of a complex mix of direct funding, contributions from participant organisations, and government incentives for achieving certain targets and key performance indicators. Not meeting the 2010 target would thus also directly affect the resources of the TPSC. The TPSC wished to explore more effective and efficient ways to achieve their teenage pregnancy rate targets and agreed to focus on the budget prioritisation process as a useful mechanism to achieve this.

Ewan Lord, an MSc student at the time, was looking for an opportunity to work on a real-world complex issue for his MSc thesis. He was acquainted with the Newham TPSC coordinator, and they discussed the possibility to work with TPSC as part of a short MSc research project. While the client organisation had much experience in using and participating in research, they were less familiar with model-driven interventions to support team decision making. An initial meeting in 2009 between Lord, Franco and the TPSC coordinator was held to explore the possibility of conducting a research project with the TPSC. Initially, a system dynamics simulation (Forrester, 2007; Sterman, 2000) was proposed as the way forward. Computer-supported group causal mapping would provide the basis of the simulation model. Parameters would be estimated on the basis of literature and expert estimation, perhaps using the delphi method (Dalkey, 1969). Historical reference data would validate the model, followed by a workshop on policy simulations that were expected to create an opportunity for organisational learning. This approach was, however, rejected early on for several reasons. Capturing the structure responsible for the issues at TPSC was considered too ambitious for a three-month research project. Some of the feedback loops involved were deemed to play out on a too long time scale to be relevant to the 2010 targets. Stakeholders' lack of alignment regarding their interests was seen as a central factor in this issue, and an alternative approach was chosen that focused more directly on interests.

After some discussions, it was mutually agreed that focusing on the budget prioritisation process would be potentially beneficial to the TPSC. Thus it was agreed that the TPSC coordinator would act as the sponsor of a research project that would enable Lord to complete his MSc thesis. Lord would be supervised by Franco, and both would act as facilitators in the modelling sessions. Lord had been trained in the use of the intervention approaches to be applied in the project, but he was less familiar with the software that would be used to build the decision model. In addition, he did not have extensive experience as a facilitator.

The intervention was designed as a mixed-method approach comprising two phases. The first phase was to consist of problem structuring, using cognitive mapping and group causal mapping to help the TPSC achieve a shared and improved understanding of the issues related to teenage pregnancy. The second phase would entail a portfolio evaluation using decision conferencing. The purpose of the second phase was to highlight a portfolio of projects which would produce the highest value in relation to the aims of the TPSC. There was an acceptance that this could only be conditionally prescriptive. We describe the process and products of the first phase later, leaving the discussion of the process and products of the second phase for Chapter 11.

9.2   Process

In preparation for the group causal mapping and decision conferencing sessions, suitable participants were identified using a power–interest grid (Ackermann & Eden, 2011; Bryson, 2004). Due to lack of time, this was done backroom rather than with the client. People with the highest combination of power and interest were targeted for participation in both group causal mapping and decision conferencing sessions; those high in interest only were targeted for the group causal mapping session; and those high in power only were targeted for the decision conferencing session. The resulting grid is shown in Figure 9.1; the list of participants across the different project phases are shown in Table 9.1. Interviews with available participants were scheduled prior to the group causal mapping session, and these are described next.

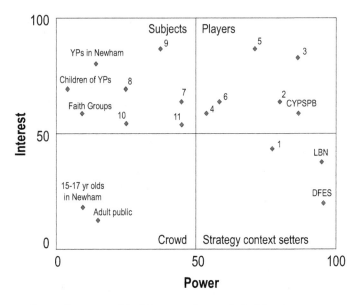

FIGURE 9.1 Power-interest grid of intervention stakeholders.

9.2.1 Individual interviews

The main aims of the interviews were twofold. First, the interviews would enable Lord, the interviewer, to learn about the situation of concern as perceived by the participants. Second, the participants' views would inform the design of the group causal mapping session, as well as provide preliminary input to the decision model (see Chapter 11). For this, the cognitive mapping technique[1] (Eden 1988) was used as an interview elicitation procedure. Mapping would help to identify causal chains of argument between ongoing TPSC projects to tackle teenage pregnancy and goals (see Chapter 11). Making these chains of argument explicit would not only justify existing projects but also trigger the generation of new projects.

Eight available interviewees were identified from the power–interest grid. One-hour interviews were conducted by Lord and scheduled over a period of two days. Where possible the order of interviews was scheduled such that those with highest power were interviewed first, so that any prompts required by the interviewer when guidance was necessary were framed by earlier interviews. Interviews were mapped on A3 paper with pencil and eraser and recorded on audio with the interviewees' consent. The audio recordings allowed Lord to check maps later, as a backroom task. Interviewees were informed that transcription of the interview would be confidential, except that the content would be merged with content from seven other interviews and presented to others in and around the TPSG and included in the final report. At the close of the interview, participants were asked whether they

TABLE 9.1 Participants in the intervention

	Interview	Group causal mapping	Decision conferencing
1. Civic representative on LBN strategy board		X	
2. Assistant director of Community Care (Primary Care Trust) Co-chair of Teenage Pregnancy Strategy Group		X	X
3. Children and young people's commissioning manager (LBN) Co-chair of Teenage Pregnancy Strategy Group	X		
4. Family planning lead Chair of prevention subgroup	X	X	
5. Teenage pregnancy strategy coordinator	X	X	X
6. Principle services manager for continuing professional development at LBN Learning and schools representative	X	X	
7. Children's rights and sex education representative	X	X	
8. Support to parents personal advisor	X		
9. Young parents forum representative	X		
10. Prevention subgroup project manager			X
11. Communications subgroup representative	X		X
Total	*8*	*6*	*4*

wanted to leave anything out or wanted to change any of the language in the interview in case they were worried about being identifiable in the merged content.

The starting question for the interviews was 'What do you think will be the issues in and around teenage pregnancy in Newham until 2010?' This was intended to focus interviewees on the period from the time of the interview up until 2010 which is when TPSG's final objectives were set and the organisation's existence may come into question. They had to focus their strategy and policy on this period of time. Interviewer and interviewee sat at a 90-degree (or less) angle, allowing the map to be seen by both. In order to elicit goals, questions were posed to allow laddering up from the interviewee's most important issues (e.g. why is this issue important to you?). Laddering down was used to identify factors or actions that would influence issues (e.g. what causes this issue? or, what could you do to resolve this issue?). Interviewees were asked to accompany the expression of goals and actions with action verbs in order to produce an action-oriented map. Approximately, 15 minutes were intended for exploring issues important to the interviewee, 15 minutes for laddering up to goals, 15 minutes for laddering down to actions, and 15 minutes for clarifying and adding detail and checking the map. This schedule was not rigidly adhered to but passed quite naturally.

After completing all eight interviews, the resulting material was entered into the Decision Explorer™² and subsequently analysed. The seventh map was from the interview with a failed recording. The shape of the resulting cognitive maps elicited immediately revealed some differences among interviewees (e.g. wider, flatter maps versus narrow, taller maps). An overall map was produced by merging the individual maps using the mapping software. Clearly, clustered teardrop chunks in cognitive maps were put into sets. Clusters relating to similar issues in other maps were put into sets with similar names so that points at which to merge the maps could be sought between these clusters. Further clusters were defined as sets on each map based on central concepts in each of them. These concepts were identified by a 'centrality' analysis in the software. Sets were allowed to overlap. Clusters were grouped into the following nine themes:

1. Funding (defence, integration, generation)
2. Intelligence (funding influence, prevention, customers)
3. Promotion (advertising, word of mouth)
4. Support to young parents (housing, education, life skills)
5. Prevention (contraception, vulnerability, confidentiality, termination of pregnancy)
6. Self-esteem (choice, stigmatism, confidence, opportunities)
7. Sex and relationship education (schools, non-school)
8. Involving young people (in decision making, in support)
9. Health (sexual, general)

Figure 9.2 shows an excerpt from the overall map, with ovals indicating themes. Analysing and merging the individual cognitive maps helped to prepare for the group causal mapping session in a number of ways. The software allowed for accommodating similar views by merging map nodes without altering the underlying map structure. Differences in views were preserved (but kept anonymous), so that they could be aired during the session.

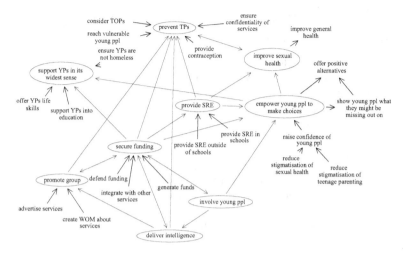

FIGURE 9.2   Excerpt from the overall map.

Following Eden's guidelines (2004), analysis of the individual maps revealed the different multi-organisational tensions present within the TPSC. These mainly originated from strongly held views within the TPSC about how to tackle teenage pregnancy issues. The merged map also showed which goals and values were shared among TPSC members.

9.2.2   Group causal mapping session

Table 9.2 shows the agenda developed for the group causal mapping session. The intention was to use the group causal mapping approach until the early part of the afternoon (except for the prioritisation step). The rest of the afternoon would be devoted to implementing the first stages of the decision conference approach (see Chapter 10).

Six people were invited to the session four of whom had been interviewed. These four individuals had not been shown their cognitive maps before the meeting, so as not to further lock them into their own frames. Reinforcing their own views could have been a further obstacle to achieving an open discussion in the session. Participants were not shown the merged map before the session either. This team of six included one participant who was not from TPSG but from the borough's Strategy Board. He was included as he had influence over the TPSG and borough's funding stream, and also because he had a role as a faith group representative whose input was important for considering the issue.

TABLE 9.2 Group causal mapping agenda, products and procedure

Agenda, products and procedure

Session (14 July 2006, 9.30–17.30h)
- 09.30h arrival of client team and introductions (1)
- 09.45h begin building group causal map (2, 3)
- 10.30h develop selected clusters further (4)
- 11.30h identify and rate central issues (5, 6)
- 12.00h develop goals system (7)
- 12.30h begin generation of options (8)
- 13.00h lunch – allows reflection for further option generation (9)
- 14.00h continue option generation (9)
- 14.30h build first iteration of benefits and how to measure them
- 16.00h agree on categories of options (project areas) for decision model
- 17.00h adjustments, questions, what's next?
- 17.30h close

After meeting: *workbook with individual cognitive map, merged map, and map analysis results*

Procedure group causal mapping
1. Introduce topic
2. Gather issues
3. Develop clusters of issues
4. Develop means-ends structure of clusters
5. Identify central issues
6. Rate central issues
7. Develop goals system
8. Identify potent loops and options
9. Develop solutions
10. Prioritise solutions and agree on actions (not included here but covered in the next two chapters)

The group causal mapping session took place at the University of Warwick (UK) away from the workplaces of the participants. The session was supported by the use of a group decision support system (GDSS) with map building and analysis capabilities called *Group Explorer*.[3] The room for the session had laptops, one for each participant and facilitator, a projector and very large projector screen, and tables arranged in a U-shaped layout. The room was set up and tested on a previous day. Unfortunately, the room was the third choice for various practical reasons and was not ideal. Although a U-shaped set up closed by the projector was achievable it was only just. The windows were boarded up due to building works going on behind them, further not only enclosing the space and adding a noise distraction but also removing a visual distraction from the projected group map. It was a hot day, and there was no air conditioning. The poor quality of the room was explicitly criticised by the client. Franco acted as the main facilitator and operated the system Lord took notes and co-facilitated.

The following question was written on a whiteboard so that team members could refer back to it during the divergent phase: what issues must TPSG consider in trying to achieve its targets by 2010? As with the interviews, this question was crucially influential in framing the context. This question was changed from that posed for interviews because this was for a group rather than a one-to-one interview, and also because facilitators wanted to emphasise action. Anticipating that team mebers would contribute a lot of material, 'must' was chosen to focus on what was most important rather than 'should' or 'could'. The projection was left off as team members used the GDSS to enter issues anonymously. The intention was to proceed with a second round of issue gathering with all the issues previously gathered shown on the screen. In 25 minutes, 144 issues were gathered. Thus the use of the GDSS enabled the group to be very productive in generating issues. This activity took longer than planned but as the team were still generating issues the facilitators agreed between themselves to let them continue. The number of issues contributed varied among team members, with one contributing 32% while another only contributed 4%. The participant who contributed few ideas was the non-TPSG member so this low contribution may legitimately been from a lack of ideas or an acceptance of the relative expertise of the other team members. The participant stated concern, however, that some of their contributions were repetitive. The facilitators also noted some difficulty with the technology.

The large number of issues gathered and the free format in which they appeared on the screen made the first visual depiction of collected issues rather complex. To the team, the surprising mess presented once the projection was subsequently switched on may have been impressive but was certainly not clear. It was decided that there was no need for a second stage of issue gathering and the facilitators moved the team to the next phase of untangling the mess. This was done by summarising emergent clusters of similar issues and developing a means-ends structure for these clusters, asking team members to link issues within and across clusters. By lunchtime, there were five well-developed clusters and two of which were hardly begun. The seven working clusters were as follows: (1) funding, (2) support to parents, (3) clinical services, (4) sex and relationship education, (5) strategy and communications, (6) workforce development, and (7) young people's involvement.

Discussion had been reasonably intense with four out of the six participants sharing most of the conversation. Of the other two, one was tired, probably compounded by the environment, and the other was the non-TPSG member. When one of these two participants had something to say the facilitators made sure they were heard. Being aware of which issues these two participants were expected to have expertise on, the facilitators encouraged them to contribute when these issues were discussed. However, the facilitators deliberately, tried to avoid steering the discussion towards these two participants to avoid taking a position on content. As such, any steering was done as much as possible discreetly and via body language. In deciding where to focus his efforts, the facilitation team tried to balance several needs. On the one hand, they wanted to ensure the team would see the results of the session as legitimate, and for that to happen they needed to avoid 'polluting' the group causal map too much with expressions representing their own interpretations. On the other hand, because of the large number of issues generated, they wondered if the aims of the session could still be met in the remaining time available. While preferring to keep to the original agenda to avoid confusing the team their concern grew that a change in the schedule might be needed to accommodate both the large set of issues gathered and the need to meet the session aims.

To ensure the best possible use of the remaining time, team members were asked to rate the central issues (i.e. issues with a high number of in-arrows and out-arrows) in terms of their relative significance to resolve the teenage pregnancy problem. The rating results raised much debate about which issues were most important, and the team were also concerned that the results would influence the outcome of the decision model. Team members could not be reassured that the rating exercise was simply a mechanism to select which issues to discuss within the time limitation. This illustrates the notion that despite the capabilities offered by the decision support technology used in an intervention, it is ultimately the perceptions of how such technology affords team members to pursue their individual agendas that determine how the technology is actually used and evaluated on the ground (Franco, 2013; Poole & DeSanctis, 1992).

After about half an hour debating the relative importance of 'improve data analysis' and 'uptake of contraceptive services', with only about an hour left for the session, the facilitators decided to drop the development of the goals system and the generation of options from the agenda. Although the goals system is the essential link between the results of group causal mapping and the decision model that would be built in the next session, there was no time for this. As for the generation of options, these could be drawn from relevant documentation, elicited from team members off line, or developed during the final session. Consequently, the facilitators moved the team to the direct elicitation of benefits. This is described in more detail in Chapter 11.

9.3 Final product

The group causal map consisted of about 160 concepts, 31 of which remained orphaned. The merged map constructed on the basis of the eight individual maps contained over 600 concepts of which nearly all were linked. However, although the eight cognitive maps were a rich source of material, they were merged by the interviewer. The group causal map on the other hand was constructed in a facilitated team discussion and is owned much more by the team than the merged map. Apart from the differences in the maps, they were also complementary in that they validated each other to some extent, especially as the list of team members was not identical to the list of interviewees. The results of the merged map, group causal map, the issue ratings, and draft value tree were compared in the following way. First, the clusters identified in the merged map were compared to those named in the group causal map. The maps matched on most clusters. Second, the issues with the top 20 centrality scores (calculated by the mapping software) in the merged map and group causal map were compared. Results again showed large overlap between the content of the two maps. Third, a comparison was made between the 20 most potent options (also calculated by the mapping software) on each map. This revealed more differences than in the prior analyses. Although it was possible to find actions in similar areas of both maps, the actions were not the same. This suggests that perhaps there were many more options to be gathered than were possible in the time available for constructing the group causal map.

In conclusion, the group causal mapping session did not provide as solid and sure results in as much depth and variety as the merged map. In addition, group causal map was not complete. This, however, does not make it invalid as the team was more likely than not to have focused first on the issues they considered to be a priority. Although the portions of the merged map were provided to the interviewees along with their individual cognitive maps with some explanation and analysis, there was probably more ownership of the group causal mapping results than the interview outputs due to the experience of working together. Team members probably had a better understanding of the group causal map (compared to the cognitive maps) as they were involved in co-construction of the map, and were confronted with each other's arguments explicitly and visually. By expressing themselves in front of the whole team they had also committed themselves, at least to a degree, to the resulting group causal map.

In the map in Figure 9.3, colour and shape are used to highlight concepts which were shown to be significant by the analysis, or stressed as significant during the interviews. Light grey ovals indicate goals expressed as specific to TPSG. The dark grey oval on the left-hand side represents a primary goal for an organisation other than TPSG. Dotted ovals on the upper right-hand side stand for higher or meta-goals to which TPSG contributes. Other ovals are goals that support the achievement of TPSG or higher goals. The statement shown in bold italics font on the lower left-hand side indicates an option that is potent in achieving goals.

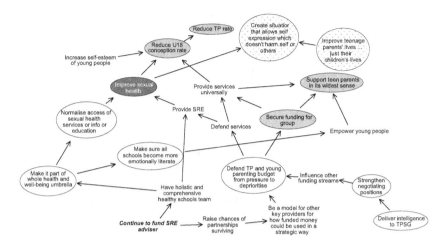

FIGURE 9.3 An excerpt from the merged map showing central issues

In conclusion, the teenage pregnancy problem, as perceived by the TPSG, could be characterised as follows: TPSG needs to provide services universally in order to reduce, before 2010, the under 18 conception rate by normalising access to sexual health services. In order to increase the uptake of confidential, young people friendly, contraceptive services, people at risk need targeting and signposting improving. These services are under threat and funding needs securing. There is recognition that good research is powerful in improving effectiveness by understanding the mechanisms of cause and effect better, identifying people at risk, and defending services by demonstrating need and success.

9.4 Implementation and results

The cognitive mapping interviews and group causal mapping session reported here constitute the first half of a mixed-method intervention. Chapter 11 reports on the second half of this intervention, which uses decision conferencing. This will include a description of the implementation of recommendations and results.

Notes

1. Cognitive mapping is essentially the same technique as group causal mapping (see Chapter 8), but applied with an individual, rather than a team.
2. Available from Banxia Software Ltd. (www.banxia.com)
3. *Group Explorer* is a predecesor of *Strategyfinder* (see Chapter 8).

References

Ackermann, F., & Eden, C. (2011). Strategic management of stakeholders: Theory and practice. *Long range planning*, 44(3), 179–196.

Bryson, J. M. (2004). What to do when stakeholders matter. Stakeholder identification and analysis techniques. *Public Management Review*, 6(1), 21–53.

Dalkey, N. C. (1969). *The Delphi Method: An experimental study of group opinion.* RAND Corporation.

Eden, C. (2004). Analyzing cognitive maps to help structure issues or problems. *European Journal of Operational Research*, 159(3), 673–686.

Forrester, J. W. (2007). System dynamics—the next fifty years. *System Dynamics Review, 23*(2–3), 359–370.

Franco, L. A. (2013). Rethinking soft OR interventions: Models as boundary objects. *European Journal of Operational Research*, 231(2), 720–733.

Franco, L. A., & Lord, E. (2011). Understanding multi-methodology: Evaluating the perceived impact of mixing methods for group budgetary decisions. *Omega, 39*, 362–372.

Lord, E. (2009). *Group modelling with equity and causal mapping to improve resource allocation in the public sector.* Unpublished MSc thesis University of Warwick, Coventry, UK.

Poole, M. S., & DeSanctis, G. (1992). Microlevel structuration in computer-supported group decision making. *Human Communication Research*, 19(1), 5–49.

SEU. (1999). *Bridging the gap: New opportunities for 16–18 year olds not in employment, education or training.* The Stationary Office.

Sterman, J. D. (2000). *Business dynamics: Systems thinking and modeling for a complex world.* Irwin McGraw-Hill.

10

DECISION CONFERENCING

Articulating value preferences and trade-offs

In this chapter, we describe a participative approach to team decision making known as decision conferencing. This approach offers a clear way to compare options or portfolios against multiple (and often conflicting) objectives. Decision conferencing is most concerned with selection and prioritisation. It is therefore well suited to the action planning phase of interventions, where solutions have to be formulated and then chosen. As with the other intervention approaches discussed in previous chapters, we will provide here only a brief description of the approach. For more detailed accounts of decision conferencing the interested reader is advised to consult the relevant literature (e.g. Belton & Stewart, 2002; Montibeller & Franco, 2011; Phillips, 2007; Phillips & Bana e Costa, 2007).

10.1 Background

Chapter 4 described how the shortage of detention capacity in the Netherlands became increasingly urgent in the late 1990s. In reaction, the Dutch prison administration developed a policy of early release, which freed up capacity for newly convicted persons. When learning about this, judges decided to increase sentence duration because their main concern was that sentences were served to completion. This illustrates that two decision makers who are involved in one and the same situation may see two different problems because either their perception of what is going on or their goals are different. Note that even if a complete description of the current situation could be made, we would still not have the full picture of a problem. Imagine we use the methods outlined in the preceding chapters and develop a causal model of the situation capable of explaining observed behaviour. Let us say

DOI: 10.4324/9781003404200-12

we also build plausible scenarios of how the situation may develop in the future. While this would take a lot of time and energy and would certainly help us to understand better what is going on, it still ignores part of the relevant information. Without also understanding the *desired* situation (i.e. the objectives to be achieved), we still do not know what the problem really is. In our example, what does adequate capacity mean for prison administrators? Probably, it would include to have enough room available to house those convicted for serious crimes immediately. Is it acceptable that others wait for a month, or several months? Can we cope with a temporary lack of capacity, knowing that the gap will be closed in a year? Is there a level of early release that is still acceptable to a judge? In the Dutch criminal justice system in the late 1990s, one-third of a sentence would regularly be subtracted for good behaviour. This seems to indicate there is some room for not serving a sentence to full completion.

Interestingly, decision makers in this case may not have readily available answers to these questions. A study by Bond et al. (2008) showed that even in important situations, decision makers find it difficult to list all the objectives that are relevant. Zajonc (1980) found that people have an immediate affective reaction to situations, objects, or persons, but need to find out and articulate why. The title of his paper captures this beautifully: 'preferences need no inferences', or in other words: you do not need to think before you have an emotional reaction, rather it is the other way around. As Belton and Stewart (2002, pp. 80, 119) note, values and preferences are not already present and waiting to be elicited, but rather they are constructed by decision makers, possibly with the help of an analyst (see also Slovic, 1995). This brings us to an important distinction between capturing the perceived situation versus the desired situation. Where in the first condition opinions of team members can in principle be checked against other data sources (documents, information systems), there is much less room for triangulation in assessing the desired situation. Ultimately, the desired situation is *hypothetical* and exists in people's minds. Once it is made explicit, it can be checked against the 'official' organisational policy or against decisions made in the past, but these are in effect consistency checks with other statements of opinions and not observations of the real world.

There is a range of quantitative methods available to help decision makers establish and compare preferences and trade-offs about options or portfolios. Some of these methods express resources spent (costs) or objectives realised (benefits) in monetary terms. For example, cost-benefit analysis (Adler & Posner, 2006; Boadway, 2006) requires the analyst to first determine all the monetary costs and benefits associated with a particular option. Then the option with the highest net benefit (benefit minus cost) will be chosen. Central to this procedure is that all benefits and drawbacks need to be expressed on a financial scale. However, in applying (societal) cost–benefit analysis, monetising effect is a major problem (Mouter, 2014). Another monetary method is cost-effectiveness analysis (Edejer, 2003). This approach is similar to cost–benefit analysis but allows effects to be expressed in non-monetary terms. These quantitative methods do not specify a process to involve teams and are not designed with more complex decision problems in mind. By contrast, multi-criteria decision analysis (MCDA) (Belton & Stewart, 2002) is a method[1] that can make use of non-monetary and qualitative information, and has been developed into a facilitated approach called decision conferencing (Phillips, 2007; Phillips & Bana e Costa, 2007).

The origin of the decision conferencing approach goes back to the late 1970s (Phillips, 2007; Phillips & Bana e Costa, 2007). It was developed by decision analyst Cam Peterson, a technical director at a US-based consultancy firm called Decisions and Designs Incorporated (Phillips, 2007). According to Phillips (2007), after over 25 years of use in over 15 countries, the following elements seem to be central to decision conferences: attendance by key players, impartial facilitation, on-the-spot modeling with continuous display of the developing decision model, and an interactive and iterative facilitated group process. Team members are chosen so that all main perspectives on the issues linked to the decision problem are represented. The facilitator's role is to guide the team process while remaining neutral with regard to content. The role of the decision model is to feed back to the team the implications of their input (Phillips, 2007). Additions to the model are made on the basis of the team discussion, and because contributions need to be clarified and linked to the rest of the model, the model also informs the discussion (Belton & Stewart, 2002; Salo & Hämäläinen, 2010). Teams use decision conferencing to evaluate a set of options (Phillips, 1989, 1990) or assess portfolios of options (Montibeller & Franco, 2011; Morton et al., 2011; Phillips & Bana e Costa, 2007).

10.2   Procedure, techniques and tools

Two simple example will clarify the main issues in supporting evaluation and prioritisation. The first might be seen as a very early use of process consultation in prioritisation. In a letter in 1772, Benjamin Franklin attempts to help his nephew in choosing whether or not to switch to a new job. Franklin does not advice on which option to follow (an advice on content), but on a method to follow (process advice). His recommendation is to list arguments in favour of the new job and list arguments contra the new position. The decision maker should then choose two arguments of about equal weight, one pro and one contra, and take both off the list. After following this procedure, one of the two lists will be empty and the answer to the problem will be clear. This letter is one of the first examples of an explicit procedure to arrive at decisions (Figueira et al., 2005). Note that arguments may be of different strengths or weights, in the sense that a strong argument pro may remove two or more weak contra arguments.

The second example concerns a straightforward decision making situation presented by Wijnmalen (2009). The decision maker initially wants to choose two options based on only one objective. How much of this objective is achieved by any option is measured by an *attribute or criterion* (Keeney & Gregory, 2007). Even in this simple situation, the decision can reach a deadlock in which the decision maker is unable to choose. Imagine there is an option A that scores 2 on an objective measured by criterion *a*, and an option B that scores 1 on the same criterion. In this case, we are still unable to make a choice because we would need to know first what the score stands for: positive or negative impacts. If the score is taken to mean a positive impact, we would choose option A. The situation can be made slightly more complex by adding a second objective measured by criterion *b*, on which the score of options is reversed (option A scores 1, option B scores 2). Adding up scores over all criteria would result in an equal score for both options: 3. Two pieces of additional information may help in choosing: either has more specific scores (knowing that option A, respectively, scores 2.05 and 0.97, while option B scores 1.45 and 2.30 may help you in choosing) or adding weights to criteria. Weights represent how much must be gained in the achievement of one objective to compensate for a lesser achievement of a different objective. Introducing weights makes it possible to calculate weighted scores for each option which helps to prioritise them. For each option, we multiply the score on the first criterion with the weight of the first criterion, doing the same for criterion two and add up the results. If positive scores represent positive outcomes, the option with the highest weighted score is the best alternative, and so on. Table 10.1 shows a worked example in which the weights assigned to the first and second criterion are 0.40 and 0.60, respectively. In this example, option B would be prioritised over option A.

Calculating scores in this way follows an additive aggregation rule, which is a simple and widely used approach (but others rules are also available, see Belton & Stewart, 2002, p. 120). Two additional considerations should be taken into account when conducting this type of multi-criteria evaluation. First, suppose that there is an option that scores equal or less than another option on all criteria. This means that the option is dominated by the second option, and thus one way to limit the options under consideration is to remove all dominated options from the analysis. The second consideration relates to the simplification in the example above that scores directly represent the decision maker's preferences. Imagine that a decision maker has to choose between several job options. She does not want to move and considers alternatives that require less than 90 minutes of travel per day, with longer travel times less preferred. It is likely that her preference for five minutes travel time is not much higher than for 15-minute travel time. But

TABLE 10.1 A multi-criteria evaluation example

	Weights	Option A	Option B
Criterion a	0.40	2.05	1.45
Criterion b	0.60	0.97	2.30
Aggregated weighted score		1.40	2.96

TABLE 10.2 Elements of decision conferencing

Procedure

1. Introduce decision context and intervention approach
2. Identify resource allocation areas and options
3. Identify benefits
4. Evaluate costs and benefits of each option
5. Determine within-criterion weights
6. Determine across-criteria weights
7. Calculate overall benefits and identify efficient frontier
8. Explore feasible portfolios
9. Conduct sensitivity analyses
10. Recommend portfolio

Activity/technique:
• Multi-criteria decision analysis techniques

Tool:
• Board and pens, decision analysis software such as *EQUITY*, decision model, decision model results

a difference between 30 and 40 minutes may make a much larger difference in preference. In other words, the score of an option on a criterion is different from the value attached to that score. Though it is possible for decision makers to communicate their preferences for different scores directly, often a formal procedure is required to communicate preferences transparently and consistently (see, for example, Montibeller & Franco, 2007).

Constructing the decision problem in such a way that it is suited for a decision conferencing intervention requires a number of steps. In what follows, we describe decision conferencing for the case of evaluating portfolios of options. In this case the decision model that is developed represents a prioritisation model for resource allocation that follows a simple value-for-money principle: choosing options on the basis of the benefit-to-cost ratio provides the best value for the available resource (Phillips, 2007; Phillips & Bana e Costa, 2007). The basic room setup for a decision conference is similar to that of a group causal mapping session. The main difference being that a decision conference always uses computer-supported technology for model building. Specifically, models are created with support of software tools that apply MCDA methods, although it is possible to build a decision model entirely in a spreadsheet. Our description below uses the *EQUITY*™ software (Phillips & Bana e Costa, 2007). Table 10.2 summarises the main elements of decision conferencing. It should be noted that although the process is presented in a linear sequence, in practice it is common to return to earlier stages as greater understanding of the issues emerges within the team.

After introducing the decision context and the decision conferencing approach, the facilitator guides the team in the identification of areas to which resources can be allocated. Money is often the main resource being considered, but other types of resource are also possible (e.g. personnel, equipment, facilities). Typical resource allocation areas might be functional areas, regional divisions, product lines, research and development projects, and so on. Options for each resource allocation area are then specified by the team. Typically, some options are already available or being currently implemented. New options may also be created (Belton & Stewart, 2002, p. 52). A key assumption in the approach presented here is that the options within or across the resource allocation areas have no dependencies. If dependencies exist, alternative methods are available (see, for example, Montibeller & Franco 2011).

Benefits and costs are then specified by the team. The aim is to make explicit which benefits and costs are important in the decision problem and how we may concretely measure these using relevant criteria. In decision conferencing, benefits and costs are often represented in the form of a value tree. An example of a value tree concerning a new plant location decision is shown in Figure 10.1. A value tree lists the overall objective at the top of the tree and breaks this down into operational objectives, which can be more easily employed to assess the performances of options.

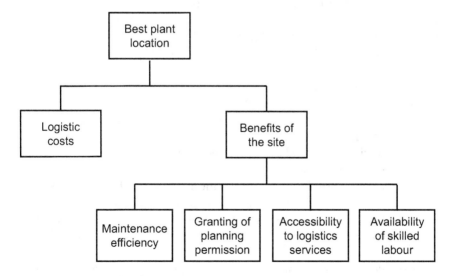

FIGURE 10.1   Example of a value tree.

Source: Adapted from Franco & Montibeller (2011, p. 6)

Value trees can be structured top-down or bottom-up. The top-down approach would start from the overall objective, the best location for the plant in Figure 10.1, and break this down into logistic costs and benefits of the site. Costs and benefits are then further subdivided if needed. The bottom-up approach starts from the options, which are grouped into different classes based on their attributes, classes can be grouped into higher-order classes, and so on.

When structuring a value tree, there is a set of properties against which each objective (benefits in our case) needs to be checked (Franco & Montibeller, 2011, p. 7):

- *essential:* capture all essential organisational objectives relevant to the decision;
- *understandable:* their meaning should be clear to all team members;
- *operational:* it should be possible to measure the performance of options against each of the fundamental objectives;
- *nonredundant:* objectives should not measure the same concern twice;
- *concise:* the set of objectives should be the smallest possible required for the analysis;
- *preferentially independent:* if it is possible to measure the performance of options on one objective disregarding their performance on all other objectives, then the linear aggregation rule mentioned earlier can be used.

After identifying benefits and costs, the next question is how to measure them. This requires that for each objective placed at the bottom level of the value tree, an associated attribute or criterion is specified. This attribute is a performance indicator employed to measure the impact (or performance) of each option on the objective. Attributes also have to be checked against a number of properties (Franco & Montibeller, 2011, p. 8). Attributes should be:

- *unambiguous:* present a clear relationship between the impact of adopting an option and the description of such impact;
- *comprehensive:* cover the full range of possible consequences if the options were implemented;
- *direct:* attribute levels should describe as directly as possible the consequences of implementing an option;
- *operational:* information required by the attribute can be obtained in practice and allow for making value trade-offs between objectives;
- *understandable:* consequences and value trade-offs using the attribute can be clearly understood by the decision making team.

Next the desirability of implementing each option is assessed in relation to each benefit. For this a *value scale* ranging from 0 to 100 is used, with 0 representing the least desirable effect and 100 the most desirable. This evaluation is carried out separately for each resource allocation area. Because of this, a movement from 0 to 100 for a particular benefit in a given area might be more or less preferrable than the same movement in another area. To take this into account, it is necessary to measure these changes in benefit on a common scale. To illustrate, let's assume a municipality is considering two areas to which resources can be directed: 'road maintenance' and 'street lighting'. It is possible to launch several projects within each area but as resources are limited, the municipality must choose how many of these projects to fund within the road maintenance and street lighting areas. For the sake of simplicity, let's assume that there is only one single benefit to consider: 'community safety'. In this situation the team would be asked to make the following comparison. First, the facilitator would ask the team to imagine the contribution that all the projects in the road maintenance area would make to community safety if they were all successful. Second, the facilitator would ask the team to imagine the contribution to community safety that all the projects in the street lighting area would make, again, if they were all successful. Then the team would be asked to compare these imagined contributions. Which one is more attractive? Which contribution represents the biggest swing in value?

The above procedure measures what are known as the *within-criterion weights* by identifying the resource allocation area with the biggest swing in value on the given criterion. In this example, let's assume the most attractive swing in value on the community safety benefit is in the street lighting area. Thus street lighting would be assigned an arbitrary within-criterion weight of 100 for community safety, and the road maintenance area would be assigned a within-criterion weight relative to that standard of 100. The same procedure is applied to all the other benefits being considered. In this way each benefit has a common scale that enables the effect on that benefit of choosing a particular portfolio of options to be measured.

To assess the overall benefit of adopting a particular portfolio of options, we would now need to determine a set of weights that would allow to compare the benefits with each other. These are known as the *across-criteria weights*. In the example above, let's assume that 'community image' is a second benefit being considered in addition to the community safety benefit. The facilitator would then ask the team to compare the attractiveness of a swing in value from the worst position to the best position on the community safety benefit with a similar swing in value on the community image benefit. Let's assume the most attractive swing is on the community safety criterion. Thus this swing would be given an arbitrary weight of 100, and the other swing would be assigned an across-criteria weight relative to that standard of 100. The same procedure would be applied if there were more than two benefits.

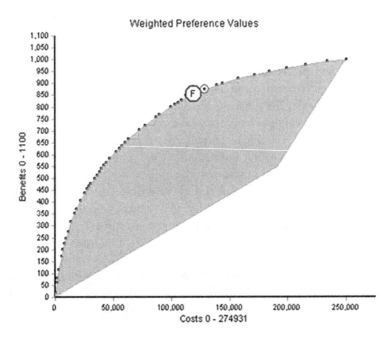

FIGURE 10.2 An efficient frontier created with EQUITY.

Source: Phillips & Bana e Costa (2007, p.59).

To summarise, the overall value *Vi* of each option *i* for a given benefit *j*, is given by a single doubly-weighted value that measures its benefits in units of preference that are now everywhere comparable (for details, see Phillips & Bana e Costa, 2007). Finally, the benefit-to-cost ratios of each option are calculated by dividing each option's overall value *Vi* by its total cost *Ci*. All options are then plotted in decreasing order of benefit-to-cost value (i.e. a value-for-money ordering) to form the efficient frontier shown in Figure 10.2.

Point F on the efficient frontier corresponds to the portfolio of options formed by the minimum requirements in all areas. The facilitator then asks the team to consider the options falling outside this affordable portfolio (i.e. options on the efficient frontier to the right of point F) to ensure that their exclusion is realistic. The shared area under the efficient frontier includes all possible portfolios, namely, all possible combinations of options.

Next, the facilitator guides the team in the exploration of alternative portfolios due to presence of operational constraints. For example, some options may be already under way and cannot be stopped; other options must be implement due to previous commitments or political reasons; and so on. Alternative portfolios typically fall below the efficient frontier, and so the facilitator uses the model to help the team undertake trial-and-error explorations of new portfolios with a view to find a solution that sits closer to the frontier. As the team explores different portfolios team members develop an appreciation that what is best for individual areas might not necessarily be for the whole. The last step involves a sensitivity analyses of the weights, although it is often the case that models are robust to these changes. After these analyses are completed, the team then decides on or recommends a final portfolio.

10.3 Versions

Decision conferencing may be used in different ways depending on the intervention purpose (evaluation of options or portfolios), and the the the method used for articulating and measuring the value of benefits and costs (e.g. Keeney, 2007, 2012; Keeney & Gregory, 2005), assessing weights or value trade-offs (e.g. Keeney, 2002; von Winterfeldt & Edwards, 1986), and calculating the total value of options (e.g. Belton & Stewart, 2002). For example, simple approaches that have been used over the years include the following: SMART (Edwards, 1971), SMARTS and SMARTER (Edwards & Barron,1994), and MACBETH (Bana e Costa et al., 2012). There is also a range of approaches to involve stakeholders in value measurement and weighting (Marttunen et al., 2015). These include questionnaires, basing criteria weights on information about stakeholders' values and interests, individual interviews, and group sessions.

10.4 Applications

There is substantive evidence of the use of decision conferences in practice in both the public and private sectors. Some notable examples include the use of decision conferences for conflict resolution (Bana e Costa et al., 2001), bid evaluation (Bana e Costa et al., 2002), flood control (Bana e Costa et al., 2004), managing biosecurity threats (Montibeller et al., 2020), water resource planning (Stewart, 2003), and R&D project prioritisation (Charlish & Phillips, 1995).

Note

1. Strictly speaking, MCDA is a family of methods. In this chapter we describe the method embedded in the decision conferencing approach developed by Phillips (e.g. Phillips 2007; Phillips & Bana e Costa, 2004). A wider range of MCDA methods are described in Belton & Stewart (2002).

References

Adler, M. D., & Posner, E. A. (2006). *New foundations of cost–benefit analysis*. Harvard University Press.

Bana e Costa, C. A., Correa, E. C., J.M., D. C., & Vansnick, J. C. (2002). Facilitating bid evaluation in public calls for tenders: A socio-technical approach. *Omega, 30*(3), 227–242.

Bana e Costa, C. A., da Silva, F. N., & Vansnick, J.-C. (2001). Conflict dissolution in the public sector: A case-study. *European Journal of Operational Research, 130*(2), 388–401.

Bana e Costa, C. A., Da Silva, P. A., & Correia, F. N. (2004). Multicriteria evaluation of flood control measures: The case of Ribeira do Livramento. *Water Resources Management, 18*(3), 263–283.

Bana e Costa, C. A., De Corte, J.-M., & Vansnick, J.-C. (2012). MACBETH. *International Journal of Information Technology & Decision Making, 11*(02), 359–387.

Belton, V., & Stewart, T. (2002). *Multiple criteria decision analysis: An integrated approach*. Kluwer Academic Publishers.

Boadway, R. (2006). Principles of cost-benefit analysis. *Public Policy Review, 2*(1), 1–43.

Bond, S. D., Carlson, K. A., & Keeney, R. L. (2008). Generating objectives: Can decision makers articulate what they want? *Management Science, 54*(1), 56–70.

Edejer, T. T. T. (2003). *Making choices in health: WHO guide to cost-effectiveness analysis*. World Health Organization.

Edwards, W. (1971). Social utilities. *Engineering Economist, Summer Symposium Series, 6*.

Edwards, W., & Barron, F. H. (1994). SMARTS and SMARTER: Improved simple methods for multiattribute utility measurement. *Organizational Behavior and Human Decision Processes, 60*(3), 306–325.

Figueira, J., Greco, S., & Ehrogott, M. (Eds.). (2005). *Multiple criteria decision analysis: State of the art surveys*. Springer.

Franco, L. A., & Montibeller, G. (2011). Problem structuring for multicriteria decision analysis interventions. In J. J. Cochran, L. A. Cox Jr, P. Keskinocak, J. P. Kharoufeh & J. C. (Eds), *Wiley encyclopedia of operations research and management science*. Wiley.

Keeney, R. L. (2002). Common mistakes in making value trade-offs. *Operations Research, 50*(6), 935–945.

Keeney, R. L., & Gregory, R. S. (2005). Selecting attributes to measure the achievement of objectives. *Operations Research, 53*(1), 1–11.

Marttunen, M., Mustajoki, J., Dufva, M., & Karjalainen, T. (2015). How to design and realize participation of stakeholders in MCDA processes? A framework for selecting an appropriate approach. *EURO Journal on Decision Processes, 3*(1–2), 187–214.

Montibeller, G., & Franco, L. A. (2011). Resource allocation in local government with facilitated portfolio decision analysis. In A. Salo, J. Keisler, & A. Morton (Eds.), *Portfolio decision analysis: Improved methods for resource allocation* (pp. 259–281). Springer Science+Business Media.

Mouter, N. (2014). *Cost-benefit analysis in practice* [Trial]. Delft.

Phillips, L. (1989). People-centred group decision support. In G. Doukidis, F. Land, & G. Miller (Eds.), *Knowledge-based management support systems* (pp. 208–224). Ellis-Horwood.

Phillips, L. (1990). Decision analysis for group decision support. In C. Eden & J. Radford (Eds.), *Tackling Strategic Problems: The role of group decision support* (pp. 142–150). SAGE.

Phillips, L. D. (2007). Decision conferencing. In W. Edwards, R. Miles Jr, & D. von Winterfeldt (Eds.), *Advances in decision analysis: From foundations to applications* (pp. 375–399). Cambridge University Press.

Phillips, L. D., & Bana e Costa, C. A. (2007). Transparent prioritisation, budgeting and resource allocation with multi-criteria decision analysis and decision conferencing. *Annals of Operations Research, 154*(1), 51–68.

Salo, A., & Hämäläinen, R. P. (2010). Multicriteria decision analysis in group decision processes. In *Handbook of group decision and negotiation* (pp. 269–283). Springer.

Slovic, P. (1995). The construction of preference. *American Psychologist, 50*, 364–371.

Stewart, T. J. (2003). Thirsting for consensus: Multicriteria decision analysis helps clarify water resources planning in South Africa.(International OR). *OR/MS Today, 30*(2), 30–35.

Wijnmalen, D. (2009). *Optieselectie met Multicriteria Analyse.* Lecture, Radboud University. Nijmegen, October 2009.

Zajonc, R. B. (1980). Feeling and thinking – preferences need no inferences. *American Psychologist, 35*(2), 151–175.

11

APPLICATION

Prioritising projects to tackle teenage pregnancies in a multi-cultural neighbourhood (part II)

This chapter describes an application of decision conferencing with the London Borough of Newham's strategy group tasked with reducing teenage pregnancies in the borough. Decision conferencing was used as the second phase of a mixed-method intervention. Group causal mapping constituted the first part of the intervention and is described in Chapter 9. This chapter draws on the work by Ewan Lord and L. Alberto Franco (Franco, 2013; Franco & Lord, 2011; Lord, 2009), who acted as facilitators in the case. As already stated in Chapter 9, 1999 the UK government recognised the severity of the problem of teenage pregnancy in the UK and set new performance targets to be achieved by 2010. In 2002, local authorities were required to establish a dedicated unit to address teenage pregnancy. The direct client in this case is the Newham team tasked with making the strategic decisions to achieve the 2010 target, hereafter referred to as the Teenage Pregnancy Strategy Committee (TPSC). The TPSC realised that although ongoing projects were effective to some extent, continuing the current way of working would not be sufficient to achieve the TPSC targets by 2010. Thus the TPSC wanted to explore more effective and efficient ways to achieve its targets. Later, we describe the motivation for starting the project, the decision conferencing session, the resulting model, and its impact.

11.1 Background and issue

The background to this case is described in more depth in Chapter 9. Here, we summarise the essential elements. Around 1999, the UK government made tackling teenage pregnancy a priority. Three years later, all local authorities in England were required to set up a Teenage Pregnancy Strategy Group,

DOI: 10.4324/9781003404200-13

hereafter referred to as the TPSG. The client of the intervention described later was one such group working for the East London borough of Newham. With one of the highest teenage pregnancy rates in the country, Newham was under high pressure to bring this rate down. The team tasked with making the strategic decisions to achieve this target was the TPSC, whose members were representatives of stakeholder groups such as medical services, local authorities, education authorities, and volunteer organisations. The TPSC wished to explore more effective and efficient ways to achieve its teenage pregnancy rate targets, and agreed to focus on the budget prioritisation process as a useful mechanism to achieve this.

The intervention was designed as a mixed-method approach. The decision conferencing intervention was built on the results of the cognitive mapping interviews and group causal mapping session described in Chapter 9. The overall goal of the intervention was to highlight a portfolio of options (in this case projects) that would produce the highest value in relation to the aims of the TPSC.

11.2 Process

11.2.1 Results of group causal mapping and preparation for meeting

Mapping was useful in managing some of the complexity of the problem, stimulating understanding, cooperation, and commitment, and identifying goals and actions. This made the problem context explicit which is probably best summarised by the overview map shown in Figure 9.2. However, in the main due to a lack of time, the link between problem structuring and the decision model was not as seamless as originally intended as described later. To change the focus of the team after the conflict over rating (see Chapter 9), the elicitation of benefits was moved from the projected screen to a whiteboard. The jump in process from map building to a structure that required serious consideration and resulting confusion proved difficult to overcome. Although eliciting the benefits was not completed by the scheduled finish time, the structure shown in Figure 11.1 was produced. It should be noted that due to the rush to achieve a result, this was probably influenced too much by the facilitator.

Despite the draft structure, at the end of the first session, there was no agreed and specified set of benefits' measurements for use in the decision model and no agreed set of projects to be evaluated. In anticipation of time constraints in the decision conference, it was decided to include only a handful of benefits around four or five. Without opportunity for another group causal mapping session before the decision conference, it had to be decided whether to begin the conference with a set of benefits or to specify them with

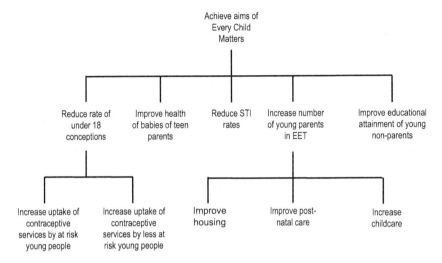

FIGURE 11.1 Initial structure of benefits.

the team. It was decided that the team's time in the conference would be best spent on populating the decision model. The team included two members who had been in the group mapping session, one of whom had been interviewed, a third member who had also been interviewed, and a fourth who was familiar with the ongoing intervention but had not been involved until that point. The one member who had been involved throughout all stages of the intervention was the TPSC coordinator, who was also the intervention sponsor. In recognition of the complex situation's need for joined-up working, a coordinator positioned for a strategic overview was deemed central to each TPSG. As he had been involved intensively in analysing the problem context, the coordinator participated in the final structuring of the benefits together with the facilitators prior to the decision conference.

The following benefits, against which each project would be evaluated, were agreed upon and checked against the technical standards required of a multi-criteria decision model (Keeney, 2007; Keeney & Gregory, 2005):

1. Number of conceptions among 15–17-year-olds in Newham (minimise)
2. Number of young parents into education, employment, and training in Newham (maximise)
3. Extra benefits other than included in the first two criteria (maximise)
4. Speed of impact (maximise)
5. Sustainability of impact (maximise)
6. Confidence in achieving benefits (maximise)

Benefits could be refined or adjusted during the decision conference. Costs are necessary to calculate the benefit-to-cost ratios (see Chapter 10). Although other costs could be included, costs were defined as amount of yearly funding for each project.

A list of 28 projects was constructed before the conference, 20 of which could be implemented at more than one level, and four of them at five or more levels. These are organised in funding areas, which are shown as 'horizontal towers' in Table 11.1. Each funding area contains projects that are either mutually exclusive or cumulative. For example, the Clinical Services area (first row from top) has mutually exclusive projects, so if we choose to fund the Clinics project, we would also be funding the EHC Prog and CCard projects. On the other hand, the TPSG Events area (third row from top) has cumulative projects, so funding 3 TPSG events would imply that 1 and 2 TPSG events are also funded as part of this. Cumulative and exclusive areas are marked on the far left of Table 1.1 with a 'C' or an 'X', respectively. In this initial model structure, there are seven Cs and two Xs.

The order of the areas was chosen for the following reasons:

- *Clinical Services*: three of the team members would have ample knowledge and opinions on this area so it was seen as a good introductory area.
- *Media*: although the Communications sub group deputy had knowledge and opinions on the Clinical services area, the other three had relatively more expertise in this area. Media was put second to bring her into the group more and because it had few options so could be passed relatively quickly.
- *TPSG events*: this was put third to introduce an X area once the groups were familiar with scoring C areas. This unfamiliarity was useful in raising the level of thinking about the construction of the model. It was more tangible than the other X area which was left to later.
- *Young People's Involvement*: small area to move things on.
- *Sex and Relationship Education* and *Support to Parents*: central issues in the problem structure were put here to remind the participants of the importance of what they were doing at a point anticipated that they might be flagging.
- *Youth Projects* and *Workforce Development*: small areas of cheaper options to move on.
- *Strategy*: this was really a judgement of staffing although two of the four posts were not yet filled. Whether to fund posts is a major consideration for the TPSG in setting its budget. Care over human resources when considering strategy was also mentioned in the maps. This is why the facilitators left it until last when the team should have become familiar with the technique and able to give maximum concentration to the issues. It was also aimed at restimulating in case the team would be tired by this point.

Options were included in the initial model according to the following reasoning: existing spending should be represented, intended future spending

TABLE 11.1 Initial list of options. (SRE: sex and relationship education; S2P: support to parents).

Area		Options					
		Do nothing	EHC programme	CCard	3 Clinics	LAC nurse	SHINE workers	SHINE website
C	Clinical services	Do nothing	EHC programme					
C	Media	Do nothing	Annual newsletter	Current campaign				
X	TPSG events	Do nothing	1 TPSG event	2 TPSG events	3 TPSG events			
C	Young People involvement	Do nothing	Y Parents involvement	Y Peoples involvement				
C	SRE	Do nothing	SRE adviser	School conference	Faith work	Peer ed. projects		
C	S2P	Do nothing	Housing audit	Goody bags	Y Parents directory	Y Fathers project	YPs adv wrkr PT	Violence work
X	Youth projects	Do nothing	1 Youth project	3 Youth projects	9 Youth projects			
C	Workforce development	Do nothing	2 TPSG training	1 WFD session				
C	Strategy	Do nothing	TPSC	Y Parents Dev off PT	TPSG Intel offcr	TPSG Proj offcr		

should be included, and at least some imaginative but feasible projects should be included. As it was not clear exactly how much time populating the model would take, the facilitators chose to start simple, reflect and reiterate if time allowed. The TPSG could predict a budget range for the next couple of years within comfortable confidence limits. Further iterations of the model could then be made more useful by refining projects that appeared on the efficient frontier (see Chapter 10) around this reasonable budget level. At the same time, the model could be kept simple by removing projects that were clearly scoring lower than others.

11.2.2   Decision conference

The decision conference was conducted about three weeks after the group causal mapping session (see Chapter 9) on premises in London familiar to the team members but removed from any of their workplaces. The environmental conditions were far improved from those in the mapping session mainly by the amount of space available. Only four members of the intended team were available, one of whom had not participated in the intervention so far, one who was involved in the group causal mapping session, and one who had been interviewed. Only the sponsor, the TPSC coordinator, had been involved in all the stages of the intervention until this point (see Table 9.1). The decision conferencing approach described in Chapter 10, which uses *EQUITY* as the main software support tool (Phillips & Bana e Costa, 2007), was adopted. Lord would both facilitate the team and operate the software. The agenda shown in Table 11.2 was developed for the session.

After a very brief introduction of how the intervention had progressed so far and what the aim of decision conference was, the initial model was introduced. The facilitator explained that each row represented an area of spending and each box in a row a spending option for TPSG. The difference between C and X areas was also explained. In anticipation of uncomfortableness over the layout arrangement of the areas it was stressed that the team would build the model so that during the course of the day all was adjustable, that this was just a starting point and that the areas were where they were for the purpose of managing the complexity of the decision problem.

Benefits were checked for understandability within the team and the assesments begun. Projects within the Clinical Services area were introduced, and team members were asked: *which project in this area would have the greatest impact on reducing the number of conceptions among 15–17-year-olds in Newham (the first benefit)?* The EHC Programme was chosen and given a value score of 100. They were then asked if any of the projects in the Clinical Services area would have less of an impact than the 'Do nothing' option. None was judged to do so, and 'Do nothing' was given a value score of 0. The team was then asked to rank the remaining projects in terms of their impact on reducing the number of conceptions. Each of these projects was

TABLE 11.2 Decision conferencing agenda, products and procedure.

Agenda, products and procedure

Session (15 August 2006, 9.30–16h)
- 09.30h introduction (1, 2, 3)
- 09.40h score areas (4)
- 11.00h within-criterion weighting (5)
- 11.30h across-criteria weighting (6)
- 12.00h first iteration; consider a feasible package under next years expected budget (7)
- 12.30h explore the first iteration: examine nearby frontiers, sensitivity analysis, trade-offs (8, 9)
- 13.00h lunch
- 14.00h SWOT analysis for further option generation (3)
- 13.00h second iteration (4, 5, 6, 7)
- 15.00h explore the second iteration and highlight best portfolio (8, 9, 10)
- 16.00h close

After meeting: *final report*

Procedure decision conference
1. Introduce decision context and intervention approach
2. Identify resource allocation areas and benefits
3. Specify options available for each area
4. Evaluate costs and benefits of each option
5. Determine within-criterion weights
6. Determine across-criteria weights
7. Calculate overall benefits and identify efficient frontier
8. Explore feasible portfolios
9. Conduct sensitivity analyses
10. Recommend portfolio

then given value scores between 0 and 100, where each value score given representing a proportion of the difference in impact between 'Do nothing' and doing the EHC Programme. The results of these assessments are shown in Table 11.3.[1]

The same procedure was then followed for the next four criteria.

The same procedure was followed for the next four benefits. A different procedure was used for the sixth benefit, 'confidence of achieving benefits'. This benefit was included to account for different sources of uncertainty surrounding the decision problem (Friend & Hickling, 2005). For instance, there was uncertainty about the values of different cultural groups in the borough. Political agendas might also change which could impact a public-sector organisation like the TPSG. Finally, although the team acknowledged that issues associated with teenage pregnancy were complex and interrelated,

TABLE 11.3 Project costs and benefits (in value scores) in the Clinical Services area.

	Project Criterion: U18 conception rate	Cost	Value
1	Do nothing	0.0	0
2	EHC programme	23.0	100
3	LAC nurse	35.0	40
4	2 Clinics	52.0	75
5	4 SHINE workers	72.0	50
6	CCard	10.0	20

the nature of these relationships was not fully understood. Thus there was uncertainty in this respect as well. The confidence benefit was thus a measure of the perceived risk of each project achieving the expected benefits in full.

Thus the team was asked to estimate the probability of each project achieving their expected benefits. All input probabilities were converted to subtractive penalty scores by a logarithmic mapping that results in corresponding value scores (for details, see Bernardo & Smith, 1994; Phillips, 2007).

As with the group causal mapping session (see Chapter 9), despite the initial model being designed for simplicity with unrushed speed of the first iteration in mind, the schedule still proved optimistic. Not all areas were value scored by lunchtime, and one of the team members had to leave at 15.00h. Although it never became as rushed as the mapping session, it was necessary to move things along as much as possible while still fostering dialogue and the facilitator not polluting the model by bringing in own opinions. The team was keen to remodel the options in the third area of TPSG events to a more sophisticated set. Instead of the choice in this area between the options of one, two, or three TPSG events at a cost of £5,000 each, four exclusive and realistic options were defined:

1. two small events at a cost of £5,000 each
2. one big event plus a small event at £10,000 and £5,000, respectively
3. three small events
4. one super event at £15,000

At lunchtime, the seventh exclusive area of Youth Projects was removed and the lowest level of this was added to the Sex and Relationship Education area. This would make it clear if any Youth centres at all, none of which was funded from the previous year's budget, would be included in a recommendation. These changes are shown in Table 11.4.

TABLE 11.4 Adjustments resulting from removal of Youth Projects area

Area	Options					
C Young People Involvement	Do nothing	Y Parents involvement	Y Peoples involvement			
C SRE	Do nothing	SRE adviser	School conference	Faith work	Peer ed. projects	1 Youth project
C S2P	Do nothing	Housing audit	Goody bags	Y Parents directory	Y Fathers project	YPs adv wrkr PT	Violence work

Value scoring of the benefits was completed around 15.00h, after which the team turned to the weighting of criteria. Despite the increased importance of this being stressed, team members were quick to reach consensus on both within-criterion and across-criteria weights (see Chapter 10). They had no problem grasping the swing weighting concept and quickly turned to weighting differences in the moves between 0 and 100 for within-criterion weighting between areas. First, they were asked to imagine a situation in which for all areas, the project with the lowest value score on the conceptions benefit was implemented. *On which area would you like to improve first?* This area would receive a within-criterion weight of 100 as it represented the biggest swing in value on this benefit from 0 to 100. Projects with a score of 100 in the remaining areas were then given each a within-criterion weight as a proportion of that 100. Next, across-criteria weights were elicited using the procedure described in Chapter 10.

The decision conference continued past 16.00h, and there was about half an hour left for using the model to explore alternative portfolios. Unfortunately, this left no time for the planned option generation via a SWOT (strength, weaknesses, opportunities, and threats) or merged model analysis (see Chapter 9), or for further iterations. Having sorted all the projects in order of priority according to benefit-to-cost ratios to form an efficient frontier, the team was asked to select a portfolio of projects P that they might fund with the current budget of £490,000. The proposed portfolio, shown in Figure 11.2, is below the efficient frontier, indicating that it could be improved. For example, portfolio C provides roughly the same benefit as portfolio P but a lower cost. On the other hand, portfolio B provides a marginally higher benefit but costs a little more.[2]

As the TPSG was facing budget cuts in the following year, a realistic portfolio of projects was identified at a lower cost. This is represented by portfolio F in Figure 11.2. The budget for the following year was expected to be £254,000 (a 52% cut), and portfolio F is the efficient portfolio that is closest

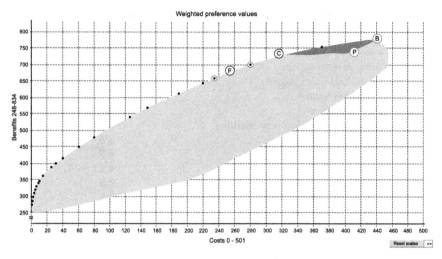

FIGURE 11.2   The area of all possible portfolios.

TABLE 11.5 Alternative portfolios (benefits and costs × £1,000)

Portfolio	Benefit	Cost	Benefit/Cost
Proposed (P)	490	412	1.19
Better (B)	532	440	1.21
Cheaper (C)	483	316	1.53
Realistic (F)	434	253	1.72

to this figure (£253,000). The benefits and costs of the four portfolios is sum-marised in Table 11.5.

Compared to the proposed portfolio P, the realistic portfolio F suggested not funding several projects in the Clinical Services area: sacrificing most of the SHiNE-related services and the LAC nurse, as well as the domestic violence work. On the other hand, it also meant upgrading one of the small TPSG events to a big TPSG event. Overall, portfolio F presented somewhat of a shock to the team as SHiNE services were an important part of TPSG's identity. The implications of adopting alternative and more efficient port-folios were intensely discussed by the team, and the model was adjusted to reflect the discussions. Sensitivity analysis showed that the portfolio was fairly robust to changes. In addition, several trade-offs between projects were explored with the team. For instance, if two SHiNE clinics were chosen as part of the portfolio, the TPSG intelligence officer post and the Media cam-paign would have to be taken out.

TABLE 11.6 Frontier portfolio (realistic) at budget of £253,000

	Benefit/Cost
Young parents forum	35.0
2 TPSG training sessions	16.3
Annual newsletter	13.5
1 Youth project	9.3
2 Workforce development sessions	8.8
Faith work	8.6
Goody bags	4.7
Housing audit	4.2
Young fathers project	2.9
1 large TPSG event followed by 1 small event	2.2
1 School conference	1.9
Young parents' directory	1.8
SRE advisor	1.7
Part-time young parents development officer	1.7
TPSC	1.4
EHC programme	1.2
Peer education projects	1.2
TPSG project officer	1.1
Part-time young parents advisory worker	1.0
Current level of media campaign	1.0

The contents of portfolio F are shown in Table 11.6. Implementing this portfolio would have serious implications for TPSG. It includes, for example, no SHiNE-related projects that were core to the TPSG strategy. This suggests that TPSG may have been prioritising projects based on their expected benefits only, rather than on their value-for-money contribution (i.e. benefit-to-cost ratio). Put differently, big projects are selected first, and small projects are then added to the portfolio until all the budget is used. Thus small but high value projects may not be funded with this approach.

11.4 Implementation and results

In a subsequent budget planning meeting of the TPSC, and counter to what the model results had indicated at the decision conference, it was agreed that the SHiNE-related projects in the Clinical Services area were still going to be funded, albeit from a mix of sources within and outside the TPSC. It was noted, however, that the actual impact of these projects would be closely monitored and the decision to fund them revisited in the following annual budget cycle. Although the recommendations following from the model were not implemented, the model in this case served a purpose as a tool for dialogue. This is evident from team members' evaluation of both the intervention process and the impact beyond the intervention. On the basis of interviews with all team members, Franco (2013) concludes that the model helped to create a shared language for discussing the issue and contributed to developing shared meanings. As the Prevention subgroup project manager commented after the intervention:

> I certainly haven't had those conversations with the department before . . . . it's not often that we sit down and really look in a very, very structured way as we did then, you know with all those different partners.
> *(Franco, 2013, p. 725)*

One such shared insight was, for instance, the realisation that the TPSG must focus on their core objectives in order to achieve them under limitations of time and resource (Lord, 2009). Despite the need for joined-up working, the team should not be distracted by goals outside of their direct area of responsibility. The selection of the first two benefits (reduction in the number of conceptions; number of young parents into education, employment and training) clearly reflects this focus on core objectives. Nevertheless, time limitations in both modelling sessions meant that some discussions were started but could not be finished

Beyond the modelling sessions, the main contribution of the decision model was its role in beginning to discuss difficult choices faced in an environment of increasing budget cuts (Lord, 2009). This started having an impact on a small scale. The TPSG, for instance, decided to disband the Support to Parents subgroup for being little more than a 'talking shop'. As the subgroups' members all worked in other capacities, this was not a direct criticism of the individual members but of the effectiveness of this grouping for these purposes.

In conclusion, the combined use of group causal mapping (Chapter 9) and decision conferencing in this case clearly resulted in improved communication and new and shared insights about the situation of concern.

Notes

1. This procedure is known as 'direct rating' as employed by SMART (Edwards, 1971) and is simple to implement. There are alternative procedures that require the construction of value scales representing the strength of preference for the achievement of different levels of benefits (von Winterfeldt & Edwards, 1986). The use of value scales avoids subjectivity but they take time to build. The team seemed to find it acceptable that they were evaluating value scores according to their own subjective judgments.
2. When the PCB triangle is orthogonal, portfolio B would provide higher benefit at the same cost. The fact that the triangle is not right angled highlights that portfolios of exact equal benefit or of exact equal cost do not always exist in practice.

References

Bernardo, J. M., & Smith, A. F. M. (1994). *Bayesian theory*. Wiley.

Franco, L. A. (2013). Rethinking soft OR interventions: Models as boundary objects. *European Journal of Operational Research, 231*(2), 720–733.

Franco, L. A., & Lord, E. (2011). Understanding multi-methodology: Evaluating the perceived impact of mixing methods for group budgetary decisions. *Omega, 39*(3), 362–372.

Friend, J., & Hickling, A. (2005). *Planning under pressure: The strategic choice approach* (3rd ed.). Elsevier.

Keeney, R. L., & Gregory, R. S. (2005). Selecting attributes to measure the achievement of objectives. *Operations Research, 53*(1), 1–11.

Keeney, R. L. (2007). Developing objectives and attributes. In W. Edwards, R. F. Miles, & D. von Winterfeldt (Eds.), *Advances in Decision Analysis* (pp. 104–128). Cambridge Unniversity Press.

Lord, E. (2009). *Group modelling with equity and causal mapping to improve resource allocation in the public sector*. Unpublished MSc thesis, University of Warwick, Coventry, UK.

Phillips, L. (2007). Decision conferencing. In W. Edwards, R. Miles Jr, & D. von Winterfeldt (Eds.), *Advances in Decision Analysis: From foundations to applications* (pp. 375–399). Cambridge University Press.

Phillips, L. D., & Bana e Costa, C. A. (2007). Transparent prioritisation, budgeting and resource allocation with multi-criteria decision analysis and decision conferencing. *Annals of Operations Research, 154*(1), 51–68.

PART III
Performing interventions

The approaches discussed in the precedent part have been designed to be deployed in a manner that is consistent with their purpose, that is, as intended by their developers. In practice, however, it is possible to have some degree of variation in how an intervention is implemented while remaining consistent with the intervention's intended purpose. Consequently, those with extensive experience and expertise with an intervention approach are likely to conduct the intervention differently from those who are relatively new to the approach. In this part, we discuss important practical issues that need to be considered by those tasked with conducting and guiding an intervention designed to support team decision making. These issues apply to any intervention approach chosen and thus are general in nature.

We begin Part III by discussing issues related to the design of a team decision support intervention. These are typically negotiated between those tasked with delivering the intervention (the analyst) and those who have a leadership position regarding the intervention (the client). There are some leverage points that analysts and clients must consider for increasing the chances of a successful intervention. First, the scope and roles pertaining to the decision task must be jointly defined and mutually agreed. Next, the composition of the team can be jointly designed not only to ensure that key stakeholders are included but also contingent on the requirements of the decision task. Equally, analysts and clients should discuss how to establish a team environment that is conducive to candid and effective communication, as well as the choice between adopting a simple (Chapter 3) or a more sophisticated (Chapters 4 to 11) approach to team decision making. In sum, the aim of this earlier part is to provide practical guidelines regarding making choices about intervention design.

DOI: 10.4324/9781003404200-14

The next chapters of Part III take a closer look at the intervention process, that is, at the nitty-gritty of facilitating a model-driven team decision making process. We will cover issues regarding team facilitation and managing team conflict and emotions. We will draw on extant research and our own experience to provide examples from actual decision support practice, so that the reader can get a sense of its interactional and situation-specific aspects.

12

DESIGN CHOICES

The opening chapters made clear why teams can sometimes find it difficult to make high-quality decisions. We then presented a collection of practical intervention approaches, simple and more sophisticated, designed help to improve team decisions. Taken together, these approaches can help to make unbiased judgments, stimulate appropriate levels of productive conflict, and use all the relevant knowledge and information needed to make the decision. This chapter takes a closer look at key choices in creating the conditions for an effective team decision support intervention and introduces a conceptual framework to help analysts and their clients think about the impact of these choices. We use the term 'client' when referring to the individual who seeks help from an analyst regarding a problem of concern[1] and to whom the analyst is accountable for conducting the intervention and producing the intervention deliverables. The client is often a leader in the organisation who is the problem owner. Sometimes, the client is also the budget holder who sponsors the intervention.

Choices about intervention design shape and influence how an intervention process will unfold in practice, either enhancing or limiting the quality of the solutions or responses developed by the team to tackle the problem. Analysts and their clients make four important choices that create the conditions for an effective intervention process. First, the *scope* of the problem and the roles that analysts and consultants will play in the intervention process must be mutually agreed upon. What is the problem that needs to be addressed? How will the analyst direct the intervention process? And what tasks will the client perform during team discussions? Second, the *membership* of the team tasked with developing a response to the problem must be established. Who should have the opportunity to participate in the process? What should

DOI: 10.4324/9781003404200-15

drive this choice? Third, the *environment* in which team discussions will take place needs to be discussed. What principles and norms will regulate the interactions? Finally, the choice about *how* team members will think and talk about the problem should be considered. How will team members share and exchange issues, assumptions, facts, and opinions about the problem? How will they structure the problem and generate and evaluate alternative responses to address the problem?

Preceding these four choices, however, is what kind of expertise the analyst and client contribute to the decision making effort. Simply speaking, the client knows about the *what* and is responsible for delivering information pertaining to the problem. The analyst is responsible for the *how* by proposing a procedure and attending to process. In the remainder of this chapter, we turn to this division of labour first.

12.1 Content, process, and procedure

Before introducing our conceptual framework about intervention design, it is important to clarify the meaning of the terms 'content', process', and 'procedure' used in this book. *Content* refers to what people know and say about the problem or decision of concern. Content is typically communicated via talk during team meetings. In principle, if we audio record a meeting and then transcribe what was said, we end up with a complete report on the meeting's content. Content can be not only found in documents but also captured and represented in artefacts such as visual displays and models. *Process* refers to how team members work together to complete their tasks or achieve their goals. During team meetings, process is about who speaks for how long, intonation, bodily posture, whether some speakers always get a reaction from other team members or their contributions are largely ignored. Thus, process has a large role in how content is interpreted. The following is an example of how content and process interact to shape interpretation.

Case nitrogen

In June 2022, the Dutch government announced a new policy on nitrogen emissions. Nitrogen deposits were held responsible for depletion of the soil, groundwater, and surface water and degradation of ecosystems. The main aim of the policy was to reduce emissions by 50% by 2030. Since agriculture and livestock are responsible for about half of nitrogen depositions, this has grave consequences for farmers. Reductions in livestock of about 30% were foreseen. In particular, farms close to natural habitats would be effected, and the government published a map indicating regional reduction targets.

Needless to say, for the farmers concerned, the new policy would have an immediate impact on their livelihood, a livelihood that was part of their core identity and occupation often going back generations. Immediately after the government plans were made public, farmers started protests across the country. They blockaded roads, dumped manure, and visited politician's homes to vent their anger. The Dutch flag hung upside down, with the blue stripe on top, became the symbol of the protests and could increasingly be seen not only in villages and the countryside but in inner cities as well.

In response to the protests, the Dutch government asked a former politician and round table organiser, Johan Remkes, to meet with farmers and representatives of farmer's organisations. These meetings took place over summer. In September 2022, the secretary of Agriculture stepped down because, as he said, he had not succeeded in his task of formulating a new perspective for the agricultural sector. In October 2022, Remkes presented his report to an audience of politicians and farmer organisations (Remkes, 2022). The 60-page report contained 25 concrete recommendations to make progress in the nitrogen discussion. These included concrete measures such as taking the proposed map off the table as a policy instrument as well as 'creative' solutions such as keeping to the 2030 deadline but reconsidering in 2025 and 2028 whether the time schedule needed updating. The report, however, did not propose changes to the core policy of reductions in emissions and livestock.

The response immediately after the presentation and later in the press was very positive. Political parties from left to right indicated that this gave them new hope, a near-unanimous reaction which is unusual in times of increased polarisation. What is telling is how often reactions referred to the tone of the report. In his presentation, Remkes mentioned that in his talks over the summer he saw despair in the faces of very reasonable people. A dairy farmer's reaction was: "That sentence touched me. And now that I repeat it, it touches me again. That recognition is what we needed so badly. That we are no criminals or polluters". "C'est le ton qui fait la musique" (Smouter, 2022). Some reactions plainly recognised that the content had not changed significantly yet were still positive: "The secretary . . . speaking after Remkes more or less had the same story. But for some reason you trust her less. There is a sense of 'sorry for the map, but now let's stop being difficult'". In a press conference later that day, a politician did not realise his microphone was still open and commented that the cabinet would need to come up with a reaction to the report fast, "before the farmers have a chance to read it and get back on their tractors again". "Everything they were angry about stays in place" (Smouter, 2022).

The reactions clearly show that process matters in how information is interpreted, even if the topic is very important to stakeholders and they recognise that the content of the message is essentially the same. Finally, *procedure* is what the analyst uses to guide the process. A procedure is often a method or technique deployed as part of an intervention approach. For example, causal mapping is a procedure used to guide the elicitation of team members' knowledge about the problem or decision, which is part of the group causal mapping intervention approach (see Chapter 8). Beyond well-established procedures (e.g. brainstorming), the analyst can design new procedures to achieve a particular goal (e.g. a new way of asking questions to increase the number of team members' contributions; a new method for collecting team members' preferences).

It is worth noting that we typically refrain from trying to intervene in the process directly. Team members are likely to feel that interpretations of and direct recommendations on the team process are out of bounds (Phillips & Phillips, 1993, p. 546). We prefer to monitor the team process and the content of team discussions, and if these are not developing as desired, adapt the procedure. For instance, if a particular agenda item results in few reactions by the team, the facilitator would note that. She then can choose to share that observation in terms of content (e.g. 'this question does not seem to generate a lot of ideas') or in terms of process (e.g. 'it seems we have little energy to work on this particular task'). While we think observations on process can be helpful, we would refrain from making the process the topic of conversation, by turning to an interpretation of process. This means we would avoid questions such as 'does anyone have suggestions on why the team has little to say about this topic?' Instead, the analyst could reformulate the question to be addressed (changing the prompt with the aim to generate additional comments) or decide to move to another agenda item.

12.2 Scope and roles

Decision support interventions involve several people whose interactions and behaviours shape the decision process and outcome. Whether the decision under consideration is simple or complex, it always pays off to be clear on what the analyst and client see as their role in the intervention, and what both parties envision the results of the intervention should be.

12.2.1 The client

Every intervention typically starts with one person in an organisation wishing to address a problem and reaching out to an analyst for help. If an intervention is feasible and agreed upon, the analyst will work for this person who then becomes the client. Typically, the client expects the analyst to have the content knowledge or methodological expertise to be able to help her with her problem. However, for the intervention approaches described in this book, the division of labour between client and analyst is agreed as follows: the analyst takes responsibility for designing the procedure and guiding the process during team discussions, and the client is responsible for providing relevant content. The source of content is varied and can include, among others, documentation, databases, models, the client herself, and a designated team of relevant stakeholders.

Before approaching the analyst, the client may have talked to her colleagues to come to some sort of consolidated idea about what the problem is. However, in our experience, neither is likely. Thus, the analyst needs to come to a preliminary understanding of how the client herself views the problem and its potential solution. Thus, a critical design choice is the *scope of the problem definition*. Scoping this preliminary problem definition is important for several reasons. First, the choice of scope clarifies the aims of the intervention to the client as well as to the analyst. Indeed, formulating the problem forces the client to make explicit what she is trying to accomplish, which helps the client to start thinking about goals (Schein, 1987, p. 49). Clarity on goals in turn makes clear where the analyst can be most helpful.

Second, the choice of scope also has implications for the sponsorship of the intervention. If the client and sponsor roles fall within different individuals, the sponsor needs to be convinced of the need to address the problem presented to her and the relevance of the proposed intervention approach before she will make the funds and organisation members' time available. And this is more likely when the initial problem description appeals to important goals or stakeholders in the organisation.

Third, the choice of scope is also important because serves as the basis for inviting others to participate in team meetings. If the problem that is going to be addressed is described too narrowly, some people may feel there is no problem, or if there is, it is not their responsibility or they have no information to add. Choosing the right phrasing for the problem to be addressed is very important in order to motivate a group of people beyond the client to spend time on the project. Failing to do so may mean that some participants with relevant information or implementation power are not present in meetings and their information is missed. Simon (1973, p. 270) notes that management attention is a scarce resource. At any moment, there are many different things going on in the organisation and its surroundings, and a manager will have to decide which are important enough to spend time on.

Another critical design choice is *when to introduce the client's definition of the problem and her preferred solution*, as it can have a critical impact on the effectiveness of team discussions. Research by Michael Roberto has shown that when leaders reveal their views too early in the decision making process, three serious adverse effects may happen (Roberto, 2013). First, team members may think that the decision has already been made by the leader and so feel that there is no genuine opportunity to influence the decision process. Second, team members' views may become framed by those of the leader's, which can constrain their thinking and thus narrow the possibilities for action that could have been considered during team discussions. Finally, when the leader reveals her position team members may feel discouraged to express minority views or challenge the leader's views.

Introducing a preferred definition of a problem or solution is one thing, but often managers go one step further and impose a solution, expecting the rest of the organisation to take action accordingly. An extensive study by management scholar Paul Nutt shows that introducing a solution early has a severely negative impact on implementation. Nutt (2002, 2011) analyses 400 decision making situations and finds that in the majority of cases the top manager conceives of a solution and imposes it on the rest of the organisation. Wanting to solve the problem fast, management prefers a top-down approach. The expectation is that it will take too long to involve others in a joint process of discovering what the problem is about and which solutions seem promising. However, in practice, a top-down approach is slower. Nutt (2002) finds that imposing a solution takes longer than a discovery process: around 22 rather than 14 months. In addition, in the first case, only half of decisions are adopted versus about 85% in the latter.

Why is idea imposition so popular and why does it fail so often? Nutt explains that while imposing a solution seems like a fast way to solve a problem; it creates delays when translating the solution into action. Implementation is slower because of the political and social forces that are stirred up (Roberto, 2013). Confronted with a top-down decision, others in the organisation may feel their interests are threatened and passively or actively block implementation. Since the decision maker has already committed to a course of action, there is little he can do to change this situation. Identifying additional arguments backing up the plan, possibly with the help of external analysts who start new research, is one option. It is, however, unlikely that this new research will be seen as neutral and convince others affected by the decision. A joint discovery process works better because the initial commitment is not to a particular solution but to a problem: the decision maker motivates why a certain issue merits attention at this moment and invites others in the organisation to look into the issue and help craft solutions. If the problem focus is set but analysis and identification of solutions are still open, people can have a voice and their input can meaningfully be taken into consideration. This expands the range of ideas considered and, as discussed earlier, builds commitment.

Thus, the analyst must warn the client about the potential risks of disclosing her views at the start of team discussions. Instead, the analyst can suggest that the client's views could be withheld until the end of the intervention process or, alternatively, the client could introduce her views to the team as only tentative, making it clear that these could change if as a result of the team discussions superior recommendations are produced.

12.2.2   The analyst

While talking to the client for the first time, the analyst will already start forming a picture of what is going on. Who is involved? What actions have stakeholders taken in the past and why? What developments outside and inside of the organisation have shaped the situation? What future developments are likely to have an impact? A critical task then is making an inventory of problem symptoms so that the analyst comes to an initial understanding of the scope of the problem. This is the basis for the project proposal, the sponsor's commitment of resources, and participants' willingness to spend time on the project.

A critical design choice for the analyst regards the *extent to which she intends to manage the process and content of team discussions*. We have already mentioned our preference for the analyst to manage process (and procedure) but not content. However, scholars are divided about whether the analyst should focus only on managing the process but not the content, or whether some content management is allowed (see also Chapters 13 and 14). For example, decision scientist Larry Phillips (Phillips & Phillips, 1993) argues that analysts should refrain from contributing to the content of team discussions for three reasons. First, contributing to content may interfere with the effective management of the process. Just as writing and talking at the same time are difficult, attending to both process and content at the same time is problematic. Second, revealing expertise in the content during discussions can cause team members to feel de-skilled, which can adversely affect teamwork. Finally, if the final recommendations include content that reflects the views of the analyst, team members' commitment to the final decision may be partial and implementation may consequently suffer. By contrast, management researchers Chris Huxham and Steve Cropper (Huxham & Cropper, 1994) posit that some content expertise is actually expected by the team and can be used to demonstrate understanding of what the team is discussing and hence, be a basis for gaining their trust and credibility.

Let us assume that Maria, a manager of a library services provider, contacted you about a situation she is facing. In the initial conversations, she mentioned several intertwined developments that were affecting the organisation: fewer people loan books, CDs, DVDs, or other materials from libraries in turn leading to less demand for support to libraries. In addition, a decline in government subsidies to libraries is imminent although its extent is highly uncertain, and the market will be opened for other service providers. You are considering how to go about helping Maria and after talking to her and others in her organisation, you may decide that more research is needed. In that case, you may opt for a round of interviews with employees and clients, find and analyse data the organisation has gathered on client satisfaction, study its competitors, and combine that information in a report to Maria and the management board. In doing so, you have taken the role of a researcher and used empirical research methods. The quality of your work is measured against well-known criteria such as validity and reliability, which are discussed in texts on empirical research methodology in the social sciences (see Appendix B). Note that methods in this field are concerned with the knowledge you produce, while what is done with that knowledge (implementation of changes) is not part of the method. As a researcher, you collect and analyse information in a neutral and objective manner and report the results and implications. Your report offers new knowledge on the problem at hand and points to solutions, but supporting implementation of solutions is not part of your role. In essence, in this role you assume that 'the facts speak for themselves'.

There are, of course, other ways to approach Maria's request for help. Let us assume you have experienced situations like this before, are of a slightly more self-confident nature, or both. After giving the situation some thought, the answer seems clear to you: the organisation should focus only on those services which are profitable and conduct transactions with client libraries on a purely commercial basis. This would constitute an advice with regard to content. Yet another way to approach the situation is the following. If your answer would be that Maria should list all the arguments for and against 'going commercial', this is an advice that specifies a process to follow. The previous answer implies you take an expert role, while the latter implies that you do not voice your own opinion but propose a procedure and leave the responsibility for finding an answer to the client.

This last approach is in line with Schein's (1987) *process consultant* role. A fundamental principle of process consultation is that the client continues to own the problem.[2] A central assumption of this book is that for most problems perceived as complex, an analyst that is an outsider and learns about the situation for the first time, is highly unlikely to come up with the best possible solution. And even if he or she did, the solution will not be accepted by those who have stake in the problem. Both the quality and acceptance of the solution are needed. A perfect solution which is not followed up is useless, while following up on bad advice does not improve the situation much either. If we intervene in a team, we hope to achieve that all team members support the conclusions reached. In a team setting, acceptance takes the form of a consensus on the way to move forward. This means that we seek to support teams in such a way that important information is brought out into the open, analysed, and integrated into a consensus view. We find that the process consultant role fits best to this goal.

Authors such as Vennix (1996, 1999), Phillips and Phillips (1993) and Bostrom et al. (1993) have built on or added to Schein's work and described in more concrete terms what an analyst does when supporting teams in this way. In designing the intervention, it is important that the analyst makes clear to the client that she will not be taking the problem off the client's shoulders. How to do that is part of the description of facilitation tasks that will be discussed in Chapters 13, 14, and 15.

A successful discussion of roles between analyst and client should ideally align each other's expectations as much as possible. This may be difficult. For example, the analyst and the client may expect the project to deliver 'scenarios' but what that term means to each of them is actually different. Thus, the analyst should be sure to check with the client and check again. Part of managing expectations is being clear on roles and responsibilities and come to an agreement on a design for the intervention, as detailed as possible in this early stage. This includes selecting and inviting others to participate in the intervention, something for which the analyst typically depends to a large extent on the client, as discussed next.

12.3 Team design

From the initial problem definition, a picture will emerge of the persons inside, and possibly outside, the organisation, whose views are important in coming to grips with the problem. Thus, one of the first tasks for the analyst is to find out how other people understand the problem. Often there are large differences of opinion on the problem, or even on the question of whether there is a problem, and this is particularly true of complex problems and decisions (Vennix, 1999). Consequently, the analyst works with the contact client in drawing up a list of individuals to invite to meetings.

A crucial design choice concerns the *size of the team* that should be assembled for taking part in the intervention. The general consensus within the group research community is that as the size of the team increases, effectiveness also increases because there are more individuals to contribute to tackling the problem at hand (Hare, 1981; Hill, 1982; Thomas & Fink, 1963). However, team effectiveness increases only up to a point, beyond which adding more participants makes the team less effective. In other words, there is an optimal level of team size. As size increases passes this optimum, differences in participation become more pronounced to the extent that a few team members come to dominate the discussions (Shaw, 1981). The optimal team size depends on the specific team and problem at hand, but the perception of scholars and practitioners is that, in general, it is rather small, typically between six and eight members (Roberto, 2013). Most of the methods covered in this book have been developed to be used with small- to medium-sized teams of up to 16 people (Shaw et al., 2004). However, tackling more complex decision problems may require that larger teams are assembled, from within or even across organisations, to provide enhanced information processing capabilities and viewpoints, in which case the same methods described in this book could be used with appropriate computer-supported technology (Eden & Ackermann, 2010).

Beyond team size, there is also a choice regarding the *type of individual* that needs to be involved in the intervention. A key consideration here is to gain access to relevant knowledge or expertise in relation to the problem at hand (Eden & Ackermann, 2010; Roberto, 2003). In practice, this requires the involvement of individuals from certain functions or roles across the organisational hierarchy. In some cases, the nature of the problem requires the involvement of individuals drawn from different organisations. The Teenage Pregnancy Group case discussed in Chapters 9 and 11 is a good example of this.

When discussing potential team members, the analyst should ask the client whether there are any individuals within the organisation who could provide information or insight related to the problem that others do not possess. However, considerations of expertise alone should not be the primary determinant of team membership when designing an intervention. Management scientists Fran Ackermann and Colin Eden argue that consultants should consider a wide range of people whose stance regarding the problem and its solution makes them key stakeholders (Ackermann & Eden, 2011b). Specifically, they advise to include those who are likely to be interested in the problem and have the power to influence, positively or negatively, the outcomes of the intervention. A grid with the two dimensions of interest and power can be built by the consultant to aid in the process of stakeholder identification. By using the grid, the consultant can help the client to prioritise who might be involved in terms of their relative power and interest. At a minimum, Ackermann and Eden suggest that those individuals categorised as both very powerful and interested should be included in the team, as this will increase the chances of implementing the outcomes of the intervention. Indeed research has shown that involvement of people responsible for implementation is associated with successful decision making in high-stakes situations (Bourgeois & Eisenhardt, 1988). Some scholars suggest that when considering who to involve, the consultant should also look at a range of potential roles that team members could adopt during discussions. The ideal team would then be one in which all roles are covered (Ackermann & Eden, 2011b; Belbin, 2010; Nutt, 2002).

Another important consideration related to team roles is the *level of team diversity* desired. If the analyst is helping the client to address a complex decision problem, it may seem obvious that forming a highly diverse team is appropriate and likely to increase the quality of team discussions due to the access to different perspectives on the problem and its solution. By a 'diverse team', we mean a team whose members exhibit differences in terms of their age, gender, history of working together, functional background, and cognitive style, among other factors. Many scholars argue that heterogeneous teams should outperform homogenous teams because the former ought to exhibit greater cognitive diversity than the latter (Van Knippenberg et al., 2011; Van Knippenberg & Schippers, 2007). Put differently, teams that possess greater cognitive diversity benefit from interactions among individuals with different points of view and expertise, because they generate the required levels of cognitive conflict that can enhance the quality of team decision making (Amason, 1996; Roberto, 2013).

The empirical evidence regarding the impact of team diversity on decision making and problem-solving performance, however, is inconclusive (Williams & O'Reilly, 1998). For example, research has shown that while diverse teams do generate higher levels of cognitive conflict, it is often the case that these raised levels of cognitive conflict lead to personal frictions, displays of heated emotions and personality clashes, the kind of affective conflict that reduces commitment to proposed solutions, and hinders the development of shared understanding (Amason, 1996; De Dreu, 2006; De Dreu & Weingart, 2003). This does not mean that forming diverse teams should be ruled out. Instead, as analyst and client start to discuss the composition of the team, they should assess the level of team diversity emerging, and then seek measures to counterbalance the pitfalls associated with high levels of either homogeneity or heterogeneity.

Finally, the analyst should highlight to their clients the possibility of drawing on people whom they trust and respect (Roberto, 2003), who can act as sounding board on key aspects of the problem or particular solutions, but who are not necessarily key stakeholders in the problem being addressed. They can also play the role of devil's advocate during team discussions, by offering constructive critique. While inviting the client's trusted individuals to participate in the intervention process is not always necessary, there are some methods that do benefit from their inclusion, such as the scenario planning method (see Chapter 6).

12.4   Context design

Ensuring that the team tasked with addressing the problem is comprised of the right mix of individuals is only a small part of designing an effective intervention. The analysts and the client must also co-design the context or environment within which team discussions will take place. A team's context both shapes and influences how an intervention process unfolds, and so careful consideration should be given to how different environmental factors can affect the team's ability to engage effectively in the intervention. There are four distinct factors to consider: organisational, situational, social, and physical. *Organisational factors* include mechanisms such as reward and punishment systems, accountability structures, and monitoring and control instruments, which can all affect team behaviours and thus decision making effectiveness (Ackermann & Eden, 2011a; Sterman, 1994; Wageman, 1995). These mechanisms tend to stay stable over time, although subtle changes can have noticeable effects on organisational behaviour. However, these mechanisms are unlikely to be changed for each problem that needs to be tackled, and so the consultant (and even the client) will have little opportunity to influence or exercise control over these factors. Nevertheless, the consultant should make the client aware of their significance, as organisational factors can affect individual and collective behaviours in very powerful ways.

Team behaviours are also affected by *situational factors* such as time pressure and sense of urgency. Clients can make time pressure more or less salient to team members by setting tight deadlines and milestones. Similarly, a sense of urgency can become salient when clients stress capabilities developed by competitors or increasing concerns by customers or stakeholders. However, increasing time pressure or a sense of urgency can lead to a need to achieve closure too quickly by the team (Kruglanski et al., 2006), or impair team performance due to undue stress, anxiety, and arousal (Janis & Mann, 1977). Consequently, the analyst should help the client consider the risks associated with heightening or lowering these factors for a particular intervention.

Social factors such as shared behavioural principles and norms also affect team behaviours and hence the intervention process. Scholars have shown that the social factors governing a decision making process can be changed at the outset of an intervention process. For example, analyst and client can co-design and implement ground rules that seek to ensure smooth and harmonious interactions during team discussions (Hackman, 2002). In addition, creating a team environment of 'psychological safety' can stimulate effective problem solving and learning (Edmondson, 1999, 2003). Team members feel psychologically safe when they share the belief that the group is safe for taking interpersonal risks. This means that individuals will feel comfortable to speak up about issues and problems at the risk of being seen as ignorant, incompetent, disruptive, or negative. A psychologically safe environment fosters candid communications about the problem at hand, which include not only raising claims about issues but also expressing dissent, admitting mistakes, and making requests for help.

Finally, intervention scholars have long recognised the importance of the *physical factors* of a team's environment (Hickling, 1990; Huxham, 1990). For example, Colin Eden argues that avoiding interruptions from day-to-day work can help team members to better concentrate on the issues to be addressed, and thus the possibility to hold team discussions away from the client's premises should be considered (Eden, 1990). Thus, the consultant must discuss with the client the advantages and disadvantages of organising team meetings on- or offsite. Eden also stresses the importance of physical aspects of room design such as layout, lighting, furniture, and equipment, as these can affect team performance during discussions (Ackermann & Eden, 2011a; Eden, 1990; Eden & Ackermann, 1998). A common room layout is a 'horseshoe' shape where team members sit around a central display, thus enabling all to read easily what is projected or written on the display, and see one another. Typical furniture includes movable tables and chairs, and sometimes plenty of wall space when a central display is not used. Equipment options vary depending on the level of structure designed for team discussions (Franco & Montibeller, 2010). In sum, by discussing choices about physical aspects of the team's environment, the analyst will help the client to create the kind of atmosphere that will stimulate team members to actively engage in the intervention process.

12.5   Communication design

Methods or procedures for thinking and talking about the problem represent the final aspect of intervention design that the analysts must consider with the client. Analysts can offer their clients a range of choices in this regard. Broadly, there are two approaches to thinking and talking about a problem: *unstructured* and *structured*, and these are discussed next.

12.5.1   *Unstructured communication*

In the unstructured approach, the consultant acts as the chair of team discussions, encouraging team members to discuss their views and ideas freely and openly without adherence to a specified procedure for how discussions should unfold. By contrast, when the structured approach is adopted, the consultant uses a well-defined script that dictates quite specifically how team members will make contributions to the discussion, prioritise issues, compare and contrast alternatives, and come to a conclusion.

Scholars have labelled the unstructured approach the 'consensus method' because of its emphasis on reaching common ground so that a solution acceptable to all team members can be found, and because it tends to foster high levels of commitment and team harmony (Murrell & Stewart, 1993; Priem et al., 1995; Schweiger et al., 1986). The consensus approach, however, may lead to premature agreement or convergence on issues or options during team discussions. In trying to reach common ground, it is also possible that dissenting voices are suppressed or that minorities are pressured to conform as a majority opinion emerges. Furthermore, early convergence may not uncover key issues and assumptions, clarify uncertainties and perspectives, and generate more innovative responses to the problem.

12.5.2 *Structured communication*

In order to foster the requisite amount of divergent and convergent thinking (see Chapter 14), together with enhanced levels of critical thinking and debate (see Chapter 15), the analyst can suggest adopting a structured approach to communication. Scholars and consultants have developed a range of structured procedures and associated techniques and tools for thinking and talking about problems, and a selected sample of longstanding model-driven intervention approaches was presented in Chapters 4 to 11. These approaches stimulate the generation of multiple issues and options, and help identify critical assumptions, uncertainties and values, as well as relationships between different aspects of the problem. Furthermore, they offer a means to foster a great deal of cognitive conflict within the team, which has been shown to enhance the quality of decision making processes (Eisenhardt et al., 1997; Roberto, 2013).

Although the use of structured approaches can offer many benefits for clients wishing to tackle messy problems, they are not free of risks. They take time to learn and master for the consultant, and often clients and their teams need some training before using a particular approach (Ormerod, 1995). In addition, the levels of cognitive conflict generated by the use of these approaches can generate affective conflict, which can reduce commitment and shared understanding within a team (Amason, 1996). Therefore, analysts must use these approaches with care, and assess whether using a structured approach is warranted for a given problem.

The argument in this book is that the complexity and ambiguity that is characteristic of situations where the stakes are high require interventions based on the use of a structured approach (e.g. Midgley, 2000; Reynolds & Holwell, 2010; Rosenhead & Mingers, 2001) such as those introduced in Chapters 4 to 11, but those new to this field will find it difficult to know which approach is best suited for their specific needs.[3] To help choose from the set of structured approaches discussed in this book, it might be useful to establish whether those involved wish to focus mainly on gaining a better and shared understanding of the antecedents and potential consequences of the decision situation of concern, or developing appropriate responses to tackle the decision situation effectively in the present. This is illustrated in Figure 12.1.

A decision situation often arises when inadequate performance on some indicator of importance to those with a stake in the situation is perceived to become an issue in the future. The left part of Figure 12.1 shows how well an organisation is doing on a particular performance indicator over time until now. For instance, think of market share or customer satisfaction for a private organisation, or the rate of teenage parents completing school monitored by a public organisation such as a ministry of education. Typically, a decision situation comes to the stakeholders' attention if performance on an indicator of interest drops below (or exceeds) an acceptable standard, or

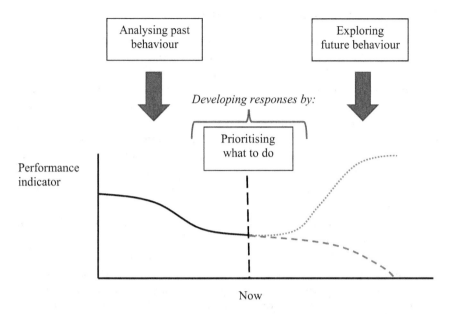

FIGURE 12.1 Primary focus of a structured approach to intervention.

is expected to do so if no action is taken. This is shown in the right part of the figure by the dashed and dotted lines. The dashed line indicates performance in the business-as-usual scenario. The dotted line is what the organisation would want the performance indicator to look like. The widening gap between the two indicates that the problem is expected to worsen over time, and thus the demand for a decision will increase.

Let us assume that at the present moment a decision situation has arisen, and that the relevant stakeholders are willing to spend effort, time, and resources, on addressing the situation as a team. Now they have choices on where to start the decision making process. Team members may choose to (i) complement their current understandings by analysing their past experiences of the situation in more depth using group model building (Chapter 4); (ii) explore alternative futures that could develop from the current situation using scenario planning (Chapter 6); or (iii) articulate their preferences, priorities, available options, responses and actions at present before selecting a particular option, response or action using group causal mapping (Chapter 8) or decision conferencing (Chapter 10). The first two choices are mainly focused on gaining a better and shared understanding of the situation in terms of its antecedents or possible consequences; the last one is intended to develop a concrete action plan to address the situation now. Of course, a decision making process that considers all three choices will increase stakeholders' confidence in the proposed action plan that results from the analysis.[4]

12.5.3 Bringing team discussions to a close

Irrespective of the approach used, *how to bring closure* to team discussions and the overall intervention is an important design choice regarding communication. Typically, the analyst will act as a facilitator (see Chapters 13, 14, and 15) and will strive to find common ground during team discussions. If the prospects of reaching a collective agreement are deemed to be challenging prior to the intervention, the client should be prepared to step in. In this case, the analyst can suggest that the client takes on the role of an arbitrator. This involves the client making clear to the team that all the arguments and proposals generated during team discussions will be carefully listened to, but that she would have the ultimate responsibility for the final decision.

The importance of spending time discussing how closure will be brought, and what will be done with the outputs of team deliberations cannot be overestimated (Edmondson et al., 2003). Team members can become frustrated and heavily disappointed if the approach to reaching closure to discussions does not conform to their expectations. Consequently, the analyst and the client must prepare and agree on a clear process roadmap, and announce it to the team at the beginning of the intervention. The proposed intervention process should in other words be transparent and offer a logical procedure for achieving the intervention goal. The role that the client will adopt in bringing team discussions to a close should be included in this process roadmap. Overall, by carefully designing and implementing a transparent process roadmap, team commitment to the final decision is more likely to be achieved because perceptions of procedural fairness will be enhanced (Kim & Mauborgne, 2003; Korsgaard et al., 1995).

Notes

1. Richard and Andersen (1995) use the term 'gatekeeper' to refer to the person who contact the analyst for help.
2. This is different from the *expert* model which comes down to giving advice with regard to content. According to Schein (1987), when calling on an expert the client expects a clear answer that will solve his problem. In this situation, the client is in fact saying 'please take the problem off my shoulders and bring me back a solution'. Schein also describes a third, intermediate, consultant role: the *doctor*. In the doctor role, the client communicates what the problem area is (the 'symptoms') without leaving out any information that is relevant. The analyst in the role of the doctor has the expertise to identify the problem behind the symptoms (the 'diagnosis') and recommends a 'cure'.
3. For studies on how expert facilitators choose intervention approaches, see Kolfschoten and Rouwette (2006) and Velez-Castiblanco et al. (2016).
4. Indeed, as each situation is unique, it may require the use of several approaches within the same intervention (Mingers & Brocklesby, 1997).

References

Ackermann, F., & Eden, C. (2011a). *Making strategy: Mapping out strategic success* (2nd ed.). SAGE.

Ackermann, F., & Eden, C. (2011b). Strategic management of stakeholders: Theory and practice. *Long Range Planning*, 44(3), 179–196. https://doi.org/10.1016/j. lrp.2010.08.001

Amason, A. C. (1996). Distinguishing the effects of functional and dysfunctional conflict on strategic decision making: Resolving a paradox for top management groups. *Academy of Management Journal*, 39(1), 123–148.

Belbin, R. M. (2010). *Management teams: Why they succeed or fail* (3rd ed.). Butterworth-Heinemann.

Bostrom, R. P., Anson, R., & Clawson, V. K. (1993). Group facilitation and group support systems. In L. M. Jessup & J. S. Valacich (Eds.), *Group support systems: New perspectives* (pp. 146–168). Macmillan.

Bourgeois, L. J., III, & Eisenhardt, K. M. (1988). Strategic decision processes in high velocity environments: Four cases in the microcomputer industry. *Management Science*, 34(7), 816–835.

De Dreu, C. K. (2006). When too little or too much hurts: Evidence for a curvilinear relationship between task conflict and innovation in teams. *Journal of Management*, 32(1), 83–107.

De Dreu, C. K., & Weingart, L. R. (2003). A contingency theory of task conflict and performance in groups and organizational teams. In *International handbook of organizational teamwork and cooperative working* (pp. 151–166). Wiley.

Eden, C. (1990). Managing the environment as a means to managing complexity. In C. Eden & J. Radford (Eds.), *Tackling strategic problems: The role of group decision support* (pp. 154–161). SAGE.

Eden, C., & Ackermann, F. (1998). *Making strategy. The journey of strategic management*. SAGE.

Eden, C., & Ackermann, F. (2010). Decision making in groups: Theory and practice. In P. C. Nutt & D. C. Wilson (Eds.), *Handbook of decision making* (pp. 231–272). Wiley-Blackwell.

Edmondson, A. C. (1999). Psychological safety and learning behaviour in work teams. *Administrative Science Quarterly*, 44(2), 350–383.

Edmondson, A. C. (2003). Managing the risk of learning: Psychological safety in work teams. In M. A. West, D. Tjosvold, & K. G. Smith (Eds.), *International handbook of organizational teamwork and cooperative working* (pp. 255–275). John Wiley & Sons.

Edmondson, A. C., Roberto, M. A., & Watkins, M. D. (2003). A dynamic model of top management team effectiveness: Managing unstructured task streams. *The Leadership Quarterly*, 14(3), 297–325. https://doi.org/10.1016/S1048-9843(03)00021-3

Eisenhardt, K. M., Kahwajy, J. L., & Bourgeois, L. J. I. (1997). How management teams can have a good fight. *Harvard Business Review*, 75(4), 77–85.

Franco, L. A., & Montibeller, G. (2010). Facilitated modelling in operational research (invited review). *European Journal of Operational Research*, 205(3), 489–500.

Hackman, J. R. (2002). *Leading teams: Setting the stage for great performances*. Harvard Business School Press.

Hare, A. P. (1981). Group size. *American Behavioral Scientist*, *24*(5), 695–708.

Hickling, A. (1990). 'Decision spaces': A scenario about designing appropriate rooms for group decision management. In C. Eden & J. Radford (Eds.), *Tackling strategic problems: The role of group decision support* (pp. 169–177). SAGE.

Hill, G. W. (1982). Group versus individual performance: Are n+1 heads better than one? *Psychological Bulletin*, *91*(3), 517–539.

Huxham, C. (1990). On trivialities in process. In C. Eden & J. Radford (Eds.), *Tackling strategic problems: The role of group decision support* (pp. 162–168). SAGE.

Huxham, C., & Cropper, S. (1994). From many to one – and back. An exploration of some components of facilitation. *Omega*, *22*(1), 1–11.

Janis, I. L., & Mann, L. (1977). *Decision making: A psychological analysis of conflict, choice and commitment*. The Free Press.

Kim, W. C., & Mauborgne, R. (2003). Fair process: Managing in the knowledge economy. *Harvard Business Review*, *81*(1), 127–136.

Kolfschoten, G. L., & Rouwette, E. A. J. A. (2006). Choice criteria for facilitation techniques. Proceedings of 39th HICSS Conference, Kauai.

Korsgaard, M., Schweiger, D., & Sapienza, H. (1995). Building commitment, attachment, and trust in strategic decision making teams. The role of procedural justice. *Academy of Management Journal*, *38*, 60–84.

Kruglanski, A. W., Pierro, A., Mannetti, L., & De Grada, E. (2006). Groups as epistemic providers: Need for closure and the unfolding of group-centrism. *Psychological Review*, *113*(1), 84–100.

Midgley, G. (2000). *Systemic intervention: Philosophy, methodology, and practice*. Kluwer Academic/Plenum Publishers.

Mingers, J., & Brocklesby, J. (1997). Multimethodology: Towards a framework for mixing methodologies. *Omega-International Journal of Management Science*, *25*(5), 489–509.

Murrell, A. J., & Stewart, A. C. (1993). Consensus versus devil's advocacy: The influence of decision process and task structure on strategic decision making. *Journal of Business Communication*, *30*(4), 399.

Nutt, P. (2002). *Why decisions fail. Avoiding the blunders and traps that lead to debacles*. Berrett-Koehler.

Nutt, P. C. (2011). Making decision-making research matter: Some issues and remedies. *Management Research Review*, *34*(1), 5–16.

Ormerod, R. J. (1995). Putting soft OR methods to work: Information systems strategy development at Sainsbury's. *Journal of Operational Research Society*, *46*(3), 277–293.

Phillips, L. D., & Phillips, M. C. (1993). Facilitated work groups: Theory and practice. *Journal of the Operational Research Society*, *44*(6), 533–549.

Priem, R. L., Harrison, D. A., & Muir, N. K. (1995). Structured conflict and consensus outcomes in group decision making. *Journal of Management*, *21*(4), 691.

Remkes, J. (2022). *Wat wel kan – Uit de impasse en een aanzet voor perspectief [What is possible – out of the impasse and towards a perspective]*. www.tweedekamer.nl/kamerstukken/brieven_regering/detail?id=2022Z18582&did=2022D39674

Reynolds, M., & Holwell, S. (Eds.). (2010). *Systems approaches to managing change: A practical guide*. Springer.

Richardson, G. P., & Andersen, D. F. (1995). Teamwork in group model building. *System Dynamics Review*, *11*(2), 113–137.

Roberto, M. A. (2003). The stable core and dynamic periphery in top management teams. *Management Decision*, *41*(2), 120–131. https://doi.org/doi:10.1108/00251740310457560

Roberto, M. A. (2013). *Why great leaders don't take yes for an answer: Managing for conflict and consensus* (2nd ed.). Pearson Education.

Rosenhead, J., & Mingers, J. (Eds.). (2001). *Rational analysis for a problematic world revisited: Problem structuring methods for complexity, uncertainty and conflict*. Wiley.

Schein, E. H. (1987). *Process consultation* (Vol. 2). Addison Wesley.

Schweiger, D. M., Sandberg, W. R., & Ragan, J. W. (1986). Group approaches for improving strategic decision making: A comparative analysis of dialectical inquiry, devil's advocacy, and consensus. *Academy of Management Journal*, *29*(1), 51–71.

Shaw, D., Westcombe, M., Hodgkin, J., & Montibeller, G. (2004). Problem structuring methods for large group interventions. *Journal of the Operational Research Society*, *55*(5), 453–463.

Shaw, M. (1981). *Group dynamics: The psychology of small group behaviours* (3rd ed.). McGraw-Hill.

Simon, H. A. (1973). Applying information technology to organization design. *Public Administration Review*, *33*(3), 268–278.

Smouter, K. (2022, October 7). De toon van Remkes slaat beter aan dan het 'toontje' van Klaver [Remke's tone has more impact than Klaver's]. *NRC Handelsblad*. www.nrc.nl/nieuws/2022/10/07/de-toon-van-remkes-zet-meer-zoden-aan-de-dijk-dan-het-toontje-van-klaver-a4144531

Sterman, J. D. (1994). Learning in and about complex systems. *System Dynamics Review*, *10*(2–3), 291–330.

Thomas, E. G., & Fink, E. F. (1963). Effects of group size. *Psychological Bulletin*, *60*(4), 371–384.

Van Knippenberg, D., Dawson, J. F., West, M. A., & Homan, A. C. (2011). Diversity faultlines, shared objectives, and top management team performance. *Human Relations*, *64*(3), 307–336.

Van Knippenberg, D., & Schippers, M. C. (2007). Work group diversity. *Annual Review of Psychology*, *58*, 515–541.

Velez-Castiblanco, J., Brocklesby, J., & Midgley, G. (2016). Boundary games: How teams of OR practitioners explore the boundaries of intervention. *European Journal of Operational Research*, *249*(3), 968–982.

Vennix, J. A. M. (1996). *Group model building. Facilitating team learning using system dynamics*. Wiley.

Vennix, J. A. M. (1999). Group model-building: Tackling messy problems. *System Dynamics Review*, *15*(4), 379–401.

Wageman, R. (1995). Interdependence and group effectiveness. *Administrative Science Quarterly*, 145–180.

Williams, K. Y., & O'Reilly III, C. A. (1998). A review of 40 years of research. *Research in Organizational Behavior*, *20*, 77–140.

13

BASICS OF FACILITATION

The previous chapter described critical factors that can affect the successful deployment and use of intervention approaches to support team decision making. This and the next two chapters build on these insights by turning to the actual delivery of team decision support interventions. In what follows, we discuss *what* the analyst does when working with teams, and *why* these 'doings' are important. 'What' is about the tasks performed by the analyst, which are grounded in a particular set of attitudes that the analyst displays during team discussions. For instance, one task is to select a problem to work on that is relevant to all team members, which is in line with a 'helping' attitude. 'Why' captures the rationale of the analyst's tasks, that is, how completing these tasks helps to bring about high-quality team decision making.

How can an analyst help a team by attending to procedure and process? In other words, how can an analyst perform the role of *facilitator*?[1] Furthermore, what is effective team facilitation? Vennix (1996) points out that much of the literature on facilitation simply states what a facilitator is supposed to do, that is, what tasks the facilitator must perform. This advice is problematic because variations in the performance of facilitator tasks can serve different purposes. For example, a facilitator often is advised to ask questions rather than state opinions. However, questions can be phrased in such a way that a particular answer is implied (Franco & Nielsen, 2018). Or a question can be asked with the intention of revealing a gap in the knowledge of the recipient (Tavella & Franco, 2015). Thus, the advice to simply ask questions is not sufficient; a facilitator also needs to understand the rationale behind asking questions.

Vennix (1996, 1999) clarifies this rationale by formulating a set of attitudes associated with different facilitation tasks. We believe these attitudes

DOI: 10.4324/9781003404200-16

represent core aspects or, to use Poole and DeSanctis' (1992) term, the *spirit* behind the use of the intervention approaches described in the previous chapters. Our assumption is that the more the facilitator's behaviour is in line with these attitudes or this spirit, the more effective they will be in supporting a team decision process. Below we describe five facilitator attitudes[2] (helping, neutrality, inquiring, relational engagement, self-reflexivity), as well as the facilitator tasks aligned with each of these attitudes.

13.1 Helping

A facilitator has a helping attitude, which means the client's problem is central and determines the overall intervention goal. The helping attitude serves at least two important functions. In Chapter 12, we discussed that an important step in designing an intervention is to choose a problem that is important to the client. Only then can we expect team members to take the time and effort to discuss the issue. Sharing and integrating information held within the team takes effort, and only motivated team members will engage in deep processing of information. Deep information processing is needed to achieve changes in team members' opinions and behaviour, which are central elements of team decision making.

Second, if the facilitator is genuinely trying to help the client and the client's problem drives the intervention process, that means the facilitator does not have an agenda of their own. In other words, there are no predetermined outcomes or preferred solutions that the facilitator is working towards. Furthermore, the facilitator must be authentic in their behaviour, and their actions are in line with their statements on their roles and responsibilities in the intervention. If the facilitator's behaviour is not in line with their professed role, this may be unethical. In addition, as Vennix (1996) notes, if the facilitator is not authentic, the participant group is likely to find out. Team members will see through tricks and find out they are led towards certain outcomes, which erodes trust in the facilitator.

13.2 Neutrality

The second attitude relates to the notion of neutrality and clarifies further how team members' input will be considered in facilitated meetings. The facilitator is neutral about the information discussed by team members. That is, they do not value certain problem dimensions more than others, or favour a particular point of view. Furthermore, neutrality means that elicitation of opinions, analysis of the resulting material and using this information to develop recommended solutions is all done by team members. In short, everything done in the facilitated meetings revolves around displaying neutrality when considering team members' input. After the meetings, whether recommended solutions are actually adopted by the client is also a question of the negotiated agreement with the responsible management on the scope and boundaries of the problem addressed. For instance, in the case of nitrogen presented in Chapter 12, recommendations in the report presented by Remkes still had to be taken over by the Dutch parliament.

Neutrality with regard to team members' input facilitates an open information search that makes possible the comparison, combination, and creation of ideas. Tavella and Franco (2015) observe that changed understanding and new knowledge are produced when team members are invited to contribute ideas, and subsequently clarify and reframe them. On the other hand, when the facilitator is not neutral and deploys authority to demarcate and fix team members' inputs, current understanding and existing knowledge remain unchanged. Black and Andersen (2012) find that the facilitator has a major role in rendering team member's contributions to the discussion explicit, by checking on their formulation and noting them down on a central screen. As the discussion proceeds, these visualised contributions can then be altered to reflect a changed understanding. Both studies show that changed understanding and new knowledge are a basis for action. Recall the case on nitrogen reported in Chapter 12, in which a novel, creative proposal was to keep to the 2030 deadline for reducing emissions, but to reconsider at earlier points in time whether the schedule needed updating. This recommendation signals to farmers and their sector organisations that their concerns are heard, and makes it more likely that they support the plan and act accordingly.

The notion that a changed understanding or new knowledge is necessary for creating action is in line with social psychological research (Chaiken et al., 1996; Petty & Cacioppo, 1986). Once participants engage in deep information processing, they will be able to analyse the information they receive to see if it supports or goes against their opinions. In essence, they will be looking for arguments: validated, high-quality messages that may persuade them to change their mind. An argument is likely to be persuasive if it is both new and relevant. In psychological research, controlled studies on persuasion usually include a preparation phase aimed at finding those arguments that are new and relevant to the particular group that is going to be involved in the follow-up study. If we take a moment to consider how this applies to decision makers working on an organisational issue, we can see why identifying convincing arguments in this setting is not easy. Decision makers are likely to have built up considerable expertise and experience in their organisation. They will feel they know all relevant information on the issue at stake, so identifying information that is both relevant and new to them is difficult (Rouwette et al., 2009). Bringing different perspectives on the issue together and ensuring a productive exchange of views increases the chance that novel insights will be created (Roberto, 2013).

Refraining from intervening with regard to discussion content, together with careful consideration of team members' inputs, gives team members the opportunity to use their contributions to influence the decision making process, which helps to build decision commitment (Kim & Mauborgne, 1993; Korsgaard et al., 1995). However, since the facilitator actively guides the group process there are clear boundaries around neutrality, of which we highlight at least three. First, the facilitator influences discussion content by specifying a particular *format* in which to exchange information. In group model building (Chapter 4), for instance, any element of the issue at hand can be raised and discussed, but the issue needs to be formulated as a variable, that is, something that can change over time. In decision conferencing (Chapter 10), objectives need to be formulated in such a way that they exhibit particular properties such as being operational, concise, and nonredundant, among others.

Second, the facilitator and the particular intervention approach employed focus team members' attention on specific *elements* of the issue. In group causal mapping (Chapter 8), actions are connected to issues which are in turn linked to goals. Issues that appear relatively isolated in a causal map because they show few connections to other material are singled out for further discussion. Similarly, when intermediate versions of the model are discussed in group model building sessions, most attention goes out to central feedback loops. These are all examples of how building a visual representation of an issue helps a team to direct its attention to underdeveloped areas of the model. It makes problem understanding more consistent and coherent and guides the team to unique, unshared information. Thus, while it is up to the team members to bring in ideas for discussion, the facilitator shapes the information exchanged by setting a format and directing attention.

Third, facilitators influence discussion *content* when they reflect back to the team what they heard. As Franco and Nielsen (2018) note, facilitators produce various formulations to make sense of team members' contributions to the discussion. Although these formulations are delivered on behalf of the team and require confirmation from the team members, their impact on the trajectory of the team discussion cannot be underestimated. The extent to which these formulations shape discussion content depends on various factors, such as whether facilitators use their 'substantive expertise' (Huxham & Cropper, 1994; Tavella & Franco, 2015) to produce a formulation, whether team members are given the opportunity to co-produce a formulation, and which contributions are chosen by the facilitator to be formulated. Similarly, as will be discussed in the next section, the type of questions produced by the facilitator also influences discussion content.

13.3 Inquiring

There are two sides to an inquiring attitude: asking questions and active listening. The former boils down to overcoming the natural tendency to give answers rather than ask questions. The latter means reflecting back what you have heard using phrases or formulations such as "so what you are saying is" or "do you mean that" (Franco & Nielsen, 2018; Vennix, 1996). By asking questions reflection is encouraged, which helps to increase insight into the subject being discussed. Already in the 1950s, Bales started to observe discussions in small groups. He coded verbal contributions (content) into four categories: questions and attempted answers, positive and negative reactions. The first two help the group to achieve its task and are information-oriented; the second two help to manage the social aspects of the group discussion including the emotions that arise. His conclusion after extensive research is that questions account for only a limited part of the discussion: 7% of contributions are questions, 56% attempted answers, 26% positive reactions, and 11% negative reactions (Bales, 1951, 2002). Why are so few questions asked in group discussions? Bales points out that by asking a question, a person makes room for another group member. The sender gives up his speaking turn and with that the opportunity to strengthen his position.

Questions, however, serve a number of important roles. Questions are likely to be asked more often after a period of tension, for example, when team members disagreed with premature proposals to define or solve the problem. As they will probably not lead to strong emotional reactions, they help the team to establish common ground again and refocus on the task. Questions are a way to raise an issue without expressing a strong commitment to it (McCardle-Keurentjes & Rouwette, 2018). Nevertheless, asking a question in a team discussion means intervening in the decision making process, in a way that influences others' behaviour, thinking and feelings. "Every question or inquiry is . . . an intervention and must be treated as such" (Schein, 1997, p. 207). In this way, they are a way to attend to and steer the meeting process.

By (re)focusing on a topic, questions help to elicit information. In Chapter 2, we saw that teams do not automatically share all relevant information. Before joining the discussion, team members may feel they already have a clear idea of the direction in which a solution can be found. The research on hidden profiles (Stasser & Titus, 2003) showed that this may bias the discussion towards focusing only on the preferred alternative, while sharing information would have shown that the best solution lies elsewhere. Bales also finds that groups do not use their information effectively. What is needed is a "better orientation to the problem and more information about the facts at the beginning of meetings, if not all the way through" (Bales, 2002, p. 239). This is all the more important in complex situations. As in the hidden profile situation, team members deciding on a complex issue each have unique information that needs to be brought together to identify the best way forward. However, even if information is brought up in the discussion, its meaning and significance to the overall issue may not be immediately clear. In Chapter 2, we described two reasons for this. First, functional backgrounds colour interpretations of a term, and differences in interpretations often go unnoticed. Franco (2013) gives the example of a project brief that is understood very differently by project managers and architects. Second, certain actions may have beneficial consequences in one department but undesired consequences elsewhere. Chapter 2 presented the example of the Dutch criminal justice chain. Prison services introduced a policy of early release of prisoners to solve the problem of crowded prisons. However, for judges this meant that sentences were not served to completion and as a result started passing longer sentences. Longer sentences in turn increase prison crowding again. In short, to appreciate the significance of an idea or action, it is worthwhile to explore how it is interpreted by different team members and how it connects to other elements of the issue at stake.

Clarifying ideas and their interrelationships helps team members to assess the value of new information and to contrast it with their own understanding. As we saw before, social psychological research shows that people only take the effort of analysing information in depth, when the issue is important to them (motivation) and when new, relevant information is available (arguments). There is a third factor that also needs to be present: *ability* (Petty & Cacioppo, 1986; Chaiken et al., 1996). Team members need to be able to attend to information. This goes beyond having expertise or experience in the problem at hand. In fact, expertise may even colour understanding concepts and relations in a way that makes it more difficult to grasp an alternative way of looking at things. A facilitator can increase the ability of a group to attend to information by, for instance, ensuring that team members' communications are understood by everyone in the room and attended to (Vennix et al., 1996).

A final reason for a facilitator to ask questions is that it provides a role model to the team members. Questioning is something that is both observable and (usually) implementable. Our experience is that in many team discussions, participants start to mimic the facilitator's behaviour, often without being directly aware of this. A colleague gave the following example. In a project on quality of life in a city district, a representative of the municipality grew impatient with the discussion on the problem and repeatedly tried to steer the discussion towards policies to improve the situation. Other participants listened politely to her suggestions but then continued their previous discussion, not taking her suggestions on board. Midway through the second meeting the civil servant got ready to suggest a solution again but then seemed to collect herself and said: "Oh, I think at this point I need to ask a question".

13.4 Relational engagement

In team decisions, the content under discussion and the relations between team members are intimately linked. Content may influence relations, for instance, when the discussion reveals past decisions associated with less-than-optimal outcomes. In this case, those involved might seek to justify their past decisions, to avoid being blamed. Imagine if over the course of the meeting, the discussion seems to concentrate more and more on problems in one specific team member's area of responsibility. This may have repercussions for the team member's status and power, their future responsibilities, and interactions with others.

Vice versa, relations also influence content. A study on team development over time illustrates this (Van Oortmerssen et al., 2014). The study describes a newly formed board with members drawn from schools, local governments, and companies which was charged with deciding on their future cooperation and realising a new building. When comparing the initial meetings of the board to the final ones, after meeting every month for a year, there were some remarkable differences. In the initial meetings, board members tended to make long statements, with little or no interruptions by others, followed by a statement by another participant. Statements were relatively unrelated; team members seemed to want to share their own opinion without necessarily building on what was said before. Over the course of the year, turn-taking became faster, people interrupted each other more and communication was more open. Van Oortmerssen et al. (2014) relate these changes in interaction to the trusting relationship between board members that developed over time.

The close interplay of discussion content and team members' relations in decision making is substantiated by other research and highlights the crucial role of particular ways of communicating during team discussions. When facilitators say something to the team, they tacitly convey an attitude to the kind of relationship they want to have with team members, as well as the kind of relationship they want team members to have with each other. The attitudes discussed so far (helping, neutrality, inquiring) are in the main concerned with the content of the team discussion rather than with its relational aspects. Research shows that when the modality of interaction fostered by facilitators and adopted by team members is that of *relational engagement*, team discussions are more likely to be productive and conducive to new knowledge creation (Tavella & Franco, 2015; Tsoukas, 2009). In relational engagement, individuals take active responsibility for both their joint tasks and the relationships they have with each other (Tsoukas, 2009). Consequently, when team members are relationally engaged, they feel psychologically safe to make themselves more open to one another (Edmondson, 1999, 2003), take interpersonal risks, and be open to mutual influence. This in turn enables team members to self-distanciate from previous ways of thinking, which facilitates the generations of new understandings and knowledge (Tsoukas, 2009).

It is often claimed that teams are able to make productive use of their differences in understanding and expertise. However, this is not always the case. In Chapter 2, we described the danger of escalating task conflict, which may turn into interpersonal conflict that not only blocks progress on the team decision but threatens to stop team cooperation altogether. Even before tensions rise, differences in knowledge and expertise complicate team decision making. Different training backgrounds, terminology, and taken-for-granted assumptions raise problems for communication in interdisciplinary teams (Edmondson, 2003). In coming to a decision, team members need to share information and reflect on routines while not knowing exactly where the discussion will take them. This brings with it significant interpersonal risk. Team members are more likely to take this risk when they perceive it is psychologically safe to do so (Edmondson, 1999, 2003), which is more likely when they trust each other (Van Oortmerssen et al., 2014). The Campus Connect case described earlier highlighted the role of trust between team members. Team members pointed to two specific instances that built trust among the team members. One was an interpersonal conflict that was resolved successfully, leading to more clarity on team member values and commitment to the joint task. The second was achieving a tangible outcome in the form of the completion of the new building. The former occasion indicates that interpersonal conflict should not be avoided at all costs. Rather, successfully steering through an episode of interpersonal conflict builds trust, which in turn leads to more and better information exchange.

What, then, can the facilitator do to foster a modality of relational engagement that can help maintain or build positive relationships in a decision making team? Keeping in mind that the intended outcome of decision support is both a high-quality decision and commitment to actions, the facilitator does two things. To foster decision quality, he needs to ensure that all relevant information is brought to the table, even if that turns out to be sensitive and potentially reflects negatively on one or more team members. For this to happen, team members need to speak up and share information openly. On the other hand, if shared information damages team members' reputation and limits the willingness to work together in the future, commitment to solutions will be reduced. In other words, the facilitator needs to be aware that what is discussed may have a personal impact on team members present and ensure that this does not hamper sharing of information or working relations. When an interpersonal conflict develops, it should not be sidestepped as it may be an integral part of the issue at hand, and because working through the conflict builds trust among team members. Trust in turn fosters psychological safety so that people are willing to speak up and resolve task conflicts, as relational engagement between participants supports the creation of new knowledge.

13.5 Self-reflexivity

The preceding description of facilitator attitudes, in particular, helping and neutrality, hopefully make clear that the facilitator is not in a privileged position versus team members in terms of shaping discussion output and conclusions. The inquiring attitude emphasises that it is not the facilitator but the team members who have intimate understanding of the subject matter, and the job of the former is to elicit this understanding so that others in the team can build on it. Although the facilitator clearly has a voice in designing the process of team interaction, this actually comes down to co-design as proposed steps have to make sense to, and be accepted by, team members. Although he shapes the format of information exchanged, guides the trajectory of team interaction and reflects back what is said, the facilitator is neutral with regard to the content raised in the discussions.

The description so far may paint a picture of the facilitator as an outsider, remaining aloof from the team discussion, unaffected by anything that is said or implied. The facilitator is a supervisor of the execution of team tasks, not a member of the team, a black box (Veltman, 2023). This, however, does not come close to our experience of facilitating teams discussing issues that matter to them. Typically, rather than remaining aloof, we find that a facilitator is highly engaged with, and impacted by, the team process. Facilitation is often an intensive and exhausting task, as it requires paying close attention to what people say and how they say it. Trying to understand what is meant and representing that understanding, while avoiding own ideas from influencing a proposed formulation or a suggestion for linking ideas, takes energy.

In other words, although facilitators have a different role than team members, they are very much engaged in, and affected by, the moment-by-moment development of the team discussion (Franco & Greiffenhagen, 2018). The facilitator is clearly impacted by what happens in the team. Importantly, this impact is as much about ideas, so cognitive, as about emotions. The team process has a cognitive impact on the facilitator when the topic discussed brings to mind own expertise or beliefs. Similarly, there is cognitive impact when the discussion connects to knowledge that may come from a previous engagement where a team talked about a similar issue. For instance, Bleijenbergh and Van Engen (2015) report on two facilitated modelling projects on women's careers in academia. In both projects, the topic of masculine norms came up. In the first case, masculine norms included an emphasis on fulltime work and a culture of overwork. It is likely that when masculine norms came up as a point for discussion in the second project, the facilitator was reminded of the work-related dimension encountered in the earlier case. Neutrality and an inquiring attitude require the facilitator to try to elicit the interpretation of masculine norms that is relevant in the present situation, and avoiding 'filling in' the concept for the team. Realising that a concept raised in the discussion brings to mind own ideas and trying to keep these from influencing the conversation is not always straightforward, as described in the section on neutrality.

Although less obtrusive, the emotional tone of the team interaction also has an impact on the facilitator. Phillips and Phillips (1993) note that teams express the full range of emotions experienced by individual team members. For instance, teams may feel frustrated and threatened because they are not meeting their goals or deadlines. Or a team may feel happy or elated if an important milestone has been met. Phillips and Phillips give the example of a senior manager, who has called the meeting, leaving midway in the session. The other team members are left feeling angry, which is not the best motivation to continue working on the goals agreed on with the manager. While it might happen that such an event immediately leads a team member to express his or her anger in words, what occurs more often is that emotions build up from more unobtrusive signals such as facial expressions and bodily movements, to a reluctance to take up the task, eventually making a discussion on the lack of progress unavoidable. The emotional state of the team, including its level of energy, clearly influences how the task gets done.

Perceiving the emotional state of the team as a whole is complicated by the fact that emotions observable in a team are expressed by individual team members, but at any one time not all team members will experience the same emotion, or to the same extent. It may happen that individuals give every sign of going along with the team, but privately feel different. There is, however, evidence that emotions expressed by others, even unobtrusively, have a clear influence on people. Emotions are said to have a communicative function (Oatley & Johnson-Laird, 2014) or even be contagious (Hatfield et al., 1994). This also means that the facilitator shares in the emotional experience of the team. Phillips and Phillips (1993, p. 544) give the following example:

> A group was struggling to discuss the difficult issues it faced in considering a new strategy for the group. The facilitator began to feel dreary and tired, and anxious that he was not competent to deal with this group. Observing that many participants also seemed inattentive and distracted, the facilitator reflected back to the group that there seemed to be a mood of dreariness about.

In the ensuing discussion, team members admitted that they did not feel up to their task.

In this example, the facilitator realises how he is feeling and reports this back to the team, which then leads to a conversation on the task and possibly a revised agenda. However, precisely pinpointing the cause of a feeling is notoriously difficult. It may also happen that a facilitator, seeing the discussion range widely and the topic seemingly becoming more and more complex, grows increasingly concerned about his ability to help the team and begins to experience high levels of anxiety and uncertainty. Phillips and

Phillips (1993) note that in this case it will often be necessary to hold and tolerate these feelings.

In conclusion, observing emotions expressed by a team may be difficult as team members are likely to react differently and signals may be weak. Initial cues to a change in emotions such as facial expressions, and bodily movements are open to different interpretations. Alternatively, facilitators can monitor their own feelings to get a sense of the emotional state of the group (Phillips & Phillips, 1993). *Self-reflexivity* is, in our view, a crucial attitude in this regard. This fits with the broader concept of reflexivity, which refers to questioning what is taken for granted in one's own and other's beliefs and actions (Bleijenbergh et al., 2018). As discussed in earlier chapters, we see these beliefs and actions as shaped by social and organisational factors and see benefit in a collective process of eliciting ideas underlying them (Ripamonti et al., 2016). Researchers often emphasise dimensions of reflexivity such as choice of methodology and the impact of personal characteristics on data collection and analysis (Amis & Silk, 2008; Brannick & Coghlan, 2007). Others, however, suggest that the importance of emotions and relations in work in organisations means that understanding and reflection on these dimensions is important as well (Reedy & King, 2019). While we agree that choice of methodology and being aware that own ideas can influence the team process are important, we think that in facilitating an ongoing conversation the emotional dimension of reflexivity plays a crucial and underappreciated role. An important reason for this is that the emotional channel is often faster than the cognitive: 'preferences need no inferences' (Zajonc, 1980). Table 13.1 summarises our description of facilitator attitudes.

TABLE 13.1 Summary of facilitator attitudes, tasks, and their rationale

Attitude	Tasks (what)	Rationale (why)
Helping	Select problem important to client Demonstrate authenticity	• Problem importance fosters motivation to contribute and process information • Authenticity creates trust in facilitator
Neutrality	Encourage open information search without contributing to content, but set format, focus attention and reflect back the content of the discussion	• Open information search allows for the combination of team members' inputs, which helps generate new information (arguments) that in turn changes minds and positively impacts decision quality • Refraining from contributing to content, together with careful consideration of team members' inputs, gives team members the opportunity to use their contributions to influence the final decision, which increases commitment to resulting decision

Attitude	Tasks (what)	Rationale (why)
		• Open information search ensures productive cognitive (task) conflict, which in turn enables participants to process information
Inquiring	Ask questions and listen actively	• Questions relieve tension • Asking questions and listening actively promotes open information search, which helps to identify and share all relevant information • Questioning and listening provide a role model for other team members
Relational engagement	Limit but do not sidestep interpersonal conflict	• Resolving interpersonal conflict builds trust but high levels impede progress on group task • Trust and team psychological safety help team members speak up and share information
Self-reflexivity	Attend to own and others' emotions	• Highlights ideas that go against own taken-for-granted beliefs and actions • Indicates level of motivation for particular steps in process, which is a basis for updating agenda

Notes

1. It is worth highlighting that depending on the intervention approach chosen, a *facilitation team* may be required to conduct the intervention. In that case, the facilitator team comprised various individuals in specific roles, for example, facilitators, modellers, recorders.
2. The helping, neutral, inquiring and authentic (which we discuss under helping) attitude are described by Vennix (1996, 1999). Relational engagement and self-reflexivity are our additions.

References

Amis, J. M., & Silk, M. L. (2008). The philosophy and politics of quality in qualitative organizational research. *Organizational Research Methods, 11*(3), 456–480.

Bales, R. F. (1951). *Interaction process analysis: A method for the study of small groups.* Addison-Wesley.

Bales, R. F. (2002). *Social interaction systems: Theory and measurement.* Transaction.

Black, L., & Andersen, D. (2012). Using visual representations as boundary objects to resolve conflict in collaborative model-building approaches. *Systems Research and Behavioral Science, 29*(2), 194–208.

Bleijenbergh, I., Korzilius, H., Rouwette, E. A. J. A., & Van der Wal, M. (2018). *Quality criteria for action research: The importance of usefulness and relevance.* Academy of Management.

Bleijenbergh, I., & Van Engen, M. (2015). Participatory modeling to support gender equality: The importance of including stakeholders. *Equality, Diversity and Inclusion, 34*(5), 422–438.

Brannick, T., & Coghlan, D. (2007). In defense of being "native": The case for insider academic research. *Organizational Research Methods, 10*(1), 59–74.

Chaiken, S., Giner-Sorolla, R., & Chen, S. (1996). Beyond accuracy: Defense and impression motives in heuristic and systematic information processing. In P. Gollwitzer & J. A. Bargh (Eds.), *The psychology of action: Linking cognition and motivation to action* (pp. 553–578). Guilford.

Edmondson, A. C. (1999). Psychological safety and learning behavior in work teams. *Administrative Science Quarterly, 44*(2), 350–383.

Edmondson, A. C. (2003). Speaking up in the operating room: How team leaders promote learning in interdisciplinary action teams. *Journal of Management Studies, 40*(6), 1419–1452.

Franco, L. A. (2013). Rethinking soft OR interventions: Models as boundary objects. *European Journal of Operational Research, 231*(2), 720–733.

Franco, L. A., & Nielsen, M. F. (2018). Examining group facilitation in situ: The use of formulations in facilitation practice. *Group Decision and Negotiation, 27*(5), 735–756.

Franco, L. F., & Greiffenhagen, C. (2018). Making OR practice visible: Using ethnomethodology to analyse facilitated modelling workshops. *European Journal of Operational Research, 265*(2), 673–684.

Hatfield, E., Cacioppo, J. T., & Rapson, R. L. (1994). *Emotional contagion*. Cambridge University Press.

Huxham, C., & Cropper, S. (1994). From many to one – and back. An exploration of some components of facilitation. *Omega, 22*(1), 1–11.

Kim, W. C., & Mauborgne, R. A. (1993). Procedural justice, attitudes, and subsidiary top management compliance with multinationals' corporate strategic decisions. *Academy of Management Journal, 36*(3), 502–526.

Korsgaard, M., Schweiger, D., & Sapienza, H. (1995). Building commitment, attachment, and trust in strategic decision making teams. The role of procedural justice. *Academy of Management Journal, 38*, 60–84.

McCardle-Keurentjes, M. H. F., & Rouwette, E. A. J. A. (2018). Asking questions: A sine qua non of facilitation in decision support? *Group Decision and Negotiation, 27*, 757–788.

Oatley, K., & Johnson-Laird, P. N. (2014). Cognitive approaches to emotions. *Trends in Cognitive Sciences, 18*(3), 134–140.

Petty, R., & Cacioppo, J. (1986). The elaboration likelihood model of persuasion. *Advances in Experimental Social Psychology, 19*, 123–205.

Phillips, L. D., & Phillips, M. C. (1993). Facilitated work groups: Theory and practice. *Journal of the Operational Research Society, 44*(6), 533–549.

Poole, M. S., & DeSanctis, G. (1992). Microlevel structuration in computer-supported group decision making. *Human Communication Research, 19*(1), 5–49.

Reedy, P. C., & King, D. R. (2019). Critical performativity in the field: Methodological principles for activist ethnographers. *Organizational Research Methods, 22*(2), 564–589.

Ripamonti, S., Galuppo, L., Gorli, M., Scaratti, G., & Cunliffe, A. L. (2016). Pushing action research toward reflexive practice. *Journal of Management Inquiry, 25*(1), 55–68.

Roberto, M. A. (2013). *Why great leaders don't take yes for an answer: Managing for conflict and consensus* (2nd ed.). Pearson Education.

Rouwette, E. A. J. A., Vennix, J. A. M., & Felling, A. J. A. (2009). On evaluating the performance of problem structuring methods: An attempt at formulating a conceptual model. *Group Decision and Negotiation, 18*(6), 567–587.

Schein, E. H. (1997). The concept of "client" from a process consultation perspective: A guide for change agents. *Journal of Organizational Change Management, 10,* 202–216. https://doi.org/10.1108/09534819710171077

Stasser, G., & Titus, W. (2003). Hidden profiles: A brief history. *Psychological Inquiry, 14*(3–4), 304–313.

Tavella, E., & Franco, L. A. (2015). Dynamics of group knowledge production in facilitated modelling workshops: An exploratory study. *Group Decision and Negotiation, 24*(3), 451–475.

Tsoukas, H. (2009). A dialogical approach to the creation of new knowledge in organizations. *Organization Science, 20*(6), 941–957.

Van Oortmerssen, L. A., Van Woerkum, C. M. J., & Aarts, N. (2014). The visibility of trust: Exploring the connection between trust and interaction in a Dutch collaborative governance boardroom. *Public Management Review, 16*(5), 666–685.

Veltman, J. A. (2023). *Assignment for modelling for stakeholder engagement II*. Radboud University.

Vennix, J. A. M. (1996). *Group model building. Facilitating team learning using system dynamics*. Wiley.

Vennix, J. A. M. (1999). Group model-building: Tackling messy problems. *System Dynamics Review, 15*(4), 379–401.

Vennix, J. A. M., Akkermans, H. A., & Rouwette, E. A. J. A. (1996). Group model building to facilitate organisational change. An exploratory study. *System Dynamics Review, 12*(1), 39–58.

Zajonc, R. B. (1980). Feeling and thinking – preferences need no inferences. *American Psychologist, 35*(2), 151–175.

14

MANAGING PROCESS AND CONTENT

The previous chapter described a set of facilitator tasks, their rationale, and a set of facilitator attitudes that altogether represent the fundamentals of facilitating team discussions. This chapter addresses the facilitation tasks in more depth by unpacking the various ways in which they can be performed when supporting team discussions.

One broad aspect to consider before facilitating a team discussion is the general approach to managing the process. When team discussions begin, analysts may or may not intervene actively to guide the pattern of participation and interaction. The intervention literature distinguishes between a *directive* and a *laissez-faire approach* to facilitating team discussions (Edmondson et al., 2003; Larson et al., 1998; Nadler, 1998; Schwarz, 1994; Webne-Behrman, 1998). In the directive approach, analysts guide the timing and extent of participation by team members during their discussions. They invite specific team members to offer their views, and they inquire repeatedly as to where individuals stand on specific topics. They ask questions of clarification and playback team members' contributions to ensure that they have been understood correctly by either summarising them or drawing out their relevant implications (Heritage & Watson, 1979). Furthermore, analysts that adopt a directive approach emphasise points in the discussion that they deem important but which perhaps have been overlooked or misinterpreted. By contrast, analysts adopting a laissez-faire style take a more hands-off approach for guiding the team discussions, allowing team members to enter and exit their discussions more freely, and they deliberately try not to influence where people focus their attention.

Research has shown that a directive style is more effective when there is asymmetry of information within the team. That is, when there is information that is not accessible to all team members or, put differently, when team members

DOI: 10.4324/9781003404200-17

possess a great deal of private information, which they even may not be aware that exists. Research by Garold Stasser and colleagues has shown that teams are more likely to repeat commonly shared information during discussions while paying less attention to privately held data (Stasser & Davis, 1981; Stasser & Titus, 1985). Failure to reveal this private information can lead to suboptimal and even flawed solutions to the problem at hand. By adopting a more directive approach, consultants can create opportunities for team members to disclose unshared information, as well as recognise when privately held data are revealed during discussion. On the other hand, a laissez-faire approach would be more adequate when there is symmetry of information within the team. In this case, all team members possess commonly shared information that is likely to surface during discussions without the need for active prompting by the analyst.

Another aspect to consider is the how to structure the interaction process of the team discussion. Researchers have shown that while teams may follow a variety of paths towards making a decision (e.g. Poole, 1983; Poole & Roth, 1989), successful teams tend to break their process into two broad phases that can be cycled many times through their discussions. They start a cycle with a divergence phase where team members either search for possible issues or solutions, and then move to a convergence phase, where they select either the core issue or problem to address, or the best solution to adopt. Effective search and selection processes can address some of the shortcomings of team decision making discussed in Part I. For example, an enhanced searching process can reduce poor information processing, and a selection process that considers the future impacts of adopting various solutions can counteract the tendency to escalate commitment to a losing strategy.

All the intervention approaches described in earlier chapters are comprised of divergent and convergent tasks that are completed within one or more divergence–convergence cycles. For example, when using the decision conferencing intervention approach, team members search for relevant objectives (divergence) before classifying them into means and fundamental objectives (convergence).

In the remainder of the chapter, we discuss how the facilitator sets the stage for a team meeting by working towards agreement on the goal, roles, and agenda of the session. We then turn to supporting the team through a divergence–convergence cycle, which particular emphasis on the management of the team discussion content and process. This chapter ends with recommendations on how to close an intervention.

14.1   Opening

Imagine you have been invited by a colleague in your organisation to reserve time in your agenda for three meetings of three hours each. The topic is something you have been concerned about for quite some time. You understand that other departments will be present in the meetings too. Apparently, some novel procedure is going to be used and an outside analyst will facilitate the sessions. Balancing the substantial amount of time this will take with the expected chance of actually making progress, you decide to give it a go and attend. You do not really expect the issue will be solved after these meetings – how could it, after people have been working on it for months already – but hey, hearing what is on the mind of the other meeting participants would be a useful exercise in itself. After all, if the first meeting goes nowhere you can always find a reason that prevents you from taking part in the next meeting. And the next.

We expect that the above roughly captures the state of mind of the majority of attendants at the start of a first session, before going into the divergence phase of a divergence–convergence cycle. The expectations participants have at that point in time are based on an invitation specifying the topic and task, the proposed way of working, and who else will be involved. Other than that, team members will have their own ideas on the topic matter and on the reputation of the sender of the invitation, as well as possible previous experiences with similar intervention approaches. The first meeting typically starts with a welcome by the client of the intervention, who will remind the team of the topic to be addressed in the session, why it is relevant now, introduce the facilitator briefly and then hand over. The facilitator then introduces her role, the general design of the intervention and the expected end result. The expectations which were initially agreed upon with the team leader are now also discussed with the participating team. The facilitator will again emphasise that she is responsible for the intervention procedure and process, and the team members for the content of the discussion.

While the problem focus is agreed with the client and stated in the invitation to participants, it is always wise to check at the start of the first meeting if team members agree this chosen focus is a relevant topic to spend their time on. In a small number of cases, we experienced that team members did not find the issue that important and were reluctant to engage with the agenda. Alternatively, the relevance of the chosen focus can be raised by highlighting the different perspectives in the room, as illustrated in the following example.

The case relates to the articulation of the business model of a regional economic board in The Netherlands. This cooperation brought together regional education institutes, municipalities and large firms. Its general aim was to grow the economy in the region. The first item on the agenda was to discuss the value proposition of the board. Initially, there was little response from the participants in the room and no ideas were suggested. Then, one participant voiced his surprise with this question as 'we have discussed this in the past and we all have the same idea'. Others indicated their support, leading the cooperation's leader and daily manager to indicate that she thought there might be less agreement on the value proposition of the board than expected.

One participant then stepped in and said: "OK, let me be the one to give a first answer. To me the board is about bringing new firms into our region". This led to an immediate response by someone else: "I thought the board's goal was to grow the existing businesses". This started off a lively discussion and got the group to engage with the first item on the agenda. In this example, we see that highlighting disagreements is a way to raise the relevance of the issue to be discussed. Typically, if people in the room need to work together, a shared understanding of core aspects such as the goal and way of working is needed. Showing that these are understood differently will get people's attention.

Not only the problem focus but also the proposed agenda needs to make sense to team members. Throughout the sessions, the facilitator will have to guide participants through a procedure that to them is a useful approach to the task at hand. That means it gives them relevant and new information, conflicts are not sidestepped and an agreement on future steps is reached. Team members will allow some time for introduction and setting the scene, but after that some of these outputs will have to materialise otherwise frustration will slowly make itself felt. If the team is not active and working on their problem within 20–30 minutes after starting the meeting, then the agenda may need to be adapted in line with the team's need (Andersen & Richardson, 1997; Bryson, 2004).

14.2   Divergence phase

After both the problem focus and proposed agenda make sense to the team, the first agenda item typically asks for active contributions from team members. Irrespective of the intervention approach used, team members are invited to generate ideas using a simple procedure such as brainstorming or the nominal group technique (NGT). On the other hand, depending on the approach chosen, team members' contributions may take various forms, such as variables, trends and developments, issues, options, evaluation criteria, preferences, or actions. The facilitator asks open questions such as "what are issues the organisation is currently phasing?", "which trends do you see in the environment of our firm?", "what is the best software to design and produce?" and the like

The facilitator can support the process by helping team members to express ideas as clearly as possible, using active listening. When using the approaches described in the previous chapters, we are often looking for contributions in a particular format: variables, means or ends, trends or developments, options, objectives, criteria, and preferences. What happens regularly in a facilitated meeting is that team members initially phrase their ideas more broadly, and need help in clarifying their contributions. A technique that is useful here is *drawing people out* (Kaner, 2007, p. 45). Imagine a scenario session in the phase of identifying future trends or developments. This topic might lead a participant to sketch in detail a possible bleak future for companies in his sector. A basic form of drawing out is to first paraphrase the participant's contribution, and then ask an open question such as "can you say more about this?" or "what would you conclude from your example?" A more specific form of drawing out would connect to the type of information sought after. Applied to this example, the facilitator could ask "which developments would help to create the future you just sketched?" or "how could we get from the current situation to the world you describe?".

It is important to note that in the divergent phase, the person who contributes the idea determines how it is written down. Team members verbalise their ideas, the facilitator summarises them into written statements, then checks if these statements represent what was meant. For example, facilitators often paraphrase (Kaner, 2007) a team member's contribution in their own words. Then they end with a check by, for instance, asking "is this what you mean?". The facilitation task then involves active listening in the form of clarifying meaning and agreeing or affirming meaning (Tavella & Franco, 2015). The aim is that the written idea on the board or screen captures what the individual contributing to the idea tried to say. The facilitator checks with the rest of the team if the contribution is understood. Whether other team members find this idea important or not, whether it overlaps with other ideas already mentioned, can or cannot easily be related to other ideas, does not matter at this point.

Contributed ideas and solutions are collected and displayed in visual form on a board or screen for everyone to see. The facilitators ensure that each contribution is captured in the format required by the procedure being used, and carefully considered. When the team is so engaged with the topic that multiple participants start speaking at the same time, a simple way to guarantee that everyone has a chance to speak and at the same time ensuring that each contribution receives adequate attention is *stacking* (Kaner, 2007, p. 48). When using stacking, the facilitator acknowledges that multiple people want to speak, assigns a number to each person, and calls upon each when it is their turn.

Team members are encouraged to contribute anything they see as relevant, ask each other questions for clarification, but to refrain from evaluating (let alone criticising) one another's ideas. Giving everyone the chance to express their own ideas, and at the same time making everyone feel that their ideas are carefully considered during discussion is critical. For having voice without consideration often leads to team members' resentment and frustration, which affects their perceptions of fairness about how the discussion was conducted and can cause resistance to implementing the resulting decision (Garvin & Roberto, 2001; Kim & Mauborgne, 1995; Korsgaard et al., 1995). If during discussions a team member signals that the facilitator gives more attention to some individuals or ideas than to others, a good advice is to admit mistakes, as not doing so would negatively affect perceptions of fairness.

In our experience, team members engage readily with a divergent task; they find generating ideas easy and enjoyable. Hearing ideas of others is likely to generate some surprises, since (as discussed before) there is no single team member that has a complete overview over the issues under discussion. Team members have in-depth knowledge and experience based on their own role in relation to the issues, and at least some ideas from other perspectives will be novel to them. This underlines that exploring an issue by taking time for idea generation already adds benefit to the team discussion, even before ideas are related or prioritised. This is also part of showing to the team that the idea-generation procedure followed helps to make progress with the task at hand. When working with a large team that was used to long and in-depth deliberations, Jac Vennix decided to gather comments on an intermediate report by asking team members to comment one by one, without interrupting one another. One team member afterwards commented "this was the best discussion we ever had" although discussion in the sense of contrasting and building on each other's ideas clearly did not take place (Vennix, personal communication).

In sum, the role of the facilitator in the divergent phase is in the main to encourage team members to share any information that is thought to be relevant to the task at hand. Being clear about this aim and emphasising that all contributions are welcome helps the team to start sharing ideas openly.

14.3 Convergence phase

Confronted with a large set of ideas, team members often feel an urge to 'make sense of them', 'structure them' or 'put them into some sort of order'. A logical follow-up to a divergent activity is then some form of convergence. This can be a 'light' version in which team members cluster similar ideas together, or the somewhat more demanding task of combining ideas by writing a narrative or story. In our view, a quite rigorous and cognitively demanding alternative is to ask team members to identify relations of a specific type: causal, input–output, means–ends, or another.

Convergence by necessity means that a team works towards a shared understanding of their contributions. It starts with a team member proposing relations and then discussing each proposed addition with the full team. In this phase, it is no longer an individual team member who determines what is added or changed on the central board or screen, but the whole team needs to come to an agreement. As a consequence, the meaning of ideas is likely to shift. When an idea or preference is related to another, someone will have to articulate in what sense they are similar (in the case of clustering) or one impacts the other (in the case of relating). This reasoning is then checked by the team and if it is not accepted, the idea will not be put in a cluster, a relation will not be drawn, or a preference will not be established. Sometimes, the initial explanation is readily accepted by the team, but often it gives rise to comments such as "This is not exactly how I read the idea on the board. In my understanding, there is also another aspect to this, which is . . .". In this process, differences in meanings will come to the fore. Ultimately, an agreement will emerge on the shared understanding of an idea. Figure 14.1 shows the central role of convergence, in the sense of agreeing on relations between ideas, in a supported team meeting.

The left-hand side of Figure 14.1 shows the first (divergent) task for team members in a decision making meeting: generate ideas on a particular issue. Generating ideas means that out of everything that comes to mind when thinking of an issue or a potential solution, team members put their ideas in words and then, with help of the facilitator, translate them into written statements that are visualised on a board or screen that all team members can see. Black and Andersen (2012) note that this way of working signals two important principles to a participant: the facilitator hears me, and I can change the wording of an idea.

In the next (convergent) task, relations between ideas are proposed and then visualised on the board or screen. Each added relation is an incremental increase of understanding and makes it clearer what the issues or proposed solutions under discussion are all about. This in turn supports articulation of additional ideas because it further clarifies the problem focus. The captured relationships form a visual model that is always in transition as the discussion progresses (Eden, 1992). The model that team members jointly build does not only help identify other relevant content but also shape the form

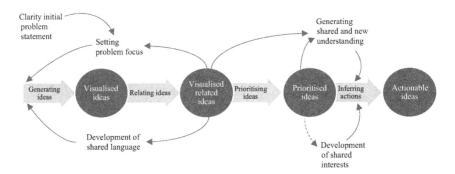

FIGURE 14.1   Transformation of ideas in team meetings.

Source: Based on Black & Andersen (2012) and Franco (2013)

in which team members exchange information. It gives them a shared language which helps them to effectively communicate their perspectives to one another (Franco, 2013).

As shown in Figure 14.1, relating ideas has a number of other effects. For example, identifying a new link from an idea to other parts of the model may change the interpretation of that idea and therefore generate new understanding. In the case of the Dutch criminal justice chain (see Chapter 2), representatives of the prison administration were well aware that early release of prisoners lowered the average duration of prison sentences. By learning that it also caused judges to pass longer sentences, the interpretation of early release is likely to have shifted. For instance, judges, to the extent that they were aware of the new early release policy, will not have fully realised the extent of prison crowding that motivated it. As all team members can suggest changes in the model and are asked to acknowledge and check proposed changes, we can expect that interpretations not only change but that these change in a particular direction: towards a new shared understanding of the ideas under discussion. Put differently, the competing and contested perspectives initially held within the team begin to converge (Cronin & Weingart, 2007; De Gooyert et al., 2022; Kaplan, 2008), which often is sufficient to generate joint action (Franco, 2013).

Sometimes, in the course of relating and prioritising ideas different interests are revealed that create barriers to joint action. What is required is a process in which team members negotiate and are willing to change their individual interests (Carlile, 2004; Franco, 2013; Tavella & Franco, 2015; Tsoukas, 2009). In the criminal justice case, at the start of the project we interviewed representatives of the Dutch police, public prosecution, judges, and prison administration. At the end of the interview, we asked about the overall goal of the criminal justice system. Although each organisation has distinct tasks and responsibilities, there was a remarkable similarity in the answers to this question. Most answers referred to the aim of keeping the Dutch citizen safe, by ensuring that a criminal act would not go unpunished. "A perpetrator will not get away with it but will serve the sentence laid down in Dutch law". Another way of saying this is that sentences need to be served in full. If serving sentences in full is the aim or common interest of all partner organisations in the criminal justice chain, the policies of increasing sentence duration and at same time lowering the time served go directly against this aim. Once these two ideas are seen to have a negative effect on serving sentences in full, their interpretation will change. They are likely to be seen in a more negative light and less likely to be chosen as policies to improve the situation at hand.

The realisation that all members of the team have a role to play in the problem, either as problem creators or as problem solvers, may make it easier to agree on how to move forward (Black & Andersen, 2012). Nevertheless, we take the view that while models may be necessary for the development of shared interests, they are certainly not sufficient. Models clarify how possible solutions or actions have consequences for particular interests. Although the intervention approaches outlined in this book emphasise collective goals over individual interests, and advocate checking for team agreement in each step of building a model, there is nothing in these methods that forces team members' goals and interests to become more aligned. As already mentioned, a possible outcome of achieving more clarity may also be that team members realise their goals and interests are incompatible (Franco, 2013). That would mean participants have consensus on the problem but do not agree on solutions to improve the problem situation, which is a result found in several modelling applications (Rouwette & Smeets, 2016, p. 141). We speculate that in this respect the person of the facilitator is more important than the method, as trust in the facilitator (e.g. Harper et al., 2021) may encourage team members to participate actively, which increases the chance of finding common ground, move beyond seeing the issue as a zero-sum game and identify actions that benefit everyone.

How can a facilitator help a team to generate, relate and evaluate ideas, and agree on actionable ideas? First, we first note that a number of facilitator actions that were important in the divergence phase also need attention in the convergence phase. For instance, transparency on task aims and outputs of each step on the agenda is also still important, as is the clarification of roles with regard to process and content, and the willingness to freely admit mistakes. Similarly, paraphrasing and drawing people out are also appropriate in the convergence phase. However, while open questions are also used in the convergence phase, these have a different purpose: to invite contributions about relations between ideas, or between the strength of preference of different solutions. Furthermore, these relationships are captured using the format required by the procedure being used (e.g. cause–effect, means–ends, input–output).

A powerful way to help a team visualise relations is by using models. As shown in Figure 14.1, developing models with a group supports information exchange in a number of ways. Black and Andersen (2012) and Franco (2013) emphasise that models can serve as so-called boundary objects: visualisations that help to articulate knowledge, create shared meanings and identify common interests. They can only fulfil this role if they are supported by adequate social processes. Adequate here means that everyone in the room has a chance to change the model shown in front of the team. Ideally, speaking time is divided evenly between team members through stacking (see previous section). It also means that proposed changes to the model are visualised and checked with the whole team. Only if no one in the team objects to the proposed change, it is implemented in the model. If a suggestion by a participant cannot be implemented in the model, it is a good idea to include it in the so-called parking lot. The parking lot is an area of the group memory that functions as a 'to do list'. It serves as a reminder of topics the team still needs to attend to.

In general, we feel that it is a good rule of thumb to keep in mind that each team members' contribution needs to lead to a change on the visual display in front of the team. This can be in the model or in the parking lot. Finally, if major changes are implemented in the model, for instance, in between sessions, a good idea is to maintain visual consistency. This means that care is taken that team members still understand the model, and see how the new version relates to the last one they worked with. If modelling is indeed supported by adequate social processes, team members will focus their attention on the model and jointly develop it further. As a result, the model will be a reflection of the team's understanding of the issues and proposed solutions up until that moment. The facilitator can direct the team members' attention to parts of the model that need to be elaborated further. This might be the list of ideas that are not yet included in the model, or an area that is relatively isolated from the rest. However, it is also worth noting that convergence can be a more difficult process in which progress at times seems slow. That means it is all the more important to point out to team members how the intervention approach helps them in accomplishing their task. This for instance takes the form of publicly noting intermediate results such as agreements or new insights. It can also include pointing out to team members that convergence is more demanding than divergence. Team members usually find the divergence phase (e.g. sharing ideas without criticising one another) easy and enjoyable. By contrast, they perceive the convergence phase as difficult because convergent activities are more demanding. Specifically, in the convergence phase, the team will have to agree on how to word the ideas displayed in the model, and on which relations will be drawn. This asks team members to consider carefully how their ideas are similar or different from those of others, and this task can be challenging. Kaner (2007) has coined the term 'groan zone' for the transition between divergence and convergence.

> This period of confusion and frustration is a natural part of group decision-making. Once a group crosses the line from airing familiar opinions to exploring diverse perspectives, group members have to struggle in order to integrate new and different ways of thinking with their own.
>
> *(Kaner, 2007, p. 18)*

Warning team members that the groan zone will come, and acknowledging frustration once it is there, helps the team to move forward. In our experience, it is also useful to switch focus regularly. Imagine, for instance, that the discussion has focused on financial aspects for some time. This may lead the attention of people not working in that area to drop after a while. Focusing on another topic area helps to engage people again.

The facilitator more actively engages with the content of the discussion in the convergence phase. During the discussion, the facilitator produces formulations that summarise or project their prior talk, which team members then need to make sense of (Franco & Nielsen, 2018). This can take the form of looking backwards, as in the clarification of previous talk to determine the 'gist' of the conversation. It can also consist of looking forward, as in thinking further, building on previous talk. This is called formulating the 'upshot' of the discussion. Both the gist and upshot of a discussion can involve sentences starting with "so" or "are you saying that". What the facilitator is in effect doing is handing back information in changed form (Phillips & Phillips, 1993, p. 545). This enables team members to recognise it since it resembles the main points of what they were saying but it also brings in a new perspective that provides new meaning. When gist and upshot formulations are being produced, the facilitator is often proposing a new meaning or building on team members' contributions to develop alternative meanings (Tavella & Franco, 2015).[1] Table 14.1 gives an overview of facilitator tasks and actions.

TABLE 14.1 Facilitator tasks and actions in managing divergence and convergence

Phase	Facilitator tasks	Facilitator actions
Divergence	Demonstrate authenticity	• Be transparent on aims and intended outputs of team discussion; welcome all contributions • Discuss expectations and emphasise own responsibility for procedure and process, and team's responsibility for content • If appropriate, admit mistakes
	Select problem important to client	• Check with team members if problem is relevant to them, adapt problem focus if needed • Raise relevance of chosen problem by highlighting differences in opinion • Adapt agenda in line with team needs
	Ask questions, listen actively	• Invite and welcome each participant to contribute ideas by asking open questions • Paraphrase, draw people out, clarify, and agree on meaning of ideas

Phase	Facilitator tasks	Facilitator actions
	Encourage an open information search without contributing to content, but set format, focus attention, and reflect back the content of the discussion	• Collect and display ideas in visual form; divide speaking time equally (stacking) • Ensure that each contribution is captured in the appropriate format • Do not allow criticism of contributions and ensure they are carefully considered • Show that approach used helps to make clear progress on issue of concern
Convergence	Demonstrate authenticity	• Be transparent on aims and intended outputs of team discussion • Discuss expectations and emphasise own responsibility for procedure and process, and team's responsibility for content • If appropriate, admit mistakes
	Ask questions, listen actively	• Invite and welcome each participant to contribute with proposed relations between ideas, or strength of preference for different ideas by asking open questions • Paraphrase, draw people out, clarify and agree on meaning of ideas
	Encourage an open information search without contributing to content, but set format and guide trajectory of discussion	• Collect and display ideas and relations in a visual model; divide speaking time equally (stacking) • Ensure that each contribution about relations is captured in the appropriate format, either in model or on parking lot • Visualise proposed changes and test for consensus • Maintain visual consistency • Direct attention to underdeveloped sections of model • Show that approach helps to make clear progress on issue of concern • Acknowledge team member's emotions in groan zone • Switch focus regularly • Actively engage with content of discussion by producing formulations (gist/upshot)

14.4 Reaching closure

Using the procedures described in this book, major insights on the issues and helpful solutions will emerge over the course of team discussions. For this to happen, we need a team of knowledgeable people with a stake in the decision, supported by adequate procedures. We have seen in the previous sections that under these conditions, open communication and trust and team psychological safety will codevelop. Team decision making is inextricably bound up with differences in opinions and personalities that are bound to create conflicts. We think the facilitated procedures in this book help to make task conflict productive, avoid sidestepping interpersonal conflict, and keep process conflict to a minimum.

This also means that major insights and emotional experiences will happen in the team process and closure is not a question of writing a summary report that brings all information together. In fact, the final report should not have any surprises for the decision making team. There are a couple of reasons why the group process has implications for action (Roberto, 2013). First, the incremental nature of the procedures ensures that the problem is broken up into small, manageable parts. The group will only proceed to the next topic if the former is closed. For instance, when building a model, new relations are only added after testing for team consensus. Second, procedures alternate between divergence and convergence in a series of iterations, thereby preventing both premature convergence on a subset of the problem and polarising divergence. Third, the approaches described here capitalise on 'small wins' throughout the decision making process. Small wins can concern the process or the content of decision making (Roberto, 2013). The facilitated procedures in this book help to create process wins such as agreements on goals, assumptions, and criteria. In terms of content, they contribute to formulating alternatives and reaching agreements on actions. Agreements on actions, for instance, are invited in the formulations the facilitator uses for closing discussions by asking for the 'upshot' (Franco & Nielsen, 2018, p. 18): "So, what does the previous conversation imply for future actions?". Likewise, the previous section described in detail how effective as well as affective outcomes are created (Wardale, 2013), resulting in high-quality decisions and commitment, by considering the emotional impact of the information exchanged.

The end of an intervention is typically marked by writing and handing over a report to the client, which summarises the suggested response to the client's situation. The client will also be interested in the process underpinning the recommendations, so it is important to provide details about the methods used, as well as the participants and data sources that contributed information. In line with guidelines on reflexivity, the end report should include a motivation for the choice of intervention approach as well as a discussion of (personal and other) problems that impacted data collection and analysis (Amis & Silk, 2008; Brannick & Coghlan, 2007).

For the facilitated interventions described in this book, the choice of team members is a major influence on data collection that should be included in the reflection. As mentioned, the report should not include any major surprises. The most important insights will have been generated during the intervention process and will, to some extent, already be part of the conversations in the organisation. The intervention approaches covered in this book focus on uncovering problem structure, possible futures and comparing solutions against guiding values. They stop short of prescribing implementation steps and change plans. For this phase, particular methods are available, such as action planning and project management.

After implementing proposed changes, both the client and facilitator will be interested in establishing whether expected impacts are actually realised and whether new problems have arisen. Evaluation can be used to establish impacts and may reveal that new issues have emerged, requiring a new round of selecting and using intervention approaches. For clients, evaluation of a completed intervention is important to ensure that expectations are met and evidence-based accountability is achieved. For facilitators and analysts, intervention evaluation is important to improve their practice. As reflective practitioners, this is a good moment to test their own expectations of what worked and why. Chapter 16 will go into evaluation of intervention approaches.

Note

1. Research shows that sometimes team members refer to superior knowledge or expertise to justify the legitimacy of a proposed meaning or deploy authority to eliminate alternative meanings (Thomas et al., 2011; Tavella & Franco, 2015). In the case of the facilitator, attempts to justify or eliminate meanings often take the form of a check on the format of a contribution, to ensure that is in line with the intervention approach and type of model used (Tavella & Franco, 2015).

References

Amis, J. M., & Silk, M. L. (2008). The philosophy and politics of quality in qualitative organizational research. *Organizational Research Methods, 11*(3), 456–480.

Andersen, D. F., & Richardson, G. (1997). Scripts for group model building. *System Dynamics Review, 13*(2), 107–129.

Black, L. J., & Andersen, D. F. (2012). Using visual representations as boundary objects to resolve conflict in collaborative model-building approaches. *Systems Research and Behavioral Science, 29*(2), 194–208.

Brannick, T., & Coghlan, D. (2007). In defense of being 'Native': The case for insider academic research. *Organizational Research Methods, 10*(1), 59–74.

Bryson, J. M. (2004). What to do when stakeholders matter. Stakeholder identification and analysis techniques. *Public Management Review, 6*(1), 21–53.

Carlile, P. R. (2004). Transferring, translating, and transforming: An integrative framework for managing knowledge across boundaries. *Organization Science*, 15(5), 555–568.

Cronin, M. A., & Weingart, L. R. (2007). Representational gaps, information processing, and conflict in functionally diverse teams. *Academy of Management Review*, 32(3), 761–773.

De Gooyert, V., Rouwette, E. A. J. A., Van Kranenburg, H. L., Freeman, E., & Van Breen, H. (2022). Cognitive change and consensus forming in facilitated modelling: A comparison of experienced and observed outcomes. *European Journal of Operational Research*, 229(2), 589–599. https://doi.org/10.1016/j.ejor.2021.09.007

Eden, C. (1992). On the nature of cognitive maps. *Journal of Management Studies*, 29(3), 261–265.

Edmondson, A. C., Roberto, M. A., & Watkins, M. D. (2003). A dynamic model of top management team effectiveness: Managing unstructured task streams. *The Leadership Quarterly*, 14(3), 297–325. https://doi.org/10.1016/S1048-9843(03)00021-3

Franco, L. A. (2013). Rethinking soft OR interventions: Models as boundary objects. *European Journal of Operational Research*, 231(2), 720–733.

Franco, L. A., & Nielsen, M. F. (2018, May 29). Examining group facilitation in situ: The use of formulations in facilitation practice. *Group Decision and Negotiation*, 27(5), 735–756. https://doi.org/10.1007/s10726-018-9577-7

Garvin, D. A., & Roberto, M. A. (2001). What you don't know about making decisions. *Harvard Business Review*, 79(8), 108–116.

Harper, A., Mustafee, N., & Yearworth, M. (2021). Facets of trust in simulation studies. *European Journal of Operational Research*, 289(1), 197–213.

Heritage, J. C., & Watson, D. R. (1979). Formulations as conversational objects. In G. Psathas (Ed.), *Everyday language: Studies in ethnomethodology* (pp. 123–162). Irvington Press.

Kaner, S. (2007). *Facilitator's guide to participatory decision making* (2nd ed.). Jossey-Bass.

Kaplan, S. (2008). Framing contests: Strategy making under uncertainty. *Organization Science*, 19(5), 729–752.

Kim, W. C., & Mauborgne, R. A. (1995). A procedural justice model of strategic decision making. *Organization Science*, 6, 44–61.

Korsgaard, M., Schweiger, D., & Sapienza, H. (1995). Building commitment, attachment, and trust in strategic decision making teams. The role of procedural justice. *Academy of Management Journal*, 38, 60–84.

Larson, J. R., Jr, Foster-Fishman, P. G., & Franz, T. M. (1998). Leadership style and the discussion of shared and unshared information in decision-making groups. *Personality and Social Psychology Bulletin*, 24(5), 482–495.

Nadler, D. (1998). Leading executive teams. In D. Nadler & J. L. Spencer (Eds.), *Executive teams* (pp. 3–20). Jossey-Bass.

Phillips, L. D., & Phillips, M. C. (1993). Facilitated work groups: theory and practice. *Journal of the Operational Research Society*, 44(6), 533–549.

Poole, M. S. (1983). Decision development in small groups II: A study of multiple sequences in decision making. *Communication Monographs*, 50(3), 206–232.

Poole, M. S., & Roth, J. (1989). Decision development in small groups IV. A typology of group decision paths. *Human Communication Research*, 15(3), 323–356.

Roberto, M. A. (2013). *Why great leaders don't take yes for an answer: Managing for conflict and consensus* (2nd ed.). Pearson Education.

Rouwette, E. A. J. A., & Smeets, S. (2016). Conflict, consensus and the management of a good debate. Exploring the deliberative assumptions of group facilitating techniques. In I. Bleijenbergh, H. Korzilius, & E. A. J. A. Rouwette (Eds.), *Methods, model building and management: A liber amicorum for Jac Vennix* (pp. 129–146). Institute for Management Research.

Schwarz, R. M. (1994). *The skilled facilitator: Practical wisdom for developing effective groups*. Jossey-Bass Publishers.

Stasser, G., & Davis, J. H. (1981). Group decision making and social influence: A social interaction sequence model. *Psychological Review*, 88(6), 523.

Stasser, G., & Titus, W. (1985). Pooling of unshared information in group decision making: Biased information sampling during discussion. *Journal of Personality and Social Psychology*, 48, 1467–1478.

Tavella, E., & Franco, L. A. (2015). Dynamics of group knowledge production in facilitated modelling workshops: An exploratory study. *Group Decision and Negotiation*, 24(3), 451–475.

Thomas, R., Sargent, L. D., & Hardy, C. (2011). Managing organizational change: negotiating meaning and power resistance relations. *Organizational Science*, 22(1), 22–41.

Tsoukas, H. (2009). A dialogical approach to the creation of new knowledge in organizations. *Organization Science*, 20(6), 941–957.

Wardale, D. (2013). Towards a model of effective group facilitation. *Leadership & Organization Development Journal*, 34(2), 112–129.

Webne-Behrman, H. (1998). *The practice of facilitation: Managing group process and solving problems*. Greenwood Publishing Group.

15

MANAGING CONFLICT AND EMOTION

Since interventions involve bridging differences of opinion and interests, conflict is likely to arise within team discussions and thus the effective management of conflict becomes paramount. Earlier in the book we discussed some of the perils of team decision making, one of which was the lack of productive conflict. Productive conflict is encouraging cognitive conflict (up to a certain level) while keeping affective conflict in check (Roberto, 2004). One way in which conflict can turn unproductive is when multiple viewpoints are brought to the table but never integrated. Discussions then remain unfinished, and the same topic can reappear in discussions time and time again. Another way in which conflict can become unproductive is when conflicts on the task at hand turn personal. We saw in Chapter 2 that when progress on the team task stalls, team members find themselves repeating the same arguments over and over (Edmondson & Smith, 2006). People then become frustrated and comments can be become personal. The discussion gets heated and fuels further impulsive, emotional reactions. Escalation of emotions was another peril to team decision making discussed in Chapter 2.

The aim of this chapter is to describe ways in which the facilitator can stimulate productive conflict while avoiding emotional dynamics that could spiral out of control during team discussions. First, we start by briefly describing what the facilitator can do to stimulate adequate levels of cognitive conflict, so that the team is able to bring all the relevant information to the table. Next, we look at the role of conflict and emotion in successful team decisions. We end the chapter with concrete facilitator actions intended to manage affective (interpersonal) conflict and emotional dynamics.

DOI: 10.4324/9781003404200-18

15.1 Stimulating productive cognitive conflict

As mentioned in Chapter 2, the evidence to date suggests that moderate levels of cognitive (task) conflict are generally beneficial to team performance (De Wit et al., 2012; DeChurch et al., 2013; O'Neill et al., 2013). This is because cognitive conflict can increase team members' tendency to engage in deep and deliberate processing of task-relevant information, which in turn increases team performance. Importantly, surfacing and managing cognitive conflict is central to the intervention approaches described in this book. Cognitive conflict often arises when the model reveals inconsistencies between team members' definitions of the decision or problem at hand. When such gaps are not apparent, the model is often used as a medium to stimulate cognitive conflict by facilitating the differentiation of views. Contrasting viewpoints are then openly discussed through model-supported analysis and interaction, which can prevent conflict escalation. This is possible because team members' attention is centred on the views contained in the model, independent of where those views come from within the group. Furthermore, the model-supported process helps team members to clarify and test assumptions underpinning contrasting viewpoints in an organised and participative manner, which can reduce misunderstandings and increase perceptions of fairness within the team (Kim & Mauborgne, 1998; Roberson et al., 1999).

By enabling a collective and systematic examination of viewpoints within the team, the model-supported process can help maintain moderate levels of productive cognitive conflict throughout group discussions. In addition, model-supported processes often foster collaborative problem-solving behaviours that can facilitate the development of integrative solutions that take a diversity of viewpoints into account (Rouwette & Franco, 2021). In this way, how conflict is handled within a model-supported environment resembles the well-established 'differentiation before integration' model of effective conflict management (Walton, 1968). The procedure for these techniques is outlined in Appendix A.

However, there is some empirical evidence that model-driven support alone may not be enough to stimulate cognitive conflict in teams (e.g. Engin et al., 2023; Sambamurthy & Poole, 1992). Therefore, what can facilitators do to ensure that an intervention can effectively stimulate and facilitate the management of cognitive conflict in teams? One possible way is for facilitators to use simple conflict stimulation strategies (e.g. Okhuysen & Bechky, 2012; Van de Vliert & De Dreu, 1994) or incorporate structured conflict stimulation procedures – for example, devil's advocacy, dialectic inquiry (Schwenk & Valacich, 1994; Schwenk, 1990).

In addition, facilitators can establish communication norms about conflict (Tjosvold, 2000) that help create a climate of 'psychological safety' (Edmondson, 1999), that is, an interaction space in which team members feel it is appropriate and acceptable to openly discuss disagreements. Regarding the latter, the facilitator can also focus attention on parts of the model that would highlight disagreements, particularly in the earlier part of the discussion, to avoid the shared-information bias (Stasser & Titus, 1985) that often leads to premature consensus (see Chapter 2).

15.2 The positive cycle of trust and information exchange

The Campus Connect case (Van Oortmerssen et al., 2014) described in Chapter 13 offered an example of a successful team decision. The case follows a board that meets every month over the course of a year. In that time, the interaction among board members changed greatly. Differences in ideas and personalities emerged and clashed, leading not only to frustration and anger but also enabling the team to come together and identify a more effective way of working. In this case, both interpersonal and process conflicts were successfully managed, creating a positive interaction between trust and open information exchange. Later, we analyse the positive spiral driving the Campus Connect case and describe two negative spirals, showing how decision making teams can get stuck in interpersonal conflict or process conflict. A facilitator can help a group by nudging it onto the positive spiral, or recognising early signals of entering either of the negative cycles and then intervening accordingly.

Cognitive theories on emotion, although diverging on a number of aspects, in the main agree that emotions are caused by appraising events in terms of concerns (Oatley & Johnson-Laird, 2014). Emotions arise when personal goals become important. If a change in the environment affects personal goals, people react in two phases. The first reaction is an immediate feeling of arousal (energy) and pleasure or displeasure. In the second stage, the emotion is interpreted and labelled (Oatley & Johnson-Laird, 2014; Russell, 2003). Imagine you receive a mail saying that the training budget in your organisation is expanded. As a result, you now have five extra days each year, in which you are taken out of your primary task to instead spend time on external training. With all expenses paid, we expect this mail would make many people feel positively energised. In the secondary reaction, goals will come into play. A goal such as 'develop my skills further' may inspire happiness, with some initial plans on how to use these days already forming. On the other hand, the secondary reaction may also be negative. When the first goal that comes to mind is 'finish work in fewer days', the feeling is one of irritation, followed by plans to work around what is perceived to be a nuisance.

One of the reasons why team decision making is a complex endeavour is that one and the same piece of information can trigger different goals for different team members. An example in the Campus Connect case (Van Oortmerssen et al., 2014) occurs in a two-day session aimed at building a shared culture. In this session, it became clear that board members had very different ideas on the future cooperation while a shared vision needed to be communicated in the near future. This led one board member to propose a change in the way of working, which would give more authority to a core group. This infuriated another member of the board as he interpreted this as giving some members a higher status than others. Others, however, did not link the proposal to status differences and emphasised their mutual respect and equality. While the proposal to change the way of working led to an immediate negative emotional outburst, in the longer term it had a positive result. As board members reported, in their emotional reactions "we then all just showed ourselves as we are" (Van Oortmerssen et al., 2014, p. 678). A better understanding of each other's perspectives increased trust in the group. This seems to say that board members developed more trust because personal goals became clearer and were more similar than expected. There was a second occasion that board members deemed important in the development of trust. This was when the joint building was ready. Members felt joy and what seemed to be a sense of accomplishment when walking through the beautiful new building.

In line with emotion theory (Mandler, 1984; Oatley & Johnson-Laird, 2014; Russell, 2003), we could say that identifying or meeting shared goals means that personal goals are brought nearer to accomplishment, leading to positive emotions. Trust in turn changed the way in which team members communicated. Communication became more open, direct, and faster. Better communication builds towards more shared information, which is the basis for accomplishing the task. These two interacting positive cycles are depicted in Figure 15.1.

How can the facilitator support the positive interaction of trust and information exchange? Differences in opinions (i.e. task conflict) are unavoidable in

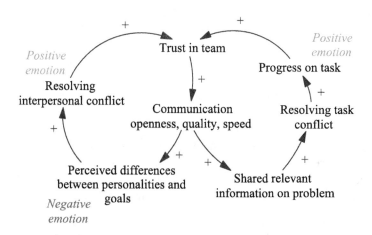

FIGURE 15.1 Positive spiral that discovers and resolves differences

team decision making. In fact, the diversity of opinions and expertise is the reason to bring the team together in the first place. Likewise, differences in personalities and goals are also an intrinsic part of working with teams. Discovering these differences may not be easy but they do serve an important role. Phillips and Phillips (1993) see the management of emotions as one of the main tasks of a facilitator. Emotions can arise not only because members have different goals but also because of personality differences or their status relative to others.

> Members wish to be accepted by the group . . . and they want the group work to go well. But to be accepted and liked, to 'fit in' to the group culture, means sacrificing much of the uniqueness that is one's self.
>
> *(Phillips & Phillips, 1993, p. 538)*

Being immersed in the team can lead to anxiety that may express itself in disengagement with the task, outbursts against other team members or against the facilitator. Sterling et al. (2019) point out that team members often have needs that they cannot articulate easily. Over the course of the team discussions they discover their motivations, 'which in some conflict situations might be related to feelings of being disrespected or undervalued, or to disparities in social power among participants' (2019, p. 8).

In summary, facilitators should be aware that in team decisions differences in personalities and goals are likely to become manifest. The facilitator can reduce tensions by paying attention to the emotional state of the group, recognising a threat against individuals if it occurs, and working with the team to change a situation in which one person's loss is another person's gain to a win-win situation (Phillips & Phillips, 1993). Identifying shared goals is a way to do this (Eisenhardt et al., 1997). A simple way to remind the group that 'we are all in this together' and to foster thinking in terms of shared goals (Eisenhardt et al., 1997), is to keep addressing the group as 'we' (Vennix, 1996).

While the Campus Connect case was an example of a positive spiral of interaction and emotion, team decision making can become trapped in a negative spiral as well. Two negative spirals are particularly dangerous. The first is a cycle of tension between individual and team goals setting off negative, person-centred communication and blaming, limiting progress on the task and feeding further tensions. The second negative spiral starts with the gradual realisation that the challenge facing the team may be too great for the time and resources available. Panic and avoiding to discuss threatening information prevent the group from effectively discussing the problem at hand, increasing the perceived challenge and fuelling further panic.

15.3 The negative cycle of lack of progress and person-centred comments

In Chapter 1, we saw that there is a clear danger that team discussions escalate from task conflicts to interpersonal conflicts. When the discussion impacts strongly held personal beliefs, participants may be keen to bring others around to their point of view by repeating the same arguments. When that does not lead to the desired result, the conversation turns to interpersonal issues and blaming the lack of progress on the other person's personal agenda or lack of expertise. Once negative personal attributions arise, emotions become the focus of the interaction and progress on the task comes to a standstill. Parties blame each other openly. The negative spiral between emotions and interactions takes over: 'Suggesting, even indirectly, that others are incompetent, ignorant, or immoral gives rise to defensive reactions that inhibit others' willingness to continue to express their views, making it all but impossible to resolve a conflict effectively' (Edmondson & Smith, 2006, p. 14).

Reasoned argumentation 'in the heat of the moment' is difficult, and impulsive 'hot' reactions take over. In the short term, repetitive argumentation and negative personal comments impede progress on the task. In the longer term, it creates so-called undiscussables. Undiscussable topics are those that are avoided because team members fear they may set off unmanageable interpersonal conflict (Argyris, 1990). If a team feels their task links to many undiscussables, conversations rarely touch on anything important and little progress is made. Undiscussables may become the 'elephants in the room' that outsiders recognise as important topics to talk about, but seem to be avoided by the team. This means differences are not discussed and resolved, and instead the discussion is dropped prematurely or ended by one side giving in (e.g. Poole & Dobosh, 2010). These interacting negative cycles are shown in Figure 15.2.

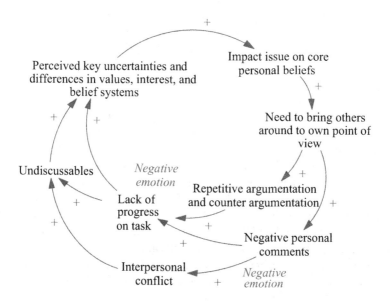

FIGURE 15.2 Negative spiral around issue touching on core personal beliefs.

When conflict and emotions are low, the facilitator can use many of the techniques described in the preceding chapter: sharing ideas and analysing information, supported by visualisation and communication techniques. There are additional actions a facilitator can take to recognise the shift from task-related to person-centred communication and prevent interpersonal conflict from flaring up. Once a heated interpersonal conflict is underway, a second set of actions may help to cool down emotions. Ultimately, as we saw in the Campus Connect case, the experience of having navigated emotional conflict also has benefits for future cooperation and the facilitator can assist in creating these benefits.

The first set of actions aims to help the facilitator note when the conversation shifts from the task to persons. This is likely to be accompanied by a change in emotional state in the group. In the previous chapter, we already discussed ways to notice weak emotional signals such as the facilitator attending to shifts in her own emotional state. Early shifts in group emotions are usually indicated by nonverbal communication. One important nonverbal cue is what participants are looking at: the model or another team member. The model represents a form of group memory, which in fact visualises the state of the team discussion up to that moment. The group memory almost automatically disconnects ideas from persons. When building a model, while model elements were suggested by one team member, relations are discussed with the whole team, making it likely that contributions are no longer associated with a particular person. In electronic brainstorming and group causal mapping, idea contribution is usually anonymous. When team members discuss while looking at the model and using model terms, we can generally conclude they are oriented to the task at hand. When they turn to face each other, this may signal a shift to person-oriented communication (Franco, 2013). A final indicator is lack of further development of content, or repetitive argumentation and counter-argumentation (Edmondson & Smith, 2006, p. 10).

A second set of actions helps the facilitator to cool down emotions. As emotions involve incompatible goals, there is one action that not only was discussed earlier but also applies here: bring shared goals back into focus (Eisenhardt et al., 1997). It is worth realising that associations between persons and ideas also exist in the wider organisation. In major organisational issues, persons may be known for their view or be seen to back one particular side of an ongoing argument. Learning and building a shared understanding means that individuals change their minds. Eden (1992) warns that changing opinions may cause a loss of face. If a sensitive issue was discussed and an agreement has emerged which implies one or more team members have made a major change in their thinking, the facilitator may deliberately choose to phrase the outcome in generic terms. Allowing for ambivalence or some level of vagueness lowers the chance that a person loses face from being seen to change her mind. The type of team leadership also has consequences for the discussion. When a team leader has a coaching style, which is supportive and non-defensive in reaction to questions and challenges rather than authoritarian or punitive, team members are more likely to discuss information openly (Edmondson, 1999). Reminding team members that their input is needed and desired increases the chance of open sharing of information (Edmondson, 2003). In addition, the team leader supports open discussion by minimising power differences in the team. Self-disclosure, or being open about own mistakes, and emphasising the need for teamwork (referring to the team as 'we'), are ways to bring this about.

Notice that a coaching style, encouraging team members to share information and minimising power differences in the team are all closely in line with facilitator attitudes discussed in Chapter 13. The discussion in Chapter 14 on managing content and process in a facilitated meeting emphasised the importance of carefully trying to capture team members' contribution to the discussion. Occasions may arise when all actions to prevent a discussion from heating up fail, and emotions run high. The aim is then to get team members out of their 'hot' emotional reactions back to 'cold' processing of information. One way to cool down emotions is by inviting participants to reflect on their reactions (Edmondson & Smith, 2006). This asks team members to step out of experiencing a reaction to turning reactions into objects of reflection, or in terms of Oatley and Johnson-Laird (2014), moving from the primary emotional reaction to the secondary interpretive stage. Once participants engage in reflection, reframing becomes possible. Two new frames are important here. The first is the realisation that, on the basis of different beliefs, one person will see things the other misses. The second new frame is that each person is responsible for discussing their views so that the other can learn what we might be missing. If the team is able to manage their conflict in this way, it will better understand what motivates each member and will likely bring team members closer together. Over time, gaining more experience with this reframing approach to handling conflicts helps teams to proceed to address undiscussables.

The third set of actions is relevant after a team has navigated an episode of interpersonal conflict. As we saw in the Campus Connect phase, a conflict is also an occasion in which team members 'show themselves as they are' and get to know each other on a more personal level (Van Oortmerssen et al., 2014). This was an important factor in the creation of trust. A similar but slightly broader factor was team psychological safety, which is the shared belief that the team is safe for interpersonal risk-taking (Edmondson, 1999, 2003). If the team has successfully worked through an interpersonal conflict, it will have explored the underlying beliefs, emotions, and both task and interpersonal conflicts. Speaking up on these matters involves considerable personal risk. In the Campus Connect case, team members were more likely to take such a risk if they had trust in the team. As one of the board members indicated, if team members feel they can express themselves without the danger of being ridiculed, they will share their thoughts and feelings more freely (Van Oortmerssen et al., 2014, p. 680). Therefore, the facilitator can assist a group by handling interpersonal issues in a respectful and impartial manner. This will contribute to creating trust and team psychological safety. As indicated in Figure 15.3, this in turn makes it more likely that the most sensitive issues, or undiscussables (Edmondson & Smith, 2006) will be raised.

15.4 The negative cycle of panic and avoiding discussion of the problem

Even when a team avoids the trap of spiralling off into interpersonal conflict, it may fall into a second trap involving excess process conflict. The negative cycle around process conflict starts from the realisation that the team may not succeed in achieving its task and can also be recognised in the Campus Connect case. In the two-day meeting, when the board members realised they were in no way near a shared understanding of the cooperation's future, while such an understanding was necessary to communicate with partners in the short term, a negative mood took over. Here, it is not the mismatch between personalities or goals of team members that causes negative emotions, but the mismatch between the team's desired outcome and the perceived situation. We noted at the start of this chapter that team members need to experience some level of urgency before they will attend to a problem. Different authors referred to this as disconfirmation (Schein, 1999), problem importance (Roberts, 1978), or motivation (Chaiken et al., 1996; Petty & Cacioppo, 1986). An intermediate level of urgency leads the decision making team to mobilise resources and increase efforts in sharing and processing information. Indeed, in the Campus Connect case, the realisation that task progress might be too slow to meet deadlines was probably an important incentive to discuss team member's goals, reaffirm shared goals, and change the decision making procedure.

However, high levels of problem urgency may lead team members to switch to ineffective coping mechanisms. In situations of major disruptions and high arousal, where there seems to be no possibility or time to develop realistic solutions, decision makers become hypervigilant or use defensive avoidance (Janis & Mann, 1977). Hypervigilance refers to the panic arising when time is running out. Defensive avoidance refers to an unwillingness to address the issue and may emerge when each available solution seems to have serious negative impacts on important goals. Hodgkinson and Wright (2002) describe a scenario planning intervention in which three forms of defensive avoidance can be recognised. The decision making team was unable to find an alternative to the current, failing strategy. Realising this had a major effect on team members, and especially on the CEO:

> One of the participants went so far as to say that the effect on the CEO had been 'the psychological equivalent of thrusting a medicine ball into her stomach', and that the results of our exercise, thus far, had greatly unsettled the rest of the group.
>
> *(Hodgkinson & Wright 2002, p. 962)*

In reaction, the team first tried to delay making a decision and postpone considering the problem. This strategy of procrastination was followed by so-called buck-passing in which the responsibility for the decision was shifted to other individuals or groups. Procrastination and buck-passing are both forms of avoiding a decision. Since the team refuses to engage with the problem, it is in effect avoiding task conflict. Using the third strategy, bolstering, the team rationalised the least objectionable decision alternative. Here, we see that when major disruptions occur and a team anticipates it will fail at its main task, emotions run so high that decision making is impaired. Task conflict is not resolved because the team either refuses to address the issue at hand or does not process information adequately. Figure 15.3 summarises the processes just described.

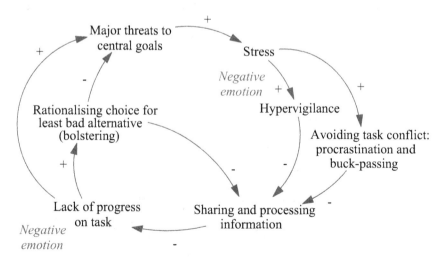

FIGURE 15.3   Negative spiral around major threats.

Again we see a downward spiral of negative emotions and slowing progress on the task, this time not caused by interpersonal conflicts but by a perceived inability to cope with an external threat. Hodgkinson and Wright (2002) note that in their case, the volatile environment of the client organisation, combined with a strong need for control exhibited by the CEO, made it impossible to start a process of open communication and the intervention ultimately did not lead to any change. In the Campus Connect case, the realisation that there was a gap between the current situation and desired outcome spurred team members into action instead of immobilising them. It seems likely that the perception of a gap increased arousal and stress, but not to such a level that it impeded decision making. Perhaps the only advice for a facilitator in addressing an issue leading to extreme stress is to recognise the perception of threat in an early stage so that effective communication is still possible and helps to defuse the situation.

Table 15.1 brings together facilitator tasks and actions discussed in this chapter.

TABLE 15.1 Facilitator tasks and actions in managing emotion and conflict

Task focus	Facilitator tasks	Facilitator actions
Emotion	Attend to own and others' emotions	• Monitor own energy level, and change to another task if relevant • Monitor own emotional state (positive–negative), and change to another task if relevant • Monitor energy level group, signal stress • Monitor emotional state group (positive–negative), signal emotional tension
	Encourage an open information search without contributing to content, but set format and guide trajectory of discussion	• Identify shared goals • Address team as 'we'
Conflict	Encourage an open information search without contributing to content, but set format and guide trajectory of discussion	• Use simple (cognitive) conflict stimulation strategies or structured conflict stimulation procedures • Disconnect ideas from individual team members to encourage a psychologically safe team climate • Move from hot to reflective interaction by using reframing

Task focus	Facilitator tasks	Facilitator actions
	Listen actively	• Note repetition of arguments and counterarguments, bring shared goals back into focus • Note when discussion shifts from model to team members, identify win-win situations
	Limit but do not sidestep interpersonal conflict	• Adapt agenda to address interpersonal conflict when it arises • Adapt agenda to address process conflict due to perception issue as threat to major goals • Prevent loss of face by allowing for ambivalence • Handle interpersonal issues in a respectful and impartial manner to help build trust

References

Argyris, C. (1990). *Overcoming organizational defenses. Facilitating organizational learning*. Allyn and Bacon.

Chaiken, S., Giner-Sorolla, R., & Chen, S. (1996). Beyond accuracy: Defense and impression motives in heuristic and systematic information processing. In P. Gollwitzer & J. A. Bargh (Eds.), *The psychology of action: Linking cognition and motivation to action* (pp. 553–578). Guilford.

DeChurch, L. A., Mesmer-Magnus, J. R., & Doty, D. (2013). Moving beyond relationship and task conflict: Toward a process-state perspective. *Journal of Applied Psychology, 98*(4), 559.

De Wit, F. R., Greer, L. L., & Jehn, K. A. (2012). The paradox of intragroup conflict: A meta-analysis. *Journal of Applied Psychology, 97*(2), 360–390.

Eden, C. (1992). Strategy development as a social process. *Journal of Management Studies, 29*(6), 799–811.

Edmondson, A. C. (1999). Psychological safety and learning behavior in work teams. *Administrative Science Quarterly, 44*(2), 350–383.

Edmondson, A. C. (2003). Managing the risk of learning: Psychological safety in work teams. In M. A. West, D. Tjosvold, & K. G. Smith (Eds.), *International handbook of organizational teamwork and cooperative working* (pp. 255–275). John Wiley & Sons.

Edmondson, A. C., & Smith, D. M. (2006). Too hot to handle? How to manage relationship conflict. *California Management Review, 49*(1), 6–31.

Eisenhardt, K. M., Kahwajy, J. L., & Bourgeois, L. J. I. (1997). How management teams can have a good fight. *Harvard Business Review, 75*(4), 77–85.

Engin, A., Franco, L. A., & Rouwette, E. (2023). Epistemic motivation in self-managing groups: Conflict patterns and group trajectories within a model-supported environment. Under Review at Group Decision and Negotiation.

Franco, L. A. (2013). Rethinking soft OR interventions: Models as boundary objects. *European Journal of Operational Research*, 231(2), 720–733.

Hodgkinson, G. P., & Wright, G. (2002). Confronting strategic inertia in a top management team: Learning from failure. *Organization Studies*, 23(6), 949–977.

Janis, I. L., & Mann, L. (1977). *Decision making: A psychological analysis of conflict, choice and commitment*. The Free Press.

Kim, W. C., & Mauborgne, R. A. (1998). Procedural justice, strategic decision making, and the knowledge economy. *Strategic Management Journal*, 19(4), 323–338.

Mandler, G. M. (1984). *Mind and body. Psychology of emotion and stress*. W.W. Norton.

Oatley, K., & Johnson-Laird, P. N. (2014). Cognitive approaches to emotions. *Trends in Cognitive Sciences*, 18(3), 134–140.

Okhuysen, G. A., & Bechky, B. A. (2012). Making group process work: Harnessing collective intuition, task conflict, and pacing. In *Handbook of principles of organizational behavior: Indispensable knowledge for evidence-based management* (pp. 309–325). Blackwell.

O'Neill, T. A., Allen, N. J., & Hastings, S. E. (2013). Examining the "pros" and "cons" of team conflict: A team-level meta-analysis of task, relationship, and process conflict. *Human Performance*, 26(3), 236–260.

Petty, R., & Cacioppo, J. (1986). The elaboration likelihood model of persuasion. *Advances in Experimental Social Psychology*, 19, 123–205.

Phillips, L. D., & Phillips, M. C. (1993). Facilitated work groups: Theory and practice. *Journal of the Operational Research Society*, 44(6), 533–549.

Poole, M. S., & Dobosh, M. (2010). Exploring conflict management processes in jury deliberations through interaction analysis. *Small Group Behavior*, 41(4), 408–426.

Roberson, Q. M., Moye, N. A., & Locke, E. A. (1999). Identifying a missing link between participation and satisfaction: The mediating role of procedural justice perceptions. *Journal of Applied Psychology*, 84(4), 585.

Roberto, M. A. (2004). Strategic decision-making processes: Beyond the efficiency-consensus trade-off. *Group & Organization Management*, 29(6), 625–658.

Roberts, E. (1978). Strategies for effective implementation of complex corporate models. In E. Roberts (Ed.), *Managerial applications of system dynamics* (pp. 77–85). Productivity Press.

Rouwette, E. A. J. A., & Franco, L. A. (2021). Technologies for improving group decision making. In S. J. Beck, J. Keyton, & M. S. Poole (Eds.), *The Emerald handbook of group and team communication research* (pp. 209–228). Emerald Publishing Limited. https://doi.org/10.1108/978-1-80043-500-120211014

Russell, J. A. (2003). Core affect and the psychological construction of emotion. *Psychological Review*, 110(1), 145.

Sambamurthy, V., & Poole, M. S. (1992). The effects of variations in GDSS capabilities on management of cognitive conflict in groups. *Information Systems Research*, 3, 224–251.

Schein, E. H. (1999). Empowerment, coercive persuasion and organizational learning: Do they connect? *The Learning Organization*, 6(4), 163–172.

Schwenk, C., & Valacich, J. S. (1994). Effects of devil's advocacy and dialectical inquiry on individuals versus groups. *Organizational Behavior and Human Decision Processes*, 59(2), 210–222.

Schwenk, C. R. (1990). Effects of devil's advocacy and dialectical inquiry on decision making: A meta-analysis. *Organizational Behavior and Human Decision Processes, 47*(1), 161–176.

Stasser, G., & Titus, W. (1985). Pooling of unshared information in group decision making: Biased information sampling during discussion. *Journal of Personality and Social Psychology, 48,* 1467–1478.

Sterling, E. J., Zellner, M., Jenni, K. E., Leong, K., Glynn, P. D., BenDor, T. K., Bommel, P., Hubacek, K., Jetter, A. J., & Jordan, R. (2019). Try, try again: Lessons learned from success and failure in participatory modeling. *Elementa Science of the Anthropocene, 7,* 9. https://doi.org/10.1525/elementa.347

Tjosvold, D. (2000). *Learning to manage conflict: Getting people to work together productively.* Lexington Books.

Van de Vliert, E., & De Dreu, C. (1994). Optimizing performance by stimulating conflict. *The International Journal of Conflict Management, 5.*

Van Oortmerssen, L. A., Van Woerkum, C. M. J., & Aarts, N. (2014). The visibility of trust: Exploring the connection between trust and interaction in a Dutch collaborative governance boardroom. *Public Management Review, 16*(5), 666–685.

Vennix, J. A. M. (1996). *Group model building. Facilitating team learning using system dynamics.* Wiley.

Walton, R. E. (1968). *Interpersonal peacemaking: Confrontations and third party interventions.* Harvard University.

PART IV

Researching interventions

The first part of this book discussed why teams often fall short of their potential and make faulty decisions. We then presented a range of basic and more advanced approaches to help teams make better decisions. The previous part addressed the design and deployment of team decision support interventions. This last part goes into two questions: what evidence do we have that these interventions actually improve team decision making? Followed by, how can I build my competencies in researching and applying team decision support interventions?

Chapter 16 reports on the evidence by first specifying the range of applications for each approach, followed by academic reviews of their use. Claims of visible and less visible products are listed. Finally, evidence for impact is addressed.

Chapter 17 closes this book by outlining how a research and practitioner in the field of team decision support can build their competencies. This is done by contrasting interventions to theory-oriented research and action research. Researchers studying interventions can choose to focus on causal explanations for observed effects (a variance approach) or analyse how interventions evolve over time (a process approach). Building competencies as an intervention practitioner can be done as part of an apprenticeship or in the classroom. Three areas of competencies are important: for conducting analysis, addressing process, and appreciating context. A sequence of building skills, from more basic to advanced, is proposed. Researching and training build on one another and are the basis for further development of the team decision support domain.

DOI: 10.4324/9781003404200-19

16

ARE INTERVENTIONS USED IN PRACTICE AND DO THEY REALLY WORK?

This chapter takes stock of what we know about the effectiveness of team decision support interventions. In Part I of this book, we identified several deficiencies of unsupported team decision making: individual and team biases, insufficient sharing of information, unproductive conflict, and escalation of emotion. Part II presented a selection of procedures for team decision support interventions. Part III outlined generic factors to consider in designing and delivering team decision support interventions, including setting up a supportive team environment and ensuring effective facilitation. These procedures and generic factors are said to remedy deficiencies in team decision making. How confident can we be of the validity of this claim? If we had evidence that particular procedures reliably result in particular products and impacts, this would be a great help in deciding whether to use a procedure and choosing between available options. In some situations, simple procedures might be adequate, in others more elaborate procedures or combinations of approaches might be needed.

In healthcare, education, consultancy, and other fields, professionals strive to make their interventions evidence-based. They recognise that at present many of the decisions taken by doctors, surgeons, educators, and consultants are not always founded on empirically tested claims but on personal experience, habits, and untested 'best practices'. They expect that grounding more of their practice in empirical evidence improves their decisions and ultimately their effectiveness. In this chapter, we summarise the evidence for effectiveness of team decision support interventions. We start by reviewing the use of approaches in practice drawing from published surveys, academic reviews, and case studies. Second, we bring together claims on products generated and impact created by team support procedures. This is followed

DOI: 10.4324/9781003404200-20

by an examination of the evidence supporting or questioning the actual achievement of the products and impacts claimed by approaches. Finally, we critically reflect on our findings and discuss what in our view are the most pressing issues in advancing research on effectiveness of team decision support interventions.

16.1 Evidence of use

In this section, we provide a short account of the practical application of team decision support interventions in two ways. First, we compare the applications reported in earlier chapters. Second, we look into published survey evidence and academic reviews, to capture actual use and the range and distribution of team decision support interventions.

16.1.1 Examples of practical applications

Chapters 5, 7, 9, and 11 reported on the background, process, products, implementation, and results of team support applications in practice. Table 16.1 summarises the main elements. Comparing the four applications immediately makes clear that there are large differences between starting questions and the process followed. The question group model building seeks to answer is explanatory, trying to find the structure responsible for past problem behaviour. All other approaches answer future- or present-oriented questions. The number of sessions and participants vary widely. With regard to visible products, applications are similar in that they all use workbooks in between meetings and deliver a final report at the end of the project. The degree of implementation differs again, with recommendations put into action and further use of the method in the Sioo case, and a relative lack of impact in the case of Nijmegen municipality.

Many more reports on applications of team support methods can be found in the literature. These include surveys and reviews of method use in particular regions, application domains, or specific academic journals. Some of these focus on a single method, including those described in this book, others extend to other approaches that support team decision making by combining facilitation and other forms of modelling. In practice, intervention approaches to team decision support are flexible, and their use is adjusted to the particular problem and team in focus. Their flexibility allows for combining approaches in practice, not only with facilitated methods but also with other quantitative and data analytic approaches used in Operational Research/Management Science, data analytics, and statistics. Combined approaches are known as *multi-methodology* (or mixed-method) interventions (e.g. Munro & Mingers, 2002). Later, we report on surveys on the use of facilitated modelling approaches (which include, among others, group model building, group

TABLE 16.1 Comparison of practical applications of four intervention approaches

	Chapter 5 *Group model building*	*Chapter 7* *Participatory scenario* *development*	*Chapter 9* *Group causal mapping*	*Chapter 11* *Decision conferencing*
Background	Which business model explains Sioo revenues between 2013 and 2018?	Is Nijmegen municipality developing the right things for 2035?	What issues must the Teenage Pregnancy Strategy Group consider in trying to achieve its targets by 2010?	
Process	Two meetings of three hours each, 12 and 11 participants	Five meetings of 3.5 hours each, about 30 participants	Interviews with cognitive mapping, eight participants One full-day meeting, six participants	One full-day meeting, four participants
Product	Workbook and final report with causal loop diagram	Workbooks and final report with scenarios and results wind tunnelling	Workbook with individual cognitive map and merged map	Final report with portfolio recommendation
Implementation and results	Proposed actions implemented, model used in further strategy meetings, use of method continued	Some indications of change of collective and individual insights, no implementation in organisation	Improved quality of communication and shared meaning, no implementation of model recommendations in organisation	

causal mapping, and decision conferencing) and also of scenario planning, and then go into academic reviews of their practical applications.

Note that the academic domains of facilitated modelling and scenario planning developed somewhat in isolation. The literature offers extensive discussions on the distinguishing characteristics of model-driven team decision support, and by extension on which approaches are or are not part of the 'family' of facilitated modelling or related groupings of methods. Franco and Rouwette (2022) propose that the core of these approaches – not surprisingly – is their use of facilitated group processes and models (see also Franco & Montibeller, 2010). Models are expressed in visual or diagrammatic form. They are transparent and accessible to team members and can describe the present as well as the future, desired or ideal situation. Different types of models may be used, expressing various kinds of relationships: between concepts, activities or stakeholders; relationships of similarity or influence; and between options (Franco & Rouwette, 2022, p. 742). Quantitative scenarios clearly use models of this kind. In its quantitative mode, scenario planning is based on statistical, simulation, optimisation, or other types of formal models. Participatory scenario development, however, often takes a qualitative form. The process of scenario construction employs visualisations of intermediate products such as ideas on trends and developments, clusters of trends, and scoring tables. Final products of qualitative scenario planning are narratives, tables such as used for comparisons of impacts of options across scenarios (wind tunnelling), and visualisations such as (rich) pictures. A narrative description of a possible future expresses relations between driving forces, possibly via needs or actions of stakeholders in the transactional environment, ultimately to performance indicators. In the latter sense, a scenario may be called a model. Nevertheless, a narrative in the form of written text is clearly a model of a different kind than a word-and-arrow diagram (as used in group model building and group causal mapping). We therefore refer to both model and narrative in the following. We start our discussion of surveys and reviews on team decision support interventions from a recent overview of published work on facilitated modelling (Franco & Rouwette, 2022) and add studies on scenario planning. We do not include simple methods in our overview as their use is ubiquitous and generic.

16.1.2 Surveys of facilitated modelling and scenario planning use in practice

Published practical applications of model-driven team decision support have grown steadily over time, as evidenced in recent surveys (e.g. Abuabara & Paucar-Caceres, 2021; Gomes & Schramm, 2021; Ranyard et al., 2015), although the bulk of applications is probably larger as most published accounts are written by scholars rather than practitioners. The earliest published study including team decision support interventions is a survey of the combined use of approaches (Munro & Mingers, 2002). Practitioners included in the survey see their use of team support approaches as successful, but an operational definition of success is not provided. More recent surveys have examined the use of methods in specific areas. O'Brien (2011), for instance, surveyed practitioners in the UK to investigate the use of approaches in strategic planning. The survey results indicate that many quantitative techniques are used to support the strategy process, but facilitated modelling is not regularly used despite practitioners being aware of this type of methods. A more positive picture is given by Ranyard et al. (2015), who report the use of various quantitative techniques, including facilitated modelling approaches. Group causal mapping (reported as SODA) is one of three model-driven intervention approaches that is being used fairly regularly in the UK, but much less frequently in the rest of the world. The results of this survey confirm a gradual increase in the use of facilitated modelling over time, although information on diffusion beyond the UK is sparse.

The use of scenarios is reported in several surveys. As described in Chapter 6, the use of scenarios for corporate strategic planning soared in the mid-1970s in the United States (Linneman & Klein, 1983) as well as in Europe (Malaska, 1985; Meristö, 1989). After a decline in popularity in the 1980s (Bradfield et al., 2005; Martelli, 2001), attention grew considerably in the period 1990–2005 (Varum & Melo, 2010). A 2023 survey of management tools by Bain & Company places scenarios in the top five of strategy support tools in terms of use and satisfaction (www.bain.com). This position has not changed much over the 30 years that this survey has been in use.

16.1.3   Academic reviews of facilitated modelling and scenario planning applications

A number of scholars have conducted literature reviews that focused on the application of particular model-driven intervention approaches. These were described in the chapters on the respective approaches but we summarise their gist here.

We should note that to identify the studies in Table 16.2 and the multi-methodology reviews later we only looked at published academic articles. This has the advantage that because we start from a search on Web of Science and other databases, we can get a complete overview of what is published in academic journals for a specific timespan and topic. Moreover, the search strategy is transparent and repeatable. The disadvantage is that much of the work on facilitated modelling and scenario planning appears in books and 'grey' literature such as unpublished dissertations or company reports. For instance, our search strategy excluded the book chapter by Phillips (2007) that mentions 16 applications of decision conferencing. It also ignores the

TABLE 16.2 Single method reviews of applications of four intervention approaches

	Reference	Number of cases	Period	Results measured
Group model building	Rouwette et al. (2002)	107	Until 1999	Communication, learning, consensus, commitment, and implementation (among others)
	Scott et al. (2015)	26	2001 to 2014	Same as previous
	De Gooyert et al. (2022)	8	2013	Cognitive change (learning) and consensus
Participatory scenario development	Varum and Melo (2010)	101 (only a small subset focused on evaluation)	1945 to 2006	The few papers that include an empirical evaluation report on policy options, ideas on long-term planning, individual, and organisational learning
	Oteros-Rozas et al. (2015)	23	2003 to 2014	Same as previous
Group causal mapping	Abuabara and Paucar-Caceres (2021)	200 (of which 19 are participatory)	1989 to 2018	No evaluation results reported
Decision conferencing	McCartt and Rohrbaugh (1989)	14 (114 individual questionnaires)	1982 to 1985	Decision process effectiveness, decision benefits, project characteristics (e.g. presence facilitator, construction action plan)
	McCartt and Rohrbaugh (1995)	26 (274 individual questionnaires)	1982 to 1989	Managerial openness to change, team size, number of decisions made, decision making effectiveness

unpublished PhD thesis by Chun (1992), who compares 22 applications, mentioned by Phillips. While this strategy will underestimate the actual use of team decision support interventions, we also need to keep in mind that reports may be biased towards successful projects. Indeed the number of failed cases reported in the facilitated modelling and scenario planning literature is very small (Hodgkinson & Wright, 2002; Rouwette et al., 2002).

The single method reviews in Table 16.2 report on method use for a broad range of organisations and look at a variety of impacts. Rouwette et al. (2002) draw on the system dynamics literature (journal, conference proceedings, and books) until 1999 and identify 107 group model building applications. Client organisations are active in a range of sectors, from private organisations in service and production, to non-profit organisations such as universities, secondary schools, and research agencies in defence or energy, to government bodies at the national or regional level. The group model building studies identified assess a large set of impacts, among which communication, learning, consensus, commitment and implementation. Several years later, Scott et al. (2015) repeat this search in a broader set of journals and identify 26 applications. The papers they identified also cover a broad range of sectors and impacts, but there is a shift in research design from qualitative case studies to quantitative assessment of impacts. Finally, De Gooyert et al. (2022) compare the impact of group model building on cognition (learning) and consensus across eight projects in the energy sector.

Abuabara and Paucar-Caceres (2021) surveyed published applications of group causal mapping, reported as SODA, from 1989 to 2018. They found a growing interest in SODA over the period of analysis, with applications reported in many sectors. Most areas where SODA had been used partially, fully, or in combination with other methods included strategic management, sustainable development, information systems, and performance evaluation. Notably, only a very small proportion of the reported applications (9.5%, or 19 papers) involve facilitated model-supported workshops. Abuabara and Paucar-Caceres suggest the lack of facilitation skills as a barrier to deploy SODA in practice as originally intended.

Decision conferencing applications were studied by McCartt and Rohrbaugh in 1989 and again in 1995. Their applications are in the main in the public sector (more than half are state government agencies, some are colleges and universities), and the remainder is about equally divided between the profit and (corporate management teams, policy-making task forces, and national professional organisations) and not-for-profit sector (social service agencies). The first study looks at 14 and the second at 26 decision conferencing applications. Both studies reserve an important role in decision process effectiveness and decision benefits, linking these to other intervention elements such as project characteristics, team size, and number of decisions made.

Other scholars have undertaken broader reviews of facilitated modelling applications. Mingers (2000) surveyed reported applications published during the 1990s in reputable, peer-reviewed journals. The review covered applications of methods used in isolation or in combination with other methods. The main areas of application were organisational design, planning, IS/IT, and health services. Schilling et al. (2007) evaluate six applications of 'socio-technical' decision analysis, a combination of multiple criteria decision analysis and decision conferencing. Client organisations are companies and public-sector organisations in Germany. Decision makers in these projects compare decision analysis to their current process of decision making in terms of information exchange, information processing, and results. In addition, Schilling et al. measure change in alignment on decision options. Marttunen et al. (2017) surveyed the peer-reviewed literature covering the 2000–2015 period, reporting on the combined use of facilitated modelling approaches with multi-criteria decision analysis methods.

The most recent review of facilitated modelling approaches to date (reporting on approaches beyond the ones covered in this book) was undertaken by Gomes and Schramm (2021), who surveyed an eclectic mix of journals covering articles published between 2010 and 2020. They found that approaches were used to support the management of problems affecting businesses, society, health care services, and the environment. Franco and Rouwette (2022) conducted a targeted review of facilitated modelling applications published during the 2010–2020 period. The authors searched in Web of Science for publications in mainstream OR journals as well as journals in the field of decision support in which facilitated modelling scholars regularly publish their work. The initial search yielded 143 papers. After excluding papers on 'desktop' applications in which authors do not involve an actual stakeholder group requesting support, 50 papers remained. In nine of these papers (group), causal mapping was used as a single method or in combination with others. The use of group model building and decision conferencing was reported less frequently, in five and two papers, respectively. Approaches were used across a wide range of domains: mining, agriculture and fishing; manufacturing and production; services; information and communication technology, education and R&D; health; government; sustainability; and community.

With regard to scenario planning approaches, a number of academic reviews are available. Cordova-Pozo and Rouwette (2023) bring together 13 of such reviews. In trying to achieve a broad overview of the literature, they used a combination of search terms in the abstract, keywords and title: various terms referring to scenarios (scenario planning, building, thinking) combined with either review, systematic, mapping, or overview. They looked for studies published until December 2021 in five databases: Web of Science, Ebsco, Embase, PubMed, and Scopus. Out of the resulting 13 reviews, only four report on empirical evaluations of the scenario approach. Another eight focus on the concept of scenarios and three on techniques for building scenarios (several reviews report on more than one category). By far the most comprehensive of these reviews is the one by Varum and Melo (2010). Their review aimed to conduct an assessment of academic publications on scenario planning. A broad search in the Science Citation Index Expanded (SCI) and the Social Sciences Citation Index (SSCI) for academic papers published from 1945 to 2006 identifies 101 publications. About one in three publications (37%) is on strategic management. The main other domains in which scenarios are used are change management (13%), technology (13%), economies, government and policies (13%) and finance (9%). Only few papers evaluate effectiveness of scenario planning, although there is no shortage of claimed impacts. Oteros-Rozas et al. (2015) analysed 23 participatory scenario planning case studies conducted by the authors in a wide range of social–ecological settings, and look at learning and shared understanding of future planning. They analyse three impacts of participatory scenario construction, in line with Varum and Melo (2010): generating and achieving legitimacy for policy options; awareness and need for long-term planning including reflection, discussion, shared understanding, and mobilisation for action; and learning.

Several products have been claimed to be the result of the use of facilitated modelling and participatory scenario building. The intended products and the mechanisms claimed to facilitate their achievement, together with supporting evidence of their attainment after use, are discussed in the following sections.

16.2   Claims of intended impact

Table 16.3 displays those products that have been claimed for model-driven team decision support and scenario planning by numerous scholars in relation to their use with single and multi-organisational stakeholder groups (e.g. Eden & Ackerman, 2004; Franco, 2007, 2009; Mingers & Rosenhead, 2004; Rosenhead & Mingers, 2001; Varum & Melo, 2010; Vennix, 1996). We use the term 'products' to refer to the visible and less visible outputs that result from using intervention approaches (Friend & Hickling, 2005). These products may be generated during or at the end of the decision support process, and their actual achievement is thought to be facilitated by specific mechanisms.

The most visible and common product is obviously the final model or set of narratives developed during the team decision process, which describes the agreed problem frame. While each intervention approach captures individual understandings of team members (i.e. how individuals have framed the problem) as well as the ensuing agreed problem frame, each type of model or narrative will represent the agreed-upon problem frame in different ways. In group causal mapping, for example, the problem frame represented by the model will contain a network of statements about issues, goals, and options.

TABLE 16.3 Products claimed for facilitated modelling and scenario planning

Mechanisms	Claimed visible products	Claimed less visible products
• Taxonomy • Model as recording device • Model as transitional object • Model as boundary object • Facilitated, participative process	• Final model or set of narratives containing agreed problem frame • Action plan to address the problem (typically in the form of 'partial commitments')	• Improved communication • Increased shared understanding • Accommodation or transformation of conflicting positions and interests • New knowledge and cognitive change, including acceptance of a wider range of uncertainty • Consensus on, and ownership of, final problem frame and action plan • Commitment to support implementation of action plan

Source: Adapted from Franco and Rouwette (2022)

In group model building, the problem frame will depict the structure underlying observed behaviour, with special emphasis on feedback loops. In scenario planning, the problem frame will be defined in terms of driving forces, alternative configurations of scenario elements, options, and scores on performance indicators.

Although facilitated modelling can be used only for structuring the problem, it must be emphasised that all approaches are intended to facilitate agreements to act (Eden & Ackerman, 2004, 2006). Consequently, a second visible product of team decision support interventions is an action plan or list of planned actions to tackle the problem. Action plans contain a mix of espoused or recommended decisions, policies, or research explorations, and which may or may not include supporting argumentation derived from the model or narratives. Typically, action plans represent only partial commitments on the part of the decision making team because, it is argued, the only way to make progress, in particular, in complex issues is by adopting an incremental approach (Eden & Ackermann, 1998; Friend, 2001; Rosenhead & Mingers, 2001). In scenario planning, this starts from the identification of robust options which subsequently can be translated into more concrete action plans (Cordova-Pozo & Rouwette, 2023).

The agreed problem frame and action plan are the consequence of achieving six less visible yet critical products during the intervention process: improved communication; increased shared understanding of the problem;

accommodation of conflicting positions and interests; new knowledge and cognitive change (including a greater acceptance of uncertainty); consensus on, and ownership of, the final problem frame and action plan; and, commitment to support implementation of the proposed action plan and, where relevant, to maintain group membership.

The achievement of these less visible products is thought to be facilitated by specific mechanisms. The model or set of narratives is built using a specific taxonomy (e.g. issues, goals, and actions in group causal mapping; variables and feedback loops in group model building). By using these taxonomies as a shared language to talk and think about the problem of concern, it is argued that communicative exchanges are more comprehensive and accurate because participants are able to better specify their different perspectives, dependencies, and knowledge about the problem (Akkermans & Vennix, 1997; Franco, 2006, 2013), which results in an improved communication among those involved.

Models and other visualisations support communication in the decision making team because they make it easier to handle a large set of information. They act as recording devices that enable to survey and trace content of team discussions 'on-the-hoof' (Franco, 2013). Better specification of group members' views, dependencies, and knowledge is also thought to be facilitated by the model and visualisations acting as a transitional object (de Geus, 1988; Eden & Ackerman, 2004; Winnicott, 1953; Rosenhead, 1996) which enables experimenting with problem structure. This means that through the analysis of relationships embedded in problem structure and the direct inputs of team members the model is constantly changing, which is thought to increase their shared understanding of the problem situation, of organisational processes and cultures, and of others' beliefs and values. Increased understanding, development of new knowledge, and cognitive change or learning are intimately linked (Checkland, 1981, 1999; Eden & Fran Ackermann, 1998; Franco, 2013; Friend & Hickling, 1997).

The role of conflict was addressed in Chapter 2 and Chapter 15. Increased shared understanding and learning can increase awareness of particular perspectives, knowledge, and interests, which often generates conflict within the team. If the conflict stays at the cognitive level, it is expected that the mutual exploration of problem structure captured by the model or other visualisations (acting as a transitional object) benefit the team in two ways: first, by creating new knowledge and fostering cognitive change (i.e. people changing their minds). A particular form of cognitive conflict is created when team members are confronted with challenging narratives on a plausible future. Given the right distance between current perceived reality and the narrative, team members can come to accept the developments sketched in the narrative as more likely (Schoemaker, 1993). Second, by building consensus on, and ownership of, the final problem frame and the recommendations for action (Eden, 1992; Rosenhead & Mingers, 2001). As described in Chapter 1, team members' anticipations of the consequences, perceived or real, of their increased understanding and learning can sometimes escalate conflict to a relational level (Edmondson & Smith, 2006), especially in complex problems or decisions. Such conflict will commonly require team members to accommodate or transform their positions and interests (Franco, 2013). This is thought to be facilitated if the model, as a transitional object, also becomes a boundary object (Black, 2013; Black & Andersen, 2012; Carlile, 2002; Franco, 2013) during team members' interactions. Chapter 13 described that a model acts as a boundary object if it is able to help group members defuse their entrenched positions and develop common interests. Achieving these accommodations also facilitates new knowledge creation, cognitive change, consensus, and ownership and, in addition, cognitive and emotional commitment (Eden, 1992; Rosenhead & Mingers, 2001) to support the implementation of action plans. Team members' active engagement in the participatory process is also argued to produce strong ownership and commitment (Franco & Montibeller, 2010; Rosenhead & Mingers, 2001).

16.3 Measuring impact

16.3.1 How to assess impact

The majority of the papers included in the reviews of applications are single case studies. These provide a rich description of the complexities facing the decision making team, in terms of problem context and stakeholders. As noted, intervention approaches are flexible and facilitators adapt the standard procedure to the client and problem setting. Studies often cover the procedure applied in the case and the process in detail. This includes the incremental development of visible products and main points of discussion in the team meetings. Claims of less visible products are often based on conversations with members of the decision making team during or immediately after the intervention process. A case study is a natural approach to studying a complex phenomenon in its real-world setting, drawing on multiple sources of data (Yin, 1984). Case studies are, however, less well suited to determine the relations between elements of a decision support intervention, (the process of creating) products, and impacts. (Appendix B gives more information on choices in empirical research concerning data collection and research designs.) In other words, while a case study results in rich information it offers little help in isolating the effective ingredient, or the factor(s) that caused observed changes over time, from the multitude of elements that were present in the case.

Nevertheless, if we are interested in the effectiveness of team decision support interventions, we need to be able to disentangle the effect of different factors. Chapter 6 showed how scenario planning was suspected of only being successful when used by gifted practitioners (Mintzberg, 1994). Finlay (1998, p. 199) levels the same criticism against facilitated modelling approaches: 'There is confounding of many things – of the facilitator him/ herself, of the methodology, of the situation in which the methodology is used, the implementation of any computer-based aid etc.'. In their study of decision conferencing applications, McCartt and Rohrbaugh (1995) find that team members' openness to change was the strongest predictor of reported beneficial outcomes, more so than characteristics of the context or method.

We can look to other academic disciplines for guidance on how to assess the effect of interventions in human or social systems. Establishing the effectiveness of methods and procedures has a long history in the medical sciences and is a more recent phenomenon in for instance education, management, and consulting. Tranfield et al. (2003, p. 210) describe a hierarchy of evidence for effectiveness of healthcare interventions (see Table 16.4). At the lowest level is personal experience: an expert in a particular procedure has found that this approach works. Experiences of a committee of experts carry slightly more weight. At the next level, we find uncontrolled experiments, cohort studies, and case studies. These types of evidence are similar in the sense that no control group is used. Either the group using the procedure is tested before and after the intervention (uncontrolled experiment) or followed through time (cohort study), or the intervention and its impacts are described in a holistic manner (case study). At the highest level of evidence is a randomised controlled trial or a variant of this. Here, the effect of the procedure is compared against a group that does not take part in the intervention.

It is probably clear why this hierarchy of evidence applies to medical studies: we need to be able to exclude other factors that might have an effect (so use control groups), would like to have a pretest and posttest (to determine changes) and test subjects that actually experience the effects of the

TABLE 16.4 Levels of evidence in healthcare

Systematic review and meta-analysis of two or more randomised controlled trials	Experiments
One or more large double-blind randomised controlled trials	
One or more well-conducted cohort studies One or more well-conducted case–control studies	Cases
A dramatic uncontrolled experiment	
Expert committee sitting in review; peer leader opinion	Personal experience
Personal experience	

intervention (without relying on the opinion of the person administering the procedure). When applying this to decision support interventions, an additional concern arises: we would like to test the intervention procedures with the team members whose input is needed to tackle the problem at hand. This creates a problem as doing a randomised trial with this team is virtually impossible. Finding two identical decision problems, addressed by two identical teams is unlikely. Asking a team to split up into two groups that each will use a different procedure to address the same decision problem is also a difficult sell (but see Huz et al., 1997). Some evaluation studies of intervention methods thus rely on situations and groups that are easier to control. Many brainstorming studies use this approach (Stroebe et al., 2010). However, they are vulnerable to the critique that results cannot be generalised as they do not apply to 'real' groups confronted with 'real' messy problems.

One of the earlier arguments against conducting systematic evaluations of the type of decision support intervention discussed in this book was based on the following notion: that any approach to their evaluation must fit the complexity of the intervention because decision support intervention approaches are complex 'technologies' dealing with complex problems (see, for example, Eden, 1995, 2000; Eden & Ackermann, 1996; Finlay, 1998). Eden, for instance, warns that controlled experiments require an extensive structuring of the problem situation in which a method is used, and may lead to a 'controlling out of the experiment' of key elements of the situation and intervention (2000, p. 219). However, these considerations do not mean that the need for evaluation has dwindled within the team decision support community. Indeed, now it is widely accepted that claims about the achievement of decision support interventions can be based not only on self-reflective or impressionistic accounts of intervention success (e.g. Sørensen et al., 2004) or failure (e.g. Houghton, 2013) but also on empirically grounded evaluations (e.g. Franco, 2008; White, 2006). Overall, then, there is clearly a role for formal, systematic evaluations of the actual achievement of claimed intervention products in the team decision support field (Midgley et al., 2013; Rouwette et al., 2009; Westcombe et al., 2006).

Ideally, we would like to conduct an evaluation that optimises both rigour and relevance. *Rigour* is concerned with being able to determine a clear link between the intervention and observed effects, and is a strong point of experiments. *Relevance*, establishing results that apply to the procedure and team we are interested in, is a strong point of case studies. Unfortunately, achieving both rigour and relevance is difficult in practice. Yet it is possible to conduct rigorous case studies (see, e.g. Gibbert et al., 2008). Once we have established expectations on the impact of particular elements of a method and particular effects, relevant experiments can be designed. Clear examples of these are the controlled study on the effect of alternative scenarios on decision making biases (Schoemaker, 1993) and various comparisons of the effect of different model formats (for a review, see Franco et al., 2021). Two approaches to non-experimental evaluation of intervention approaches have emerged in recent years, the first employing an evaluation framework, and the second drawing on social scientific theories.

One evaluation approach to team decision making support is based on the development and use of a *framework* that relates the mechanisms of the intervention to their claimed products and takes into account the context and purpose of the intervention being evaluated. An example is the framework developed by Midgley and colleagues (Midgley et al., 2013), which is based on the tradition of multi-method systemic intervention (Jackson, 2000; Midgley, 2000; Mingers & Brocklesby, 1997). Another one is the meta-framework proposed by Donais et al. (2021), which draws from Chess' (2000) environmental public participation framework. This meta-framework focuses on evaluating multi-criteria decision analysis interventions but is applicable more widely. There are at least two advantages of using an evaluation framework. First, an evaluation framework can inform the development of suitable questionnaires to elicit participants' views before and after the intervention (e.g. Huz et al., 1997), which can then be analysed to produce quantitative evidence of the achievement of intervention products from the perspective of those involved. Second, repeated use of an evaluation framework can help build a corpus of accumulated evidence from different evaluation studies, and subsequently inform the design of further evaluation studies that could add to the corpus of evidence.

The second evaluation approach is *theory-based*, and stems from the need to understand why the products claimed for team decision support interventions were achieved (or not) in a particular application context. A theory-based approach could use an established theory in a 'top-down' fashion to analyse the data generated from the intervention to assess the actual achievement of intervention products. A good example is the study by Rouwette and colleagues (Rouwette et al., 2011), who use Ajzen's (1991) theory of planned behaviour to evaluate seven group model building interventions. Overall, they found that group model building changed participants' attitudes, subjective norms, and intentions, each of which can be related to participants' problem frames, consensus, and commitment, respectively. Alternatively, a theory-based approach could analyse the data generated from the intervention to build a theory 'bottom-up'. Theories developed in this way can provide a locally meaningful evaluation based on how participants make sense of the intervention in which they are engaged (e.g. Henao & Franco, 2016). Some decision support scholars argue that bottom-up explanations must also fit into the broader patterns of interactions within which the modelling intervention is embedded (e.g. White, 2006). In this way, a 'middle-range' theory (Pawson, 2002) can be built to explain why the intervention products were realised (or not), and for whom. Such theory also recognises that using the same intervention in one situation may work, but it may not work in another situation (Franco, 2013; White, 2006).

It is our contention that the framework-based and theory-based approaches to intervention evaluation should be seen as complementary rather than as competing or opposite. Combining the insights generated from the two approaches can provide a richer understanding of the actual achievement of team decision support interventions products than any one approach can provide by itself.

Finally, it is worth noting there is very little written about impacts beyond the intervention. For example, we know little about whether the use of decision support approaches can be linked to positive organisational change or performance. This is not to say that interventions cannot contribute to long-term impacts. Indeed, the high-profile cases by Ormerod at Sainsbury's (Ormerod, 1995, 1996) and by Eden and colleagues at Bombardier (Ackermann et al., 1997; Williams et al., 2003) are a testimony that team decision support interventions can indeed make a tangible and significant difference to organisations beyond the intervention. However, published accounts like these are rare in the literature. In a few cases, team decision support scholars have gone back to stakeholder groups (or the organisations to which they belong) to identify any long-term effects following an intervention (e.g. Franco et al., 2004; Henao & Franco, 2016; McCartt & Rohrbaugh, 1989, 1995; Rouwette & Smeets, 2016). Yet, again, these are the exception rather than the rule. For example, the study of group causal mapping applications by Abuabara and Paucar-Caceres (2021) indicated that the use of the approach has been mostly limited to achieving products within, rather than beyond, the interventions they surveyed. This should not come as a surprise: it would be very difficult to claim long-term impacts given the myriad of uncontrollable factors, both within and outside the team using decision support environment, that could affect the implementation and impact of recommendations. This is unfortunate, as not being able to demonstrate the link between intervention and long-term organisational impacts can make their dissemination and take up more difficult.

16.3.2 Levels of impact

What does it mean to say a particular intervention approach creates impact? In the preceding sections, we noted that the effect of the intervention needs to be separated from that of the person doing the intervention, and from the contextual factors having to do with the problem situation, organisation, or team involved in the decision. Beyond the simple procedures described in Chapter 3, the four advanced procedures outlined in later chapters are complex interventions that lead a decision making team through various divergent, convergent, and prioritisation phases. The four methods approach problems from different angles (for instance, problem structure in group model building, uncertain futures in participatory scenario development, decision options and their impact on criteria in decision conferencing) and aim to create specific visible products. Nevertheless, they share a foundation in facilitation and visualisation using models and narratives, as described in Chapters 13, 14, and 15. They are also similar in their use of basic methods, which is most evident in the divergent phase as they all use nominal group technique or (electronic) brainstorming. This shared foundation in facilitation principles as well as similar use of basic methods is important, as it means we can establish effectiveness at three levels: at the generic level of facilitation, at the level of particular 'complex' methods, and at the specific level of basic methods that constitute some of the 'building blocks' of the latter. Table 16.5 organises the steps in the four advanced decision support intervention approaches into problem setting, divergent, convergent, and prioritisation phases.

The efficacy of nominal group technique and electronic brainstorming (in comparison to freely interacting or brainstorming groups) has been shown in a series of studies (Stroebe et al., 2010). This means that in the divergent

TABLE 16.5 Opening, divergent, convergent, and prioritisation phases and steps in four intervention approaches

	Group model building	*Participatory scenario development*	*Group causal mapping*	*Decision conferencing*
Opening	1. Identify problem variable and reference mode of behaviour	1. Formulate starting issue or question	1. Introduce topic	1. Introduce decision context and intervention approach
Divergence	2. Identify variables 6. Identify control and target variables	2. Identify trends (SEPTE) 5b. Determine policies and indicators	2. Gather issues 3. Develop clusters 7. Develop goals system 9. Develop solutions	2. Identify resource allocation areas and benefits 3. Specify options available for each area

(*Continued*)

TABLE 16.5 (Continued)

	Group model building	Participatory scenario development	Group causal mapping	Decision conferencing
Convergence	3. Identify causal relations 4. Check feedback loops 5. Check validity	3. Cluster trends 6. Translate into scenarios and write texts 7. Determine impact on transactional environment	4. Develop means-ends structure of clusters 5. Identify central issues 9. Identify potent loops and options	4. Evaluate costs and benefits of each option 5. Determine within-criterion weights 6. Determine across-criteria weights 9. Conduct sensitivity analysis
Prioritisation		4. Score clusters on uncertainty and impact 5a. Determine driving forces and elements 8. Determine robust options	6. Rate central issues 10. Prioritise solutions and agree on actions	7. Calculate overall benefits and identify efficient frontier 8. Explore feasible portfolios 10. Recommend portfolio

phase, scenario planning and model-driven team decision support rely on well-tested approaches. In the convergent and prioritisation phases, there are some similarities (e.g. the use of clustering, ranking, and voting) but overall this is where the largest differences between methods are evident.

Methods are also clearly similar in their use of facilitation. In Chapter 13, facilitator attitudes were outlined which formed the basis for a set of facilitator tasks in supporting decision making teams. Table 13.1 summarised the rationale for each attitude which was drawn from empirical research on group and organisational decision making. In the same vein, Chapter 12 presented the research by Nutt (2002), who found that in a dataset of 400 decision making situations, about one in four decisions were made in a process of joint discovery with stakeholders. Joint discovery, in comparison to top-down decisions, leads to a faster decision making process, more implementation, and better outcomes. Joint discovery is similar to facilitation in the important sense that it gives stakeholders a voice in (and the opportunity to influence) the decision making process. Nutt's study and other research into the effectiveness of facilitation provide are an empirical base for the effectiveness of the facilitator actions as outlined in Chapters 13, 14, and 15.

16.4   Evidence of impact

In this section, we discuss the evidence for claimed effects of intervention approaches to team decision support. These were listed as the less visible products in Table 16.3: communication, shared understanding, accommodation of interests, new knowledge and cognitive change, consensus, and commitment to implementation.

For two of the four approaches to team decision support, participatory scenario development and group causal mapping, few evaluation studies are available. The review of scenario planning by Varum and Melo (2010) identifies 101 academic papers of which 41% are empirical. Varum and Melo find it difficult to come to a conclusion on effectiveness due to the variety in domains of application and different methodologies that go under the name of scenario planning. After analysing applications in companies in more depth, Varum and Melo (2010, p. 365) conclude that 'there is a notable lack of research on the use and effects of scenario planning in business'. The 23 applications of participatory scenario planning analysed by Oteros-Rozas et al. (2015) provide some evidence of positive impacts. They find scenarios help to generate policy options and increase the legitimacy and acceptance of policy options across stakeholders. Second, scenario planning creates awareness, an increased need for long-term planning, and enables collective reflection and discussion. In this way, a shared understanding is built and stakeholders are mobilised into action. Third, by increasing dialogue and resolving conflicts, scenarios enhance individual and collective learning. The review on SODA by Abuabara and Paucar-Caceres (2021) identifies 200 published applications, of which only 19 are participatory and so are applications of group causal mapping. Unfortunately, Abuabara and Paucar-Caceres do not report on impacts of these applications.

The evidence on the impact of any of the group decision support approaches outlined in this book consists mostly of case studies. For example, in the case of group model building applications, Rouwette et al. (2002) note that out of 107 applications, 88 gather evaluation data in the main through observation that informs personal reflection. And although we cannot disregard the reflections of highly experienced facilitated modelling scholars and practitioners, we should exercise caution: personal reflections alone are not reliable evidence of impacts. Self-reporting as a sole basis of evaluations is fraught with difficulties, as people struggle to distinguish between subjective and objective effects associated with group decision support (De Gooyert et al.,

2022; Rouwette, 2016). In the few cases where questionnaires or interviews have been used to support the evaluation of team decision support interventions, very few or no details are given on the recruitment of the sample of respondents and interviewees, the impact of the sample on data collection, or the data analysis approach employed.

Overall, systematic evaluations are rather scarce in the literature. Exceptions are two early studies on decision conferencing by McCartt and Rohrbaugh (1989, 1995), and a limited number of more recent studies identified by Franco and Rouwette (2022). McCartt and Rohrbaugh (1989, 1995) applied decision conferences through the Decision Techtronics Group of the State University of New York. A cross section of projects representative of different types of client organisations was selected, resulting in 14 respectively 26 applications. Questionnaires were sent to all participants in these projects. Measures included elements of the context, process in terms of decision process effectiveness (including openness to change), and impacts in terms of the number of decisions made and decision making effectiveness. Key results are the following. Team members felt that in the majority of projects (60% and 70%, respectively), important decisions had been made. Most projects were also judged to be effective, in terms of both process and outcomes (only about one-third of the projects in the first study and one-fourth in the second were rated low on these aspects). In the second study, team members' openness to change, favouring a flexible, creative process over thorough analysis of all data, was the strongest predictor of reported beneficial outcomes.

More recent systematic evaluations on team decision support interventions are reviewed by Franco and Rouwette (2022). The authors searched for decision support evaluation studies in a broad set of journals, but for the 20-year period between 2000 and 2020, they only found 12 studies that assessed whether the products listed in Table 16.3 had been realised after the intervention. Notably, almost all studies evaluated group model building interventions. The remaining study evaluated decision conferencing. Overall, evaluation studies of practical group model building interventions (e.g. Rouwette, 2016; Rouwette et al., 2002; Scott et al., 2016) provide evidence for a positive impact on communication, cognitive change (learning), consensus, commitment, and implementation of results. Recent studies (e.g. de Gooyert et al., 2021; Valcourt et al., 2020) lend further support to an effect on consensus and alignment. However, it has proven difficult to reproduce these results in controlled environments (McCardle-Keurentjes, 2015). In their study on decision conferencing interventions, Schilling et al. (2007) use questionnaire data on six cases and found a positive effect on commitment and team alignment on solutions.

16.5 Critical reflection and questions for the future

Overall, surveys and academic reviews show that modelling and scenario planning for group decision support are used across a wide range of domains, in complex real-world problem settings. Moreover, over the years the number of published applications has increased (Cordova-Pozo & Rouwette, 2023; Franco & Rouwette, 2022). Decision support approaches are based on facilitator guidelines which are supported by empirical research (see Chapter 13). In particular in the divergent phase, they employ methods such as nominal group technique and electronic brainstorming that have been evaluated extensively (Stroebe et al., 2010). However, the procedures as a whole also include convergent and often prioritisation activities and use particular visualisations (types of models, narratives) that are thought to help team members in gathering and processing information. Practitioners and researchers alike claim that team decision support interventions consistently leads to certain impacts. These include visible products such as a model or set of narratives, and an action plan. More difficult to establish are less visible products such as an increase in quality of communication, shared understanding, accommodation of interests, new knowledge, consensus on problem frame and action plan, and commitment to implementation of actions.

Overviewing the literature on interventions that use scenarios and models, the evidence that these impacts materialise is accumulating. In particular, the impact on cognitive change (new knowledge) and alignment (consensus) is now shown in several studies in real-world settings, using a pretest–posttest design (e.g. de Gooyert et al., 2021; Rouwette et al., 2011; Valcourt et al., 2020). Implementation of actions has been observed in a range of case studies (McCartt & Rohrbaugh, 1989, 1995; Schilling et al., 2007). A number of in-depth studies (e.g. Franco, 2006; Rouwette, 2016) trace the impact of model-driven interventions on communication. One claimed outcome of group decision support that remains understudied is the accommodation or transformation of interests. We noted in Chapter 13 that models (or narratives, for that matter) have the potential to align interests but may not be sufficient. More research on this claimed impact of interventions is needed. It is at present not clear if results of one intervention approach can be generalised to another approach that uses a different type of model, or narratives instead of a model. We note therefore that while there are certainly many publications on participatory scenario development and group causal mapping, relatively few of these are evaluation studies.

So, all in all, do we think the intervention approaches to team decision support described in this book are evidence-based? Our answer is a careful 'yes', based on the combination of evidence from real-world applications in the form of cases and systematic evaluations of particular intervention impacts. When used by a trained facilitator, we feel confident that these intervention approaches reliably help teams working on complex issues to – among others – improve their quality of communication, build their understanding, and arrive at a consensus on what the problem is about and what to do about it.

Which directions are important for future research? We noted three topics of interest: alignment of interests as an understudied impact, differential impacts of model (or visualisation) formats, and two particular approaches (participatory scenario construction and group causal mapping) that can be evaluated in more depth. Three ways to approach this come to mind. First, the surveys and academic reviews in this chapter in the main looked at published work in academic journals. Incorporating (chapters of) books, conference papers and grey literature will expand the scope of reviews. Second, rigorous case studies or comparative field experiments, using consistent research methods, can help to explore meaningful differences between approaches or, keeping the approach constant, between contexts (e.g. Scott et al., 2015). Third, differences in model or visualisation formats can be explored in relevant experiments, building on results of controlled studies on other Operational Research/Management Science interventions (Franco et al., 2021). The approaches outlined in this book concentrate on and are most different in the convergent phase. While there is ample research on divergent processes, procedures that are effective in convergence deserve to be studied in more depth.

The next chapter gives more guidance on how to conduct and research team decision support interventions.

References

Abuabara, L., & Paucar-Caceres, A. (2021). Surveying applications of Strategic Options Development and Analysis (SODA) from 1989 to 2018. *European Journal of Operational Research*, 292(3), 1051–1065. https://doi.org/10.1016/j.ejor.2020.11.032

Ackermann, F., Eden, C., & Williams, T. (1997). Modeling for litigation: Mixing qualitative and quantitative approaches. *Interfaces*, 27(2), 48–65.

Ajzen, I. (1991). The theory of planned behavior. *Organizational Behavior and Human Decision Processes*, 50(2), 179–211.

Akkermans, H. A., & Vennix, J. A. M. (1997). Client's opinions on group model building: An exploratory study. *System Dynamics Review*, 13(1), 3–31.

Black, L. J. (2013). When visuals are boundary objects in system dynamics work. *System Dynamics Review*, 29(2), 70–86. https://doi.org/10.1002/sdr.1496

Black, L. J., & Andersen, D. F. (2012). Using visual representations as boundary objects to resolve conflict in collaborative model-building approaches. *Systems Research and Behavioral Science*, 29(2), 194–208.

Bradfield, R., Wright, G., Burt, G., Cairns, G., & Van der Heijden, K. (2005). The origins and evolution of scenario techniques in long range business planning. *Futures*, 37(8), 795–812.

Carlile, P. R. (2002). A pragmatic view of knowledge and boundaries: Boundary objects in new product development. *Organization Science*, 13, 442–455.

Checkland, P. (1981). *Systems thinking, systems practice*. Wiley.

Checkland, P. (1999). *Soft systems methodology: A 30-year retrospective*. Wiley.

Chess, C. (2000). Evaluating environmental public participation: Methodological questions. *Journal of Environmental Planning and Management*, 43(6), 769–784. https://doi.org/10.1080/09640560020001674

Chun, K.-J. (1992). *Analysis of decision conferencing: A UK/USA comparison* [PhD dissertation]. London School of Economics & Political Science.

Cordova-Pozo, K., & Rouwette, E. A. J. A. (2023). Types of scenario planning and their effectiveness: A review of reviews. *Futures, 149.* https://doi.org/10.1016/j.futures.2023.103153

de Geus, A. (1988). Planning as learning. *Harvard Business Review, 66*(2), 70–74.

De Gooyert, V., Rouwette, E. A. J. A., Van Kranenburg, H. L., Freeman, E., & Van Breen, H. (2022). Cognitive change and consensus forming in facilitated modelling: A comparison of experienced and observed outcomes. *European Journal of Operational Research, 229*(2), 589–599. https://doi.org/10.1016/j.ejor.2021.09.007

Donais, F. M., Abi-Zeid, I., Waygood, E. O. D., & Lavoie, R. (2021). A framework for post-project evaluation of multicriteria decision aiding processes from the stakeholders' perspective: Design and application. *Group Decision and Negotiation, 30*(5), 1161–1191. https://doi.org/10.1007/s10726-021-09753-y

Eden, C. (1992). A framework for thinking about group decision support systems (GDSS). *Group Decision and Negotiation, 1*, 199–218.

Eden, C. (1995). On evaluating the performance of 'wide-band' GDSS's. *European Journal of Operational Research, 81*, 302–311.

Eden, C. (2000). On evaluating the performance of GSS: Furthering the debate, by Paul Finlay (*European Journal of Operational Research*, 107, pp. 193–201) – a response by Colin Eden. *European Journal of Operational Research, 81*(120), 218–222.

Eden, C., & Ackermann, F. (1996). "Horses for courses". A stakeholder approach to the evaluation of GDSSs. *Group Decision and Negotiation, 5*, 501–519.

Eden, C., & Ackermann, F. (1998). *Strategy making: The journey of strategic planning.* SAGE.

Eden, C., & Ackermann, F. (2004). Use of 'soft OR' methods by clients, what do they want from them? In M. Pidd (Ed.), *Systems modelling: Theory and practice* (pp. 146–163). Wiley.

Eden, C., & Ackermann, F. (2006). Where next for problem structuring methods. *Journal of the Operational Research Society, 57*(7), 766–768.

Edmondson, A. C., & Smith, D. M. (2006). Too hot to handle? How to manage relationship conflict. *California Management Review, 49*(1), 6–31.

Finlay, P. (1998). On evaluating the performance of GSS: Furthering the debate. *European Journal of Operational Research, 107*(1), 193–201.

Franco, L. A. (2006). Forms of conversation and problem structuring methods: A conceptual development. *Journal of the Operational Research Society, 57*, 813–821.

Franco, L. A. (2007). Assessing the impact of problem structuring methods in multi-organisational settings: An empirical investigation. *Journal of the Operational Research Society, 58*(6), 760–768.

Franco, L. A. (2008). Facilitating collaboration with problem structuring methods: A case of an inter-organisational construction partnership. *Group Decision and Negotiation, 17*(4), 267–286.

Franco, L. A. (2009). Problem structuring methods as intervention tools: Reflections from their use with multi-organizational teams. *OMEGA: The International Journal of Management Science, 37*(1), 193–203.

Franco, L. A. (2013). Rethinking soft OR interventions: Models as boundary objects. *European Journal of Operational Research, 231*(2), 720–733.

Franco, L. A., Cushman, M., & Rosenhead, J. (2004). Project review and learning in the UK construction industry: Embedding a problem structuring method within a partnership context. *European Journal of Operational Research, 152*(3), 586–601. https://doi.org/10.1016/S0377-2217(03)00065-1

Franco, L. A., Hämäläinen, R. P., Rouwette, E. A. J. A., & Leppänen, I. (2021). Taking stock of behavioural OR: A review of behavioural studies with an intervention focus. *European Journal of Operational Research*, 293(2), 401–418.

Franco, L. A., & Montibeller, G. (2010). Facilitated modelling in operational research (invited review). *European Journal of Operational Research*, 205(3), 489–500.

Franco, L. A., & Rouwette, E. A. J. A. (2022). Problem structuring methods: Taking stock and looking ahead. In S. Salhi & J. Boylan (Eds.), *The Palgrave handbook of operations research* (pp. 735–780). Springer.

Friend, J. (2001). The strategic choice approach. In J. Rosenhead & J. Mingers (Eds.), *Rational analysis for a problematic world revisited: Problem structuring methods for complexity, uncertainty and conflict* (pp. 115–149). Wiley.

Friend, J., & Hickling, A. (1997). *Planning under pressure: The strategic choice approach* (2nd ed.). Butterworth- Heinemann.

Friend, J., & Hickling, A. (2005). *Planning under pressure: The strategic choice approach* (3rd ed.). Elsevier.

Gibbert, M., Ruigrok, W., & Wicki, B. (2008). What passes as a rigorous case study? *Strategic Management Journal*, 29, 1465–1474.

Gomes, A. D. A., Jr, & Schramm, V. B. (2021). Problem structuring methods: A review of advances over the last decade. *Systemic Practice and Action Research*, 1–34.

Henao, F., & Franco, L. A. (2016). Unpacking multimethodology: Impacts of a community development intervention. *European Journal of Operational Research*, 253(3), 681–696. https://doi.org/10.1016/j.ejor.2016.02.044

Hodgkinson, G. P., & Wright, G. (2002). Confronting strategic inertia in a top management team: Learning from failure. *Organization Studies*, 23, 949–977.

Houghton, L. (2013). Why can't we all just accommodate: A soft systems methodology application on disagreeing stakeholders. *Systems Research and Behavioral Science*, 30(4), 430–443. https://doi.org/10.1002/sres.2136

Huz, S., Andersen, D. F., Richardson, G. P., & Boothroyd, R. (1997). A framework for evaluating systems thinking interventions. An experimental approach to mental health system change. *System Dynamics Review*, 13(2), 149–169.

Jackson, M. (2000). *Systems approaches to management*. Kluwer.

Linneman, R. E., & Klein, H. E. (1983). The use of multiple scenarios by United States industrial companies – a comparison study, 1977–1981. *Long Range Planning*, 16(6), 94–101. https://doi.org/10.1016/0024-6301(83)90013-4

Malaska, P. (1985). Multiple scenario approach and strategic behaviour in European companies. *Strategic Management Journal*, 6(4), 339–355.

Martelli, A. (2001). Scenario building and scenario planning: State of the art and prospects of evolution. *Futures Research Quarterly*, 17(2), 57–74.

Marttunen, M., Lienert, J., & Belton, V. (2017). Structuring problems for multi-criteria decision analysis in practice: A literature review of method combinations. *European Journal of Operational Research*, 263(1), 1–17.

McCardle-Keurentjes, M. H. F. (2015). *Facilitated modelling and hidden profiles. An experimental evaluation of group model building*. Radboud University.

McCartt, A. T., & Rohrbaugh, J. (1989). Evaluating group decision support effectiveness. A performance study of decision conferencing. *Decision Support Systems*, 5, 243–253.

McCartt, A. T., & Rohrbaugh, J. (1995). Managerial openness to change and the introduction of GDSS – explaining initial success and failure in decision conferencing. *Organization Science*, 6(5), 569–584.

Meristö, T. (1989). Not forecasts but multiple scenarios when coping with uncertainties in the competitive environment. *European Journal of Operational Research, 38*(3), 350–357.

Midgley, G. (2000). *Systemic intervention: Philosophy, methodology, and practice.* Kluwer Academic/Plenum Publishers.

Midgley, G., Cavana, R., Brocklesby, J., Foote, J., Ahuriri-Drscoll, A., & Wood, D. (2013). Towards a new framework for evaluating systemic problem structuring methods. *European Journal of Operational Research, 229*(1), 143–154.

Mingers, J. (2000). Variety is the spice of life. Combining soft and hard OR/MS methods. *International Transactions in Operational Research, 7*, 673–691.

Mingers, J., & Brocklesby, J. (1997). Multimethodology: Towards a framework for mixing methodologies. *Omega-International Journal of Management Science, 25*(5), 489–509.

Mingers, J., & Rosenhead, J. (2004). Problem structuring methods in action. *European Journal of Operational Research, 152*, 530–554.

Mintzberg, H. (1994). *The rise and fall of strategic planning.* Prentice-Hall.

Munro, I., & Mingers, J. (2002). The use of multimethodology in practice – results of a survey of practitioners. *Journal of the Operational Research Society, 53*(4), 369–378.

Nutt, P. (2002). *Why decisions fail. Avoiding the blunders and traps that lead to debacles.* Berrett-Koehler.

O'Brien, F. A. (2011). Supporting the strategy process: A survey of UK OR/MS practitioners. *Journal of the Operational Research Society, 62*(5), 900–920.

Ormerod, R. J. (1995). Putting soft OR methods to work: Information systems strategy development at Sainsbury's. *Journal of Operational Research Society, 46*(3), 277–293.

Ormerod, R. J. (1996). Information systems strategy development at Sainsbury's supermarkets using "soft" OR. *Interfaces, 26*(1), 102–130.

Oteros-Rozas, E., Martin-Lopez, B., Daw, T. M., Bohensky, E. L., Butler, J. R. A., Hill, R., Martin-Ortega, J., Quinlan, A., Ravera, F., Ruiz-Mallen, I., Thyresson, M., Mistry, J., Palomo, I., Peterson, G. D., Plieninger, T., Waylen, K. A., Beach, D. M., Bohnet, I. C., Hamann, M., Hanspach, J., Hubacek, K., Lavorel, S., & Vilardy, S. P. (2015). Participatory scenario planning in place-based social-ecological research: Insights and experiences from 23 case studies. *Ecology and Society, 20*(4), 66, Article 32. https://doi.org/10.5751/es-07985-200432

Pawson, R. (2002). Evidence-based policy: The promise of realist synthesis. *Evaluation, 8*(3), 340–358.

Phillips, L. D. (2007). Decision conferencing. In W. Edwards, R. Miles Jr, & D. von Winterfeldt (Eds.), *Advances in decision analysis: From foundations to applications* (pp. 375–399). Cambridge University Press.

Ranyard, J. C., Fildes, R., & Hu, T.-I. (2015). Reassessing the scope of OR practice: The influences of problem structuring methods and the analytics movement. *European Journal of Operational Research, 245*(1), 1–13. https://doi.org/10.1016/j.ejor.2015.01.058

Rosenhead, J. (1996). What's the problem? An introduction to problem structuring methods. *Interfaces, 29*(6), 117–131.

Rosenhead, J., & Mingers, J. (Eds.). (2001). *Rational analysis for a problematic world revisited: Problem structuring methods for complexity, uncertainty and conflict.* Wiley.

Rouwette, E. A. J. A. (2016). The impact of group model building on behavior. In M. Kunc, J. Malpass, & L. White (Eds.), *Behavioral operational research: Theory, methodology and practice* (pp. 213–241). Palgrave Macmillan. https://repository.ubn.ru.nl/bitstream/handle/2066/178390/178390pos.pdf

Rouwette, E. A. J. A., & Smeets, S. (2016). Conflict, consensus and the management of a good debate: Exploring the deliberative assumptions of group facilitating techniques. In I. Bleijenbergh, H. Korzilius, & E. A. J. A. Rouwette (Eds.), *Methods, model building and management: A liber amicorum for Jac Vennix* (pp. 129–146). Institute for Management Research.

Rouwette, E. A. J. A., Korzilius, H., Vennix, J. A. M., & Jacobs, E. (2011). Modeling as persuasion: The impact of group model building on attitudes and behavior. *System Dynamics Review*, 27(1), 1–21. https://doi.org/10.1002/sdr.441

Rouwette, E. A. J. A., Vennix, J. A. M., & Felling, A. J. A. (2009). On evaluating the performance of problem structuring methods: An attempt at formulating a conceptual model. *Group Decision and Negotiation*, 18(6), 567–587.

Rouwette, E. A. J. A., Vennix, J. A. M., & Van Mullekom, T. (2002). Group model building effectiveness. A review of assessment studies. *System Dynamics Review*, 18(1), 5–45.

Schilling, M. S., Oeser, N., & Schaub, C. (2007). How effective are decision analyses? Assessing decision process and group alignment effects. *Decision Analysis*, 4(4), 227–242.

Schoemaker, P. J. H. (1993). Multiple scenario development: Its conceptual and behavioral foundation. *Strategic Management Journal*, 14, 193–213.

Scott, R. J., Cavana, R. Y., & Cameron, D. (2015). Recent evidence on the effectiveness of group model building. *European Journal of Operational Research*, 249(3), 908–918.

Scott, R. J., Cavana, R. Y., & Cameron, D. (2016). Client perceptions of reported outcomes of group model building in the New Zealand public sector. *Group Decision and Negotiation*, 25(1), 77–101. https://doi.org/10.1007/s10726-015-9433-y

Sørensen, L., Vidal, R., & Engstrom, E. (2004). Using soft OR in a small company: The case of Kirby. *European Journal of Operational Research*, 152(3), 555–570. https://doi.org/10.1016/S0377-2217(03)00065-1

Stroebe, W., Nijstad, B. A., & Rietzschel, E. (2010). Beyond productivity loss in brainstorming groups: The evolution of a question. *Advances in Experimental Social Psychology*, 43, 157–203.

Tranfield, D., Denyer, D., & Smart, P. (2003). Towards a methodology for developing evidence-informed management knowledge by means of systematic review. *British Journal of Management*, 14, 207–222.

Valcourt, N., Walters, J., Javernick-Will, A., & Linden, K. (2020). Assessing the efficacy of group model building workshops in an applied setting through purposive text analysis. *System Dynamics Review*, 36(2), 135–157.

Varum, C. A., & Melo, C. (2010). Directions in scenario planning literature–a review of the past decades. *Futures*, 42(4), 355–369.

Vennix, J. A. M. (1996). *Group model building. Facilitating team learning using system dynamics*. Wiley.

Westcombe, M., Franco, L. A., & Shaw, D. (2006). Where next for PSMs – a grassroots revolution? *Journal of the Operational Research Society*, 57(7), 776–778.

White, L. (2006). Evaluating problem structuring methods: Developing an approach to show the value and effectiveness of PSM interventions. *Journal of the Operational Research Society*, 57(7), 842–855.

Williams, T., Ackermann, F., & Eden, C. (2003). Structuring a delay and disruption claim: An application of cause-mapping and system dynamics. *European Journal of Operational Research*, 148(1), 192–204.

Winnicott, D. W. (1953). Transitional objects and transitional phenomena: A study of the first not-me possession. *International Journal of Psycho-Analysis*, 34(2), 89–97.

Yin, R. (1984). *Case study research. Design and methods*. SAGE.

17

BUILDING SKILLS FOR THE STUDY AND PRACTICE OF INTERVENTIONS

Team decision support intervention is an active area of research. Judging from the number of published applications, its use is growing over time. There is every reason to expect its continued usage in the future, as there is no lack of issues that are complex in both an analytical and a social sense. However, for that to happen, methods need to continue to be developed and adapted to new circumstances. New generations of practitioners will need to be supported in developing their skills in team decision support intervention. We think in this respect it is useful to consider research and intervention in combination. First, because broadly speaking, team decision support practitioners conduct 'research' in the sense of investigating a problem located within a system of interest. Similar to empirical research, their aim is to create insights that are empirically grounded and analytically sound. However, practitioners go beyond insight as they also aim to create an action plan that will be implemented. This goal is similar to action research. Second, evaluating team decision support interventions is important to practitioners, clients, and researchers. For practitioners, knowing more on what worked and what did not is a crucial basis for professional development. Clients often want to know more about the visible and less visible products of a team decision support intervention. Researchers can use insights into method effectiveness to adapt existing methods or develop new ones. Third, academics who are also practitioners want to report applications and method development in peer-reviewed journals. Clarity on how intervention research is similar or different to other types of research helps to motivate methodological choices.

We start this chapter by contrasting intervention research to other forms of research. We discuss differences and similarities in terms of data collection and research design. Theory-driven research, action research, and

DOI: 10.4324/9781003404200-21

intervention research are compared. Next, we describe different approaches to evaluating team decision support interventions. The final section offers further guidance on how to become a competent practitioner in team decision support.

17.1   Interventions as a form of research

In this section, we highlight how intervention research differs from other types of research. An important distinction is theory-driven versus practice-driven research. The quality of theory-driven research is measured against classic criteria such as validity and reliability, which indicate how much confidence we can have in the insights derived from a study. For practice-driven research, another criterion is at least as important: relevance to the stakeholders concerned. A particular type of practice-driven research, action research, offers a range of options to work towards confidence and relevance.

17.1.1   Theory-driven research

There is a wide diversity of types and aims of empirical research. A researcher can choose from three types of research designs: a survey or an experiment, typically used in quantitative research, and a case study, predominantly used in qualitative research. A researcher also needs to consider which data source to draw on: situations, texts, individuals, or groups. (Appendix B provides more information on data collection methods and research designs.) In choosing among these options, a researcher is guided by both the type of research question and aim of the study.

Research can aim to contribute mainly to theory or practice (Vennix, 2019). In the first case, the researcher is primarily interested in learning more about certain phenomena, so generating knowledge for its own sake is the ultimate aim. Her audience then primarily consists of other academic researchers, who will carefully pore over each methodological step and check the novelty of the study's results. Interestingly, checking methodology does not include defining the starting question. Methodology is about whether a claim to knowledge is justified, not about where the claim comes from (Vennix, 2019). The start of research, that is, the moment when an idea suddenly springs to mind, or a new connection between events appears, is said to be in the 'context of discovery' (Reichenbach, 1964). There are examples of researchers staring into a fire or sitting under a tree when the new insight suddenly hits them.

Methodology is not about the discovery phase but about the next steps: translating an idea into concepts, definitions, and measurements; setting up a study; and gathering data and analysing results. These next steps constitute the 'context of justification' which is of interest to methodologists. Two quality criteria are particularly important here. Validity refers to the extent to which measures represent the concept as intended. Reliability refers to the stability of measurements: will we get the same results if a test is taken again at a later time, or when administered by another person? Checking research against these criteria tells us how confident we can be in results.

Research for the sake of building understanding can of course be very relevant to practical life. Scientific discoveries have led to medical and technological breakthroughs that have changed the life of many people. Nevertheless, this form of research is 'fundamental' or *theory-driven* and whether or not results can be applied is of secondary concern. In contrast, in applied or *practice-driven* research, the practical problem is the starting point. Here, the audience is a team of people representing an organisation, multiple organisations, or societal groups. This audience has a much more pronounced role in shaping the research. It is not so much a forum to whom the researcher defends methodological choices and novelty of results after the research is completed but has an active role from the start and throughout the study. In practice-driven research, stakeholders have a say in the formulation of the research question and are a major source of information throughout the study. They have to have confidence in results, but at least as important is whether results are relevant to their issue of concern. In other words, this type of research aims not only to create novel understanding but also to enable participants to change their situation. Some forms of practice research emphasise creation of insights and employ methods similar to theory-driven studies. One particular form of practice research, action research, puts equal emphasis on achieving change.

17.1.2 Action research

The term 'action research' was introduced by Kurt Lewin (1946) to refer to his studies on social change and group relations. He saw the role of action research as helping practitioners change social reality. Lewin inspired the development of a particular approach to empirical research that has continued to develop and adapt to circumstances. Major application areas are community development and organisational decision making. Three characteristics set action research apart from other forms of research: its participatory, emancipatory, and scholarly nature (Bleijenbergh et al., 2023). Participatory means that both the researcher and the researched are involved in the research. This has consequences for the position of the researcher. Instead of being a neutral observer of the situation or of research 'subjects', the researcher is involved in the change process. The emancipatory nature of action research is illustrated by Lewin's efforts in supporting the democratisation of society by developing knowledge that improves the situation of minority groups (Bleijenbergh et al., 2023; Lewin, 1946). The aim to improve the situation of particular groups that are affected by a problem is therefore a necessary element of action research, and in an organisational context it should at least support solving problems for (groups of) individuals who are directly affected by the issue (Eden & Huxham, 1996). The scholarly nature of action research follows from the unique type of knowledge it can bring to light. It assumes that participation is necessary to really understand what is going on in any problem in which human action plays a role. Lewin summarised the basic idea behind this approach as 'if you want to understand something, try to change it'. Studies based on observations by outsiders, or even interviews with people involved in the problem, may not be adequate to find the real reason for observed behaviour in the problem.

Argyris and Schön (1974) find that if people are asked to explain their behaviour, what they will answer reveals their espoused theory. They have no direct access to their reasons for behaving as they do. Alternatively, they may be reluctant to share their opinions as they want to portray themselves in a particular way, for instance, to appear competent or knowledgeable. In terms of Argyris and Schön, real reasons for behaviour are part of the theory in use. The theory in use can only be inferred from action in the problem situation. In Chapter 1, we discussed System 1 and System 2. Not knowing the real reason for one's own behaviour is much like System 2 trying to determine why System 1 reacts in a particular way. Action research thus assumes that if we knew the real trigger for behaviour, taking away that trigger would lead to different behaviours. Without testing our understanding in this way, we are not sure about the validity of our knowledge. To achieve this level of understanding the researcher needs to work closely with stakeholders and not remain an outsider.

How are these characteristics reflected in action research studies? Bleijenbergh et al. (2023) review 317 action research papers published between 2005 and 2020 in leading management journals. A case study is the most often used research design and only very few studies use a survey or experiment. Researchers and participants work together for an extended period of time; the average duration of a study is no less than 30 months. The participatory nature of action research is apparent in the studies reviewed. In about half of the studies, participants took part in the research process based on co-production of knowledge, together with the researchers. In about one-third, the researcher took a role as a consultant, most often involving the participants as discussion partner. With regard to the emancipatory nature, apparently in management studies action research has a less radical aim than originally envisaged. Only about one in six papers discussed action research that explicitly targets giving a voice to specific groups or improving a specific group's situation; most papers (about two out of three) aim to improve organisational processes. Regarding the scholarly aim, papers focused mostly on theory development (about half) and method development (about one in three). Thus, although action research studies aim to generate knowledge relevant to participants, published studies also highlight the contribution to advances in theories or methods. Bleijenbergh et al. (2023) find that action researchers rely on a range of criteria to assess the quality of their research. Relevance and validity are among the most often used criteria (both by two out of three studies), reliability only in about one in three studies.

17.1.3 Comparison theory-driven research, action research and intervention research

Table 17.1 compares three forms of research. We see that in theory-driven research both the starting question and the researcher are placed 'outside' of the study. The research question is taken as a given and the researcher should influence the study as little as possible. All data sources are used. In the case of theory development a qualitative design and analysis method will be used. Nevertheless, we can expect most studies aim to test hypothesised relations and employ a quantitative design and analysis method. The main aim is to contribute to knowledge, which means validity and reliability of knowledge claims are the main quality criteria.

TABLE 17.1 Comparison of theory-driven research, action research and intervention research

	Theory-driven research	Action research (a form of practice-driven research)	Intervention research
Starting question	Outside of research (context of discovery)	May be given or adapted in study	Essential part of research (problem structuring)
Position researcher	Does not participate	Participates, works closely with participants	Participates, co-creates with participants, is neutral towards content
Data source	All (situations, texts, individuals, teams)	One or more teams as main source, also uses situations, texts, individuals	One or more teams as main source, additional sources (interviews, secondary data) may be used
Research design	Quantitative (survey, experiment) and qualitative (case study)	Mainly qualitative (case study), quantitative (survey, experiment) is possible	Case study

	Theory-driven research	Action research (a form of practice-driven research)	Intervention research
Data analysis	Standard quantitative analysis (e.g. statistics, simulation), process analysis (e.g. sequence analysis, optimal matching), may use qualitative analysis	Standard qualitative analysis (e.g. content analysis, discourse analysis, grounded theory analysis), may use quantitative and process analyses	Joint development of model or narrative, may be validated against other data
Quality criteria	In the main validity, reliability	Relevance, validity, less emphasis on reliability	Relevance, validity, less emphasis on reliability

The starting question is in both action and intervention research part of the research process. Both types of research give participants a say in determining the focus of the study. Team decision support interventions are, however, more explicit about the need to structure the problem in close interaction with the participant group (Franco & Rouwette, 2022). Since the problem is often interpreted differently by those concerned, finding out what the problem is all about is a major part of the intervention. In both action and intervention research, the researcher actively works with participants. Team decision support interventions, as described in Chapter 13, assign the interventionist the role of a facilitator who remains neutral with regard to content. Action researchers and interventionists see working with teams as an important part of the research. This is not only because a team is an important data source, one that allows for eliciting insights and testing these against other opinions (which can be seen as a form of validation, cf. Bleijenbergh et al., 2011), but also because of its impact on participants. Participation in the team allows one to witness firsthand the emergence of novel ideas, provide counterarguments, and shape the team process and outputs. In contrast, if a person only participates in a study by providing data, the final results will reach her later in the form of a presentation or a paper report. Chapter 13 presented several arguments as to why participation is particularly effective in fostering implementation.

In terms of research design, action research predominantly is qualitative but quantitative designs can be used (Bleijenbergh et al., 2023). Interventions seem to have much in common with case studies. The study concerns a real-life situation that is often complex, thus making it difficult to determine what is in focus and what is part of the context. This requires finding out about central factors and their interrelationships, which mainly draws on the interpretations of participants in the study. Both participants' interpretations and the observations by team members are the main data source but may be tested against other (secondary or interview) data. Using other independent datasets to check interpretations in a process of triangulation supports validation. It means the researcher does not have to work on the assumption that 'the answer is in the room' (Geurts et al., 2006). Data analysis in theory-driven research comes down to standard quantitative techniques (e.g. statistics, simulation) or more specialised process analysis techniques (e.g. sequence analysis, optimal matching), but qualitative analysis techniques may also be used. In contrast, action research mainly uses qualitative analysis techniques (e.g. content analysis, discourse analysis, grounded theory analysis), but quantitative and process analysis techniques may also be used. In intervention research, the joint development of a model or narrative is the main analysis tool. Finally, both action and intervention researches focus on relevance and validity as quality criteria. Action and intervention research place less emphasis on reliability as they are practical and situation-specific, which means that repeating a study is fraught with problems (Bleijenbergh et al., 2011).

17.2 Evaluating team decision support interventions

The discussion in this section will focus on the empirical investigation of the practice of using team decision support 'as it happens' (Franco & Greiffenhagen, 2021) on the ground. This puts the human, social and organisational challenges associated with their practical use centre stage. These challenges are well known to decision support practitioners, but their empirical interrogation is typically absent from published accounts of team decision support interventions. This can only be done by examining what practitioners and users actually do when they engage in a team decision support intervention, which places the study of intervention practice within the domain of the behavioural and social sciences. A similar concern is shared by Operational Research scholars working within the sub-discipline of Behavioural Operational Research (Brocklesby, 2016; Franco & Hämäläinen, 2016a, 2016b; Franco et al., 2021). Treating practice as a research problem demands specific competencies that are distinct from those of mainstream academics and practitioners working in this field. Here, the discussion will concentrate on what are more likely to be the main options regarding research methodology open to researchers interested in studying practice, the variance approach and the process approach, as well as the required competencies for implementing these options[1] (Franco & Rouwette, 2022).

First, researchers can adopt the so-called *variance* approach (Mohr, 1982; Poole et al., 2000) to investigate team decision support use. In general terms, variance research seeks explanations of change in terms of relationships among independent variables and dependent variables. Explanations take the form of causal statements captured in a theory-informed research model that incorporates these variables (e.g. A causes B, which causes C). The model is then tested with data generated by the team decision support intervention, and the model findings are assessed in terms of their generality. The variance approach for investigating team decision support interventions requires the implementation of quasi-experimental or 'pretest and posttest' research designs (see Appendix B). This involves careful selection of independent variables, which might be either manipulated (e.g. method, computer support) or left untreated (e.g. experience, demographics). It also requires choosing and measuring dependent variables that act as surrogates of the less visible products claimed for team decision support interventions (e.g. learning, consensus; see Chapter 16). Measurements can be taken in absolute or relative terms, and can also include perceptions about intervention outcomes (e.g. commitment, confidence) and the intervention itself (e.g. satisfaction, usefulness), which can only be measured subjectively via self-reports. Variables that act as either covariates or moderators through which independent variables influence the dependent variables (e.g. 'conflict' as moderating the relation between 'method' and 'consensus') can also be included. Once information about all variables is collected, data are quantitatively analysed using a wide range of statistical techniques (e.g. analysis of variance, regression, structural equation modelling). Generally speaking, the competencies that are required to conduct variance research align well with those of a quantitative social science researcher: review the literature and identify relevant theory, formulate hypotheses, test these empirically, and then develop a causal explanation that further specifies the theory. Indeed, the few systematic evaluation studies of team decision support interventions discussed in the previous chapter adopt have adopted a variance approach.

Despite its obvious appeal to the mainstream team decision support researcher, a variance approach will only produce explanations that contain a small number of variables, which will not always be applicable in cases where the overall intervention outcome is both complex and emergent. If the interest is in understanding how team members respond to events and circumstances within an intervention, and how their responses affect results, then team decision support researchers can adopt what is known as the *process* approach (Mohr, 1982; Poole et al., 2000). Generally speaking, process research seeks explanations of how a sequence of events leads to an outcome. Rather than using variables, a process approach considers an evolving actor (individual, group, organisation) to which events occur or who makes events happen as the unit of analysis. Process explanations provide 'thick' narratives that account for how one event led to another, and that one to another, and so on to the final outcome (Poole, 2007). Diverse and eclectic research designs are used to implement a process approach, and central to these designs is the task of identifying or reconstructing the intervention process through the analysis of activity and events taking place over time. Typically, process studies derive theory inductively from observation and ethnographic-type methods, which requires collecting and analysing large amounts of qualitative and quantitative data from which a process explanation is developed. It is also possible to test theory-informed models of the intervention process, or use theories to guide empirical observation in an 'abductive' or 'retroductive' mode (Mingers, 2012), which then further specifies the theories (Poole et al., 2000).

It might be apparent that the demands placed on the researcher wishing to implement a process approach are higher than if a variance approach is adopted. Specifically, becoming acquainted with theories from the social sciences, as well as gaining competence in social science research methodologies is not straightforward. Yet the process approach has attracted growing attention of team decision support scholars in recent years (e.g. Ackermann & Eden, 2011; Ackermann et al., 2018; Burger, 2020; Franco, 2013; Franco & Greiffenhagen, 2018; Shaw et al., 2003; Tavella & Franco, 2015; Tavella et al., 2020; Tully et al., 2018; White, 2009; White et al., 2016). It is worth noting that not all process research presents the same challenges for those wishing to adopt it. As Brocklesby (2016) notes, some types of process research represent a more feasible proposition for a wider population of team decision support researchers (e.g. Ormerod, 2014a). For those interested in pursuing more complex types of process research, there are several heuristics and systems available in the literature that include both qualitative (e.g. Langley, 1999; Pentland, 1999) and quantitative (Poole et al., 2000) process research.

17.3 How to become a competent intervention practitioner

What are the competencies required to deploy team decision support in practice? In a review of the extant literature that examines team decision support competencies, Ormerod (2014b) identifies core competencies under three broad headings: conducting analysis, designing and managing process, and appreciating context. Developing these competencies is often best done through apprenticeship, in which a novice has access to observing an expert in action, as well as applying the methods in practice. However, apprenticeship opportunities like this are not always available. Instead, university programmes that incorporate team decision support into the curriculum, as well as specialist team decision support training courses offered by expert providers, have traditionally addressed this gap. Here, there are two approaches to developing team decision support competencies. The first one aims to develop competencies via small consulting projects with a real organisation, in which participants can have hands-on experience in using team decision support under the supervision of an academic with team decision support expertise. When conducting projects is a formal part of a university programme or training course, then this approach to develop team decision support competencies is the closest to the apprenticeship model.

The second approach is to develop team decision support competencies in the classroom, but this is significantly more challenging for those teaching, and being taught, team decision support (Ackermann, 2011). The size of the challenge will depend on the specific competencies that are the target of development. For example, competence in conducting model-based analysis requires mastery of qualitative modelling techniques, which can be developed via experiential learning (e.g. Williams & Dickson, 2000), case studies, and the understanding gained from 'textbook' descriptions of various team decision support interventions, such as those presented by Rosenhead and Mingers (2001) or Reynolds and Holwell (2010). Although the use of experiential learning tasks, case studies, and textbooks cannot replicate the complex reality of team decision support practice, this approach is nonetheless effective for helping novices develop a minimum level of desk-based analytic competence in team decision support. Similarly, the need to develop competencies in appreciating the complexity of the context in which team decision support is deployed can somewhat be addressed by sharing the personal experiences of team decision support teachers and trainers with students and trainees.[2] This can be complemented by bringing former clients into the classroom to talk about their experience of facing past problem situations and discuss how useful they found team decision support interventions in tackling those situations (Ackermann, 2011).

By contrast, developing competencies in designing and managing process is significantly more challenging, particularly within the boundaries of a standard university programme or training course. This requires designing a learning environment that not only can bring the real world of team decision support practice into the classroom but also one that provides learning materials that capture the uncodified tacit knowledge of team decision support experts, which is not revealed in textbooks (Keys, 2006). To gain competence in designing and managing the process, the general approach seems to be engaging team decision support novices in meaningful tasks in which they have a stake (Ackermann, 2011; Carreras & Kaur, 2011), or tasks based on realistic consultancy projects (e.g. Hindle, 2011). Such approaches aim to provide opportunities for team decision support novices to develop experience in performing tasks that are typical of team decision support interventions such as, for example, preparing a proposal, interviewing, facilitating a group, presenting results, and recognising and justifying the added value brought by the use of team decision support interventions. This is a useful way to build competence one that can help novices to move beyond just having desktop qualitative modelling skills and an appreciation of context.

Any approach to competence building needs to carefully consider which knowledge and skills are basic and need to be built first, providing a basis for more advanced competencies, and so on. To take one example, the Business Analysis and Modelling a master programme (part of the European Master in System Dynamics)[3] aims to build students' competencies in group model building. The programme starts by building system dynamics modelling and analysis skills. This serves to familiarise students with the 'language' that will be used in group modelling sessions. After this part, students will be able to build models individually, using documents, one-on-one interviews, databases, and/or academic papers as an input. To introduce them to using a team as a data source, they first engage in a group model building session as participants. The idea here is that they are 'immersed' in the situation, and get a firsthand experience of the sometimes confusing reality of a modelling workshop. At some moments, the session seems to progress smoothly and the team is engaged in a task. At other times everything seems to be happening at once, for instance, when a difficult-to-model problem is discussed while some team members give every sign of having run out of energy. Building the model and working with the team sometimes pull in opposite directions, and the facilitator needs to decide on the spot which deserves her attention first. This is followed by several sessions in which students alternate between the role of facilitator and participant. In each session, the facilitators guide the team of participants through a series of preselected scripts (Ackermann et al., 2011; Andersen & Richardson, 1997).[4] A member of staff who is experienced in group model building is present during the session and leads a round of debriefing at the end. After having built experience with a range of scripts in a 'simulated setting' (with fellow students), in the next course period students are brought into contact with a public or private organisation that wants help in deciding on a complex issue. Students do the intake, select team members with the contact person, design and facilitate sessions, and report to the client organisation. A coach is available to discuss design choices or reflect on (intermediate) results. This way of working has been employed since 2010 and generally led to satisfied clients and positive reactions from students. Many students subsequently engage in group model building projects as part of their master theses.

It is worth noting, however, that the students' first engagement with a real-world issue, with participants from actual public or private organisations, may exhibit a high level of complexity, uncertainty, and conflict but does typically not involve interpersonal conflicts or large power differences. In this sense, even these real-world situations are still 'sanitised' versions of the situations for which team decision support interventions were developed. We feel that while scripts contain a clear and well-defined set of expected behaviours by intervention participants and are very useful didactic devices, working in situations of interpersonal conflict and power differences requires more than the use of scripts. Indeed, we feel that the third of Ormerod's (2014b) core competencies, appreciating context, is probably the most difficult to develop. It requires in-depth knowledge of the strengths and limitations of different decision support approaches, and the ability to combine elements to develop a session design that fits the situation at hand (Rouwette, 2022).

We do not mean to say that such scripts are divorced from real intervention practice. The main issue resides in their inability to capture the interactional and situated specifics of using team decision support interventions in practice, which is an aspect certainly well known to team decision support experts. In other words, scripts must be 'accomplished' on the ground, and therefore cannot determine or prescribe what intervention participants actually do *in situ* (Franco & Greiffenhagen, 2018). They need to work in a meeting in which at some moments multiple things happen at once.

To the extent that the current approach to develop competencies in designing and managing process, and its supporting learning materials, does not fully correspond to actual practice, team decision support students and trainees are at a disadvantage. An approach to competence building based on real intervention practice will need to be informed by research that collects and analyses interventions as performed by experts on the ground (e.g. Franco & Greiffenhagen, 2018; Franco & Nielsen, 2018). Analyses of multiple instances of recorded intervention practice can identify the actual organisation and trajectories of different intervention tasks and activities, with a view to identifying what works and what does not. With the knowledge accrued from these analyses it would be possible, for example, to develop facilitation 'role plays' grounded in the actual, rather than simulated, activities of anonymised facilitators. The structure of such role plays could be designed in a way that the trajectory of a given facilitated task would only be revealed after students and trainees do something at a particular point in time.[5]

In this way, building our knowledge on what works in team decision support interventions, and under which circumstances, helps to improve training for decision support facilitators and adapt decision support to new challenges. Ultimately, we hope this book contributes to combining smart analysis with stakeholder involvement. In our view, this combination is urgently needed given the many pressing challenges societies wrestle with today. The interplay of societal, ecological, and economic goals makes it likely that issues in the future will be as complex if not more complex than the ones we face today and that more stakeholders will want to have a say. To address these issues, we can build on the evidence-based approaches described in this book.

Notes

1. It is worth noting that both the variance and process approaches presented here can be adopted in theory-driven and practice-driven research (see Section 17.1).
2. Some intervention approaches also contain specific tools to gain an appreciation of context, for example, the use of 'rich pictures' and analysis I, II, and III (cultural

stream analysis) in soft systems methodology (Checkland, 2000) or the 12 questions on boundary critique in critical systems heuristics (Ulrich & Reynolds, 2010).

3. For more information on the BAM master programme, see www.ru.nl/opleidingen/masters/business-analysis-and-modelling. More information on the EMSD programme is on www.europeansystemdynamics.eu/.

4. A script is a repeatable element of process that, if used in a specified context consistently yields similar outcomes. A typical script covers 15 to 20 minutes of a session. Scripts for different phases of teamwork are accessible online via Scriptapedia (https://en.wikibooks.org/wiki/scriptapedia). See Chapter 4 for more information.

5. This approach to competence building has been pioneered in other professional fields such as mediation (Stokoe, 2014) and education (Kane & Staiger, 2012).

References

Ackermann, F. (2011). Getting "messy" with problems: The challenges of teaching "soft" OR. *INFORMS Transactions on Education, 12*(1), 55–64.

Ackermann, F., Andersen, D. F., Eden, C., & Richardson, G. P. (2011). Scripts-Map: A tool for designing multi-method policy-making workshops. *Omega, 39*, 427–434.

Ackermann, F., & Eden, C. (2011). Negotiation in strategy making teams: Group support systems and the process of cognitive change. *Group Decision and Negotiation, 20*(3), 293–314. https://doi.org/10.1007/s10726–008–9133-y

Ackermann, F., Yearworth, M., & White, L. (2018). Micro-processes in group decision and negotiation: Practices and routines for supporting decision making. *Group Decision and Negotiation, 27*(5), 709–713. https://doi.org/10.1007/s10726-018-9590-x

Andersen, D. F., & Richardson, G. (1997). Scripts for group model building. *System Dynamics Review, 13*(2), 107–129.

Argyris, C., & Schön, D. A. (1974). *Theory in practice: Increasing professional effectiveness.* Jossey-Bass.

Bleijenbergh, I., Korzilius, H., Rouwette, E. A. J. A., & Van der Wal, M. (2023). The quality of action research in the field of management: The usefulness and relevance of actionable knowledge. Under Review at European Management Review.

Bleijenbergh, I. L., Korzilius, H., & Verschuren, P. (2011). Methodological criteria for the internal validity and utility of practice oriented research. *Quality & Quantity, 45*, 145–156.

Brocklesby, J. (2016). The what, the why and the how of behavioural operational research: An invitation to potential sceptics. *European Journal of Operational Research, 249*(3), 796–805. https://doi.org/10.1016/j.ejor.2015.09.034

Burger, K. (2020). Understanding participant engagement in problem structuring interventions with self-determination theory. *Journal of the Operational Research Society.* https://doi.org/10.1080/01605682.2020.1790307

Carreras, A. L., & Kaur, P. (2011). Teaching problem structuring methods: Improving understanding through meaningful learning. *INFORMS Transactions on Education, 12*(1), 20–30.

Checkland, P. (2000). Soft systems methodology: A thirty year retrospective. *Systems Research and Behavioral Science, 17*, 11–58.

Eden, C., & Huxham, C. (1996). Action research for management research. *British Journal of Management, 7*(1), 75–86.

Franco, L. A. (2013). Rethinking soft OR interventions: Models as boundary objects. *European Journal of Operational Research*, *231*(2), 720–733.

Franco, L. A., & Greiffenhagen, C. (2018). Making OR practice visible: Using ethnomethodology to analyse facilitated modelling workshops. *European Journal of Operational Research*, *265*(2), 673–684. https://doi.org/10.1016/j.ejor.2017.08.016

Franco, L. A., & Greiffenhagen, C. (2021). Group decision support practice 'as it happens'. In D. M. Kilgour & C. Eden (Eds.), *Handbook of group decision and negotiation* (2nd ed., Vol. 2, pp. 793–814). Springer International Publishing. https://doi.org/10.1007/978-3-030-49629-6

Franco, L. A., & Hämäläinen, R. P. (2016a). Behavioural operational research: Returning to the roots of the OR profession. *European Journal of Operational Research*, *249*(3), 791–795. https://doi.org/10.1016/j.ejor.2015.10.034

Franco, L. A., & Hämäläinen, R. P. (2016b). Engaging with behavioural OR: On methods, actors, and praxis. In M. Kunc, J. Malpass, & L. White (Eds.), *Behavioural operational research: Theory, methodology and practice* (pp. 3–26). Palgrave Macmillan. https://doi.org/10.1057/978-1-137-53551-1

Franco, L. A., Hämäläinen, R. P., Rouwette, E. A. J. A., & Leppänen, I. (2021). Taking stock of behavioural OR: A review of behavioural studies with an intervention focus. *European Journal of Operational Research*, *293*(2), 401–418.

Franco, L. A., & Nielsen, M. F. (2018, May 29). Examining group facilitation in situ: The use of formulations in facilitation practice. *Group Decision and Negotiation*, *27*(5), 735–756. https://doi.org/10.1007/s10726-018-9577-7

Franco, L. A., & Rouwette, E. A. J. A. (2022). Problem structuring methods: Taking stock and looking ahead. In S. Salhi & J. Boylan (Eds.), *The Palgrave handbook of operations research* (pp. 735–780). Springer.

Geurts, J., Altena, C., & Geluk, B. (2006). Interventie door interactie. Een vergelijkende beschouwing [Intervention by interaction. A comparison.]. *M&O*, *3/4*, 322–351.

Hindle, G. A. (2011). Case article – Teaching soft systems methodology and a blueprint for a module. *INFORMS Transactions on Education*, *12*(1), 31–40. https://doi.org/10.1287/ited.1110.0068ca

Kane, T. J., & Staiger, D. O. (2012). Gathering feedback for teaching: Combining high-quality observations with student surveys and achievement gains. Research paper. MET project. Bill & Melinda Gates Foundation. 1–64. https://files.eric.ed.gov/fulltext/ED540960.pdf

Keys, P. (2006). On becoming expert in the use of problem structuring methods. *Journal of the Operational Research Society*, *57*, 822–829.

Langley, A. (1999). Strategies for theorising from process data. *Academy of Management Review*, *24*(4), 691–710.

Lewin, K. (1946). Action research and minority problems. *Journal of Social Issues*, *2*(4), 34–46.

Mingers, J. (2012). Abduction: The missing link between deduction and induction. A comment on Ormerod's 'rational inference: Deductive, inductive and probabilistic thinking'. *Journal of the Operational Research Society*, *63*(6), 860–861.

Mohr, L. (1982). *Explaining organizational behavior*. Jossey-Bass.

Ormerod, R. J. (2014a). The mangle of OR practice: Towards more informative case studies of 'technical' projects. *Journal of the Operational Research Society*, *65*(8), 1245–1260.

Ormerod, R. J. (2014b). OR competences: The demands of problem structuring methods. *EURO Journal on Decision Processes*, 2(3–4), 313–340.

Pentland, B. T. (1999). Building process theory with narrative: From description to explanation. *Academy of Management Review*, 24, 711–724.

Poole, M. S. (2007). Generalization in process theories of communication. *Communication Methods and Measures*, 1(3), 181–190.

Poole, M. S., van de Ven, A. H., Dooley, K., & Holmes, M. E. (Eds.). (2000). *Organizational change and innovation processes: Theory and methods for research*. Oxford University Press.

Reichenbach, H. (1964). *The rise of scientific philosophy*. University of California Press.

Reynolds, M., & Holwell, S. (Eds.). (2010). *Systems approaches to managing change: A practical guide*. Springer.

Rosenhead, J., & Mingers, J. (Eds.). (2001). *Rational analysis for a problematic world revisited: Problem structuring methods for complexity, uncertainty and conflict*. Wiley.

Rouwette, E. A. J. A. (2022). *System dynamics and power*. International System Dynamics Conference, Frankfurt. https://proceedings.systemdynamics.org/2022/papers/P1155.pdf

Shaw, D., Ackermann, F., & Eden, C. (2003). Approaches to sharing knowledge in group problem structuring. *Journal of the Operational Research Society*, 54(9), 936–948.

Stokoe, E. (2014). The Conversation Analytic Role-play Method (CARM): A method for training communication skills as an alternative to simulated role-play. *Research on Language and Social Interaction*, 47(3), 255–265.

Tavella, E., & Franco, L. A. (2015). Dynamics of group knowledge production in facilitated modelling workshops: An exploratory study. *Group Decision and Negotiation*, 24(3), 451–475.

Tavella, E., Papadopoulos, T., & Paroutis, S. (2020). Artefact appropriation in facilitated modelling: An adaptive structuration theory approach. *Journal of the Operational Research Society*, 1–15. https://doi.org/10.1080/01605682.2020.1790308

Tully, P., White, L., & Yearworth, M. (2018). The value paradox of problem structuring methods. *Systems Research and Behavioral Science*, 36(4), 424–444.

Ulrich, W., & Reynolds, M. (2010). Critical systems heuristics. In M. Reynolds & S. Holwell (Eds.), *Systems approaches to managing change: A practical guide* (pp. 243–292). Springer.

Vennix, J. A. M. (2019). *Research methodology. An introduction to scientific thinking and practice*. Pearson.

White, L. (2009). Understanding problem structuring methods interventions. *European Journal of Operational Research*, 99(3), 823–833.

White, L., Burger, K., & Yearworth, M. (2016). Understanding behaviour in problem structuring methods interventions with activity theory. *European Journal of Operational Research*, 249(3), 983–1004. https://doi.org/10.1016/j.ejor.2015.07.044

Williams, T., & Dickson, K. (2000). Teaching real-life OR to MSc students. *Journal of the Operational Research Society*, 51(12), 1440–1448.

APPENDIX A: BASIC INTERVENTIONS

This section outlines the procedures of a set of basic interventions: brain-storming, nominal group technique, devil's advocate, dialectical inquiry, and simple prioritisation techniques.

A1. Brainstorming

Brainstorming is a term introduced in a book by Osborn in the 1950s. In order to apply brainstorming in a group setting, a number of principles and steps are important. Osborn (1957, p. 84) describes the following principles:

1. criticism is not permitted: the participants do not evaluate each other's ideas
2. free-wheeling is welcome: the wilder the idea, the better
3. quantity is good: the more ideas there are, the better the chance of a good idea
4. we are looking for combination and improvement: by building on each other's ideas, or combining ideas, new and better ideas are created

The principles can be applied in a number of ways. One possible procedure is the following:

Discussing the problem and the rules

Participants are invited to take part in the session with a specific aim. They are experts and/or stakeholders in a specific area and are asked to use their knowledge to gather as many ideas as possible about a topic. The meeting therefore begins with a clear delineation of the problem that will be the focus of the session. As stated in the course description, every participant has already read up on a role within the case. The central problem in the session therefore involves the case, but you are free to choose a more specific problem that is important to the organisation concerned. After this, the group members will explain the aforementioned principles in their own words.

Reformulate the problem and choosing a starting question

You now refine the problem to a very specific question that you present to the group. Formulate an open and specific question in order to begin the brainstorming session. Osborn (1957) gives a number of examples. Do not formulate the question during the session, but do this beforehand.

Warming up

To help the participants become comfortable with the creative assignment, it is a good idea to let them practice briefly with a fictional problem that does not involve the organisation concerned. This warming up is also a useful exercise for practising the rules of brainstorming (especially the first one: do not evaluate).

Make notes about the flow of ideas

To make sure that people can build on each other's ideas, make notes about all ideas in a way that is visible to everyone. While making notes about the ideas, try to use the participant's own words as much as possible. Also make sure that the notes of the contributions are not too long.

'Wildest idea'

If the flow of ideas dries up after a time, you can get it going again by asking for the wildest idea that anyone can imagine. Decide beforehand how you will present this question to the group.

A2. Nominal group technique

Nominal group technique is described in the book by Delbecq et al. (1975). The full procedure includes a round of voting at the end. This is left out here so that the steps support only the divergent phase of group decision making.

Remind the group of the problem

Write the central problem in the centre of a whiteboard or blackboard.

Introduce contributing ideas

Ask the participants to write down ideas about things that involve the problem variable. Be clear about the format you are looking for, for instance, when the aim is to gather variables for group model building, the following specification of format can be used. Indicate to participants that ideas may be on causes or consequences of the problem, or any elements a participant feels are important to the issue at hand. Ask the participants to do this as much as possible in terms of variables. If it is not possible to formulate an idea as a variable, it does not really matter; the facilitator and the rest of the group can work together to find a variable.

Invite participants to note down ideas

Give the participants a few minutes to write down their own ideas.

Introduce gathering ideas

Explain that you are going to gather ideas and show them on the board or computer screen for everyone to see. Ask each participant for one idea and write this on the whiteboard or blackboard. Pay attention to the conversion into variables and check to see if the other group members know what the person contributing to the idea means. Allow a clarification of meaning, but not a discussion on the relevance or importance of the idea. Explain that in this phase, the person contributing the idea has the last word: if he or she prefers a particular formulation even if other objects, the proposed formulation will be put on the central board or screen.

Stop collecting ideas after two or three rounds. Emphasise that the aim of this phase is only to create an initial list of variables so that model building can begin, and that variables that were not written on the board for the group are not automatically discarded. During the model building process, variables from the individual lists or even entirely new variables can be added.

A3. Devil's advocacy

Devil's advocacy is an approach to improve the quality of strategic plans (Janis, 1982). The plan is attacked by one or more persons playing the devil's advocate who try to demonstrate all that is wrong with the plan. The following are the steps involved in devil's advocacy:

1. Divide the group into two subgroups; one subgroup is assigned the role of devil's advocate.

2. One subgroup (not the devil's advocate) develops written recommendations accompanied by arguments which are supported by all key assumptions, facts, and relevant data.

3. The first subgroup presents its written recommendations to the devil's advocate group.

4. The devil's advocate group develops a formal written critique in which they attempt to uncover all that is wrong with the recommendations or assumptions. The subgroup presents their critique is presented to the first group

5. The other group revises its original recommendations based on the critique.

6. These steps are repeated until both subgroups can accept the recommendations.

7. The final recommendations are written down.

A4. Dialectical inquiry

The devil's advocacy approach asks for critiquing a plan with the aim to improve it. However, using this approach runs the following risks (Mason, 1969). First, although it may help to expose some of the plan's underlying assumptions, it does so in the context of what is wrong. It does not serve to develop a new managerial world view. Second, if the negative critique prevails and the plan is rejected there is no new plan to replace it. Third, there is a tendency for the team offering the critique to have a destructive rather than constructive attitude. Fourth, in response to extended criticism, the decision maker's psychological response might be to come up only with safe plans for the future.

One way to implement dialectical inquiry is the following (Roberto, 2013):

1. Divide the team into two subgroups.

2. Subgroup 1 develops a proposal, fleshing out the recommendation, key assumptions, and supporting data.

3. Subgroup 1 presents the proposal to Subgroup 2 in written and oral form.

4. Subgroup 2 develops a detailed critique of these assumptions and recommendations. It presents this critique in written and oral form.

5. Subgroup 1 revises its proposal based on the feedback.

6. The subgroups continue in this revision–critique–revision cycle until they converge on a shared set of assumptions.

7. Based on those assumptions, the subgroups work together to develop a common set of recommendations.

A5.   Simple prioritisation techniques

A basic approach to prioritisation is voting by using sticky dots. This involves the following steps:

1. Participants are each given a set number of sticky dot stickers.
2. Participants are instructed that they can put all of their dots next to one idea, or divide them over different ideas.
3. Participants place dots next to the ideas they like.
4. Ideas are prioritised from top (most dots) to bottom (fewest dots).

A variation is to give participants dots of different colours, for instance, green dots to indicate liking and one or a few red dots indicating 'vetoes'. Another alternative is to not use 'physical' dots but a limited number of votes. When these are collected by the facilitator in front of the plenary group, an element of excitement is added ('which option will win?'). Do keep in mind that if some ideas end with a roughly equal number of votes, the last team members can swing the vote from one idea to another.

APPENDIX B: CHOICES IN DATA COLLECTION AND RESEARCH DESIGN

B.1 Data collection methods

Empirical research comes in many different forms. Data sources are a useful starting point for classifying types of research (Vennix, 2019). Some data that are relevant to a study may already exist, in either 'raw' or unprocessed form, or processed. Raw data come in various formats, for instance, as texts or visual material. Processed data are, for example, provided by various commercial and government organisations that conduct surveys, such as a polling agency that reports on approval rates of politicians or policies. If a researcher gathers new data, there are in principle three sources to turn to real-world situations, people, and texts. If we subdivide people further into individuals and groups, we come to the following overview of data sources and data collection methods.

All of these data sources can have a role in research on team decision support interventions. For instance, in their study on group model building,

TABLE B.1 Data sources and data collection methods

Data source	Data collection method	Versions
Situation	Observation	Quantitative, qualitative non-participatory, qualitative participatory
Text	Content analysis	Quantitative, qualitative
Individual	Survey	Written questionnaire or oral interview; more or less structured
Group	Group interview	More or less structured

Source: Adapted from Vennix (2019, p. 146)

Huz et al. (1997) use data from meeting observations (situations), archival analysis of meeting agendas and summary notes (texts), between meeting interviews (individuals) and facilitation team reflections (groups).

B.2 Research designs

As can be seen in Table B.1, each data collection method has a qualitative and quantitative version. At first sight, qualitative and quantitative may be taken to refer to the type of data generated: text or numbers. However, arriving at these results implies particular choices in research design at the start of the study. Quantitative (or empirical–analytical) research departs from a clear idea of central concepts and their relations. Each concept is defined and operationalised, meaning that corresponding measurements are selected. For instance, in quantitative research, observations would require an observation protocol (Vennix, 2019). If a researcher wants to observe a particular phenomenon, it will be described and operationalised into observables. A protocol will be constructed for observers to follow, so that they know which behaviours to record (code) and observations do not depend on the person doing the coding. Qualitative (or interpretative) research would not use an observation protocol but observe more freely. Researchers in this tradition might also choose to participate in the situation.

These two main types of research – quantitative and qualitative – tend to use different research designs, although a strict categorisation is a too simple representation of the large variety of research approaches that are used in practice. Qualitative research is typically associated with a case study. A case study investigates a phenomenon in its real-life context, in which the boundaries between the phenomenon and context are not clearly demarcated, and multiple sources of evidence are used (Yin, 1984). (Some of these sources may contain quantitative data.) The study by Huz et al. (1997) is clearly a case study as it contrasts data from different sources and works towards an understanding of how the modelling intervention and organisational context together shape project results. Using multiple sources of data allows for checking if an interpretation based on one data source also holds when other types of data are considered. This process of confronting several independent datasets and checking them against each other is called triangulation. Quantitative research often takes the form of a survey or experiment. A survey as a research design (not to be confused with a survey as data-gathering method) is a way to gather data on a large number of objects in a systematic manner. It is probably best known for opinion polls, in which the objects are individual people who all answer the same set of questions. But 'objects' can be anything, for instance, items on stock in petrol stations across Europe, or the number of days in a year with temperatures above 30 °C. In many ways, a survey takes the opposite approach from a case study. Where a survey results in limited data on a large set of research objects, a case study gathers a lot of data on one or a few research objects. The final research design is the experiment (Cook & Campbell, 1979). Here, the researcher manipulates a variable (the stimulus or the treatment) and observes the effect on another variable. To determine that there is an effect means, we have to find out if there is a change over time, meaning that a pretest and posttest are needed. To increase confidence that the effect was actually caused by the stimulus, additional measures can be taken. A control group can be used that does not receive the stimulus but might receive another treatment that is not effective (a placebo). If an effect is found for the experimental group but not for the control group, we have more confidence that the stimulus caused the change. Nevertheless, this so-called pretest–posttest control group design does not rule out the possibility that differences between participants that existed before the experiment influenced results. For instance, imagine we design a classroom experiment and place students in groups as they register. If we place all students registering early in the experimental group, and those who are late in the control group, we might inadvertently at the same time create a difference in motivation (to the extent that time of registration is an indicator for motivation). By using randomisation, the effect of pre-existing differences between the experimental and control groups is neutralised as far as possible. An experiment is ideally suited for research into causality (Vennix, 2019).

In Chapter 14, we looked at levels of evidence for interventions (Tranfield et al., 2003). We noted that for assessing effectiveness of medical interventions, case studies carry less weight than a randomised experiment. The preceding discussion of research designs hopefully makes clear why. An experiment is better at isolating the actual cause for change from a host of other factors in the context. Nevertheless, a case study is a logical design to research how a particular team decides on a particular, unique, complex issue. While a single-case study may not give much confidence in establishing a link between method and impact, as more case studies are added in which the method is held constant but decision makers and issues vary, confidence increases.

B.3 Choosing between research designs and data collection methods

How does a researcher choose between different research designs and data collection methods? The first consideration here is the type of research question that the researcher is interested in. In the examples of experiments earlier, the researcher is looking into cause-and-effect relations. That means she is seeking to answer an explanatory question. Before being able to provide an explanation, or put differently to establish a causal relation between factors, we need clear definitions and operationalisations of each factor. Here, we see again that an experiment fits within the quantitative tradition of research: before data are collected, we need to know exactly what we are looking for.

Definitions and measurements can be derived from theories and previous empirical research, or developed anew. In novel situations, it may not be clear whether existing theories and insights apply which makes open exploration a useful first step. Imagine a researcher in the early 2000s, at the time when social media are rapidly becoming more popular. If he wants to know more about the role of new media in the life of teenagers, he is interested in an explorative question. Once central concepts, definitions, and measurements become more clear, descriptive questions can be asked (e.g. how many hours per day does a teenager in the UK on average spent on a particular type of social media?). These could then lead to explanatory questions (e.g. does extraversion explain number of hours spent on social media?). In other words, at least three types of research questions can be distinguished: explorative, descriptive, and explanatory (Vennix, 2019).

Another distinction between types of research which is an important input into the choice for a design or data collection method is the primary aim and audience of the study. Research can be fundamental or theory-driven, which means that understanding is the main aim and the primary audience are other researchers. Alternatively, research can be applied or practice-oriented research, which means that a practical problem drives the study. The study then not only needs to deliver understanding but also provide a basis for taking action.

References

Cook, T. D., & Campbell, D. T. (1979). *Quasi experimentation: Design and analysis for field settings (H3)*. Houghton Mifflin.

Delbecq, A., Van de Ven, A., & Gustafson, G. (1975). *Group techniques for program planning: A guide to nominal group and delphi processes*. Scott, Foresman and Co.

Huz, S., Andersen, D. F., Richardson, G. P., & Boothroyd, R. (1997). A framework for evaluating systems thinking interventions. An experimental approach to mental health system change. *System Dynamics Review, 13*(2), 149–169.

Janis, I. L. (1982). *Groupthink: Psychological studies of policy decisions and fiascos* (2nd ed.). Houghton Mifflin Company.

Mason, R.O. (1969). A dialectical approach to strategic planning. *Management Science, 15*(3), B-403–414.

Osborn, A. (1957). *Applied imagination. Principles and procedures of creative problem-solving.* (Revised ed.). Scribners.

Roberto, M. A. (2013). *Why great leaders don't take yes for an answer: Managing for conflict and consensus* (2nd ed.). Pearson Education.

Tranfield, D., Denyer, D., & Smart, P. (2003). Towards a methodology for developing evidence-informed management knowledge by means of systematic review. *British Journal of Management, 14*, 207–222.

Vennix, J. A. M. (2019). *Research methodology. An introduction to scientific thinking and practice*. Pearson.

Yin, R. (1984). *Case study research. Design and methods*. SAGE.

INDEX

Note: Page numbers in *italics* indicate a figure and page numbers in **bold** indicate a table on the corresponding page.

Printed in the United States
by Baker & Taylor Publisher Services